The Capitalist Cycle

Historical Materialism Book Series

More than ten years after the collapse of the Berlin Wall and the disappearance of Marxism as a (supposed) state ideology, a need for a serious and long-term Marxist book publishing program has risen. Subjected to the whims of fashion, most contemporary publishers have abandoned any of the systematic production of Marxist theoretical work that they may have indulged in during the 1970s and early 1980s. The Historical Materialism book series addresses this great gap with original monographs, translated texts and reprints of "classics."

Editorial board: Paul Blackledge, Leeds; Sebastian Budgen, London; Jim Kincaid, Leeds; Stathis Kouvelakis, Paris; Marcel van der Linden, Amsterdam; China Miéville, London; Paul Reynolds, Lancashire.

Haymarket Books is proud to be working with Brill Academic Publishers (http://www.brill.nl) and the journal *Historical Materialism* to republish the Historical Materialism book series in paperback editions. Current series titles include:

Alasdair MacIntyre's Engagement with Marxism: Selected Writings 1953–1974
Edited by Paul Blackledge and Neil Davidson

Althusser: The Detour of Theory, Gregory Elliott

Between Equal Rights: A Marxist Theory of International Law, China Miéville

The Capitalist Cycle, Pavel V. Maksakovsky, Translated with introduction and commentary by Richard B. Day

The Clash of Globalisations: Neo-Liberalism, the Third Way, and Anti-globalisation, Ray Kiely

Critical Companion to Contemporary Marxism, Edited by Jacques Bidet and Stathis Kouvelakis

Criticism of Heaven: On Marxism and Theology, Roland Boer

Exploring Marx's Capital: Philosophical, Economic, and Political Dimensions, Jacques Bidet

Following Marx: Method, Critique, and Crisis, Michael Lebowitz

The German Revolution: 1917–1923, Pierre Broué

Globalisation: A Systematic Marxian Account, Tony Smith

Impersonal Power: History and Theory of the Bourgeois State,
Heide Gerstenberger, translated by David Fernbach

Lenin Rediscovered: What Is to Be Done? *In Context,* Lars T. Lih

Making History: Agency, Structure, and Change in Social Theory, Alex Callinicos

Marxism and Ecological Economics: Toward a Red and Green Political Economy, Paul Burkett

A Marxist Philosophy of Language, Jean-Jacques Lecercle and Gregory Elliott

The Theory of Revolution in the Young Marx, Michael Löwy

Utopia Ltd.: Ideologies of Social Dreaming in England 1870–1900, Matthew Beaumont

Western Marxism and the Soviet Union: A Survey of Critical Theories and Debates Since 1917
Marcel van der Linden

The Capitalist Cycle

Pavel V. Maksakovsky
Translated with introduction
and commentary by Richard B. Day

Haymarket Books
Chicago, Illinois

First published in 2005 by Brill Academic Publishers, The Netherlands
© 2006 Koninklijke Brill NV, Leiden, The Netherlands

Published in paperback in 2009 by
Haymarket Books
P.O. Box 180165
Chicago, IL 60618
773-583-7884
www.haymarketbooks.org

ISBN: 978-1-60846-018-2

Trade distribution:
In the U.S. through Consortium Book Sales, www.cbsd.com
In the UK, Turnaround Publisher Services, www.turnaround-psl.com
In Australia, Palgrave Macmillan, www.palgravemacmillan.com.au
In all other countries by Publishers Group Worldwide,
www.pgw.com/home/worlwide.asp

Cover design by Ragina Johnson.

This book was published with the generous support
of the Wallace Global Fund.

Printed in the United States.

10 9 8 7 6 5 4 3 2

Library of Congress Cataloging-in-Publication Data is available.

To Dušan Pokorný

Scholar, Teacher and Friend

Pavel V. Maksakovsky

Contents

Translator's Introduction: Maksakovsky's *The Capitalist Cycle* ix

Pavel V. Maksakovsky
The Capitalist Cycle: An Essay on the Marxist Theory of the Cycle

Foreword by A.S. Mendel'son 3
Introduction 5
1. Methodological Foundations of the Theory of the Conjuncture ... 13
2. The General Theory of the Cycle 48
3. The Role of Credit in the Conjuncture 106
4. The Problem of Crises in the Works of Marx 133
5. In Place of a Conclusion 143

Bibliography 145
Index 149

Richard B. Day

Translator's Introduction: Pavel V. Maksakovsky's *The Capitalist Cycle*[1]

An Essay on the Marxist Theory of the Cycle

In 1929 the Communist Academy published 3,100 copies of *The Capitalist Cycle: An Essay on the Marxist Theory of the Cycle*. The author was Pavel V. Maksakovsky. His book was published posthumously, for Maksakovsky had died on 2 November 1928. At the time of his death, he was twenty-eight years old. The Library of Congress has a copy of his book that is date-stamped 14 March 1930. It is not clear whether any other copies exist. Apart from one article, which appeared in 1928 in the journal *Bol'shevik*, I know of no further published work by this author.[2] His name and his work have been all but lost. He appears in none of the standard encyclopaedias; there seems to be no trace of him on the Internet; and apart from my own book on Soviet economic theory from 1917–1939,[3] I am not aware of any secondary source that mentions him, including *The History of the Political Economy of Capitalism*, published by Leningrad University in 1989.[4]

---

[1] For his critical help with this project, I am indebted to Dušan Pokorný of the University of Toronto.

[2] Maksakovsky 1928.

[3] Day 1981, pp. 130, 133–6, 233, 236.

[4] Demin 1989. Michael David-Fox has written a major study of the Institute of Red Professors, where Maksakovsky worked. He did not encounter Maksakovsky in his

Nevertheless, *The Capitalist Cycle* is one of the most erudite publications in Marxist economic theory to appear in the Soviet Union during the first two decades after 1917. Maksakovsky's interpretation of *Capital* and *Theories of Surplus-Value* surpasses the efforts of almost all of his better-known Soviet contemporaries. In terms of theoretical sophistication, it ranks with the best works of Isaak I. Rubin and Evgeny A. Preobrazhensky, both of whose major publications have long been available in English translation.[5] Like Rubin and Preobrazhensky, Maksakovsky was a dialectician who *studied* Marx rather than merely *quoting* him. Not only did he explore Marx's work 'from the inside', beginning with methodology and working towards concrete conclusions, but he was also familiar with the work of many other leading economists of his own day, both Marxist and bourgeois. His footnotes reveal a knowledge of M.I. Tugan-Baranovsky, Otto Bauer, Karl Kautsky, Rosa Luxemburg and Rudolf Hilferding; he commented frequently on important Russian economists of the 1920s, such as N.D. Kondrat'ev, S.A. Pervushin, V.A. Bazarov and N. Osinsky; he was also thoroughly familiar with path-breaking Western literature on the business cycle, including the work of Gustav Cassel, Mentor Bouniatian, Paul Mombert, Arthur Spiethoff and Wilhelm Röpke. In short, Maksakovsky was a scholar and an intellectual – just the sort of Bolshevik who almost certainly would have been purged, like Rubin, Preobrazhensky and countless others, in the 1930s.[6]

Besides being an impressive scholar, Maksakovsky was also the prototype of a Marxist revolutionary. What we know of his biography reads in parts like a Sergei Eisenstein film or the heroic Soviet fiction of the 1920s. He was born in 1900 in the factory town of Ilevo, located in the *guberniya* of Nizhegorod in the Volga River basin. His father and three brothers were metalworkers, but from 1912–16 the family returned to the land after the factory where they had been employed closed down. In 1916, they moved to Ekaterinoslav, in south-central Ukraine. Here his brothers became involved in strike activity, which might have contributed to his political education. When the Ukrainian Rada declared independence in June 1917, Maksakovsky was recruited into

---

research. See David-Fox 1997. The same is true of another careful study of the Institute. See Behrendt 1997.

[5] See Rubin 1973; Preobrazhensky 1965, 1973, 1979, 1985; also Preobrazhensky and Bukharin 1969.

[6] Maksakovsky's emphasis on the role of consumer demand would have been enough to cause him 'political' difficulties as the Five-Year Plan began. See Maksakovsky 1929, pp. 64–7 (pp. 68–71 in this volume).

Bolshevik-inspired underground work and joined the party in 1918. Forced into hiding by an arrest warrant, he resumed party work and served as a volunteer with the Red Army when it reached Ekatorinoslav early in 1919. He briefly attended a party school in Ukraine, but then returned to the Red Army. He fought at Ekatorinoslav and later worked in the underground in the Poltava region. In October 1919, he was taken prisoner by Denikin's forces and sentenced to execution as a 'Bolshevist commissar and spy'. After convincing the soldiers who were escorting him to defect to the Bolsheviks, he eluded the death sentence and survived to fight against the anarchist forces of Nestor Makhno, serving briefly as chairman of a military-revolutionary committee. Following a bout of typhus, in 1920 he was sent to Sverdlovsk, in Ukraine, where he worked as instructor in a party school until 1924. He subsequently taught at the Plekhanov Institute of the National Economy, and in 1925 he was invited to join the Institute of Red Professors. Illness prevented him from delivering a projected course on Marxism at the prestigious Communist Academy, but in the autumn of 1927 he participated in a seminar at the Institute of Red Professors dealing with Marxist economic theory. The notes from that seminar became *The Capitalist Cycle: An Essay on the Marxist Theory of the Cycle*.

The most obvious gap in this sparse biographical information is just where and when Maksakovsky had the opportunity for rigorous study of economics and the Marxist classics. Whatever the case, there is no doubt that he made a striking impression upon his colleagues at the Institute of Red Professors. The leader of the seminar that he attended was A.S. Mendel'son. In a brief foreword to *The Capitalist Cycle*, Mendel'son indicated that the manuscript was unfinished and that he, as editor, did take it upon himself to make minor changes. Although he also hinted at some critical reservations,[7] his preface concluded with warm praise:

> The work is written so clearly, with such talent, and at such a high level of theoretical sophistication that even comrade Maksakovsky's mistakes are interesting and instructive. The book's impressive theoretical vitality, the militant revolutionary spirit that pervades this deeply theoretical work, and its excellent form – all of these attributes cause me to regard *The Capitalist Cycle* as one of the very best works recently written on questions concerning

[7] Mendel'son's own view of conjuncture theory can be found in Mendel'son 1928, pp. 6–68.

> the general theory of reproduction. In the person of comrade Maksakovsky, who died at such a young age, we have lost a major Marxist theoretical force.[8]

The most outstanding feature of Maksakovsky's book is his exemplary grasp of Marx's dialectical method and its implications for the logical movement of *Capital*. In his first chapter, Maksakovsky deals exclusively with questions of methodology. While this may seem to have little direct connection with a theory of the business cycle, in fact it is essential to Maksakovsky's project. His theme is that bourgeois economics is characterised by a superficial empiricism that attempts to formulate *abstract* economic laws by reference to what appear to be *concrete* data, such as the volume of production, the level of employment, the rate of interest, the price of shares, etc. For Maksakovsky, however, these surface indicators are nothing but phenomenal manifestations of an essential dialectical movement that can never be grasped by mere observation and measurement, only by the logical activity of reason itself. The laws that govern the capitalist whole are not to be found simply by abstracting from the empirical; instead, the empirical must first be *conceptually* comprehended by beginning with the inner logic that forms and determines the surface of economic phenomena.

Marx understood surface manifestations of capitalist contradictions to be expressions of an inner, *dialectical necessity*. Maksakovsky follows Marx by interpreting *Capital* in terms of a dialectical movement from the abstract to the concrete by way of 'value' and the organising activity of 'the law of value'. The law of value is the fundamental law of the system, out of which spring numerous particular laws, which, in their continuous interaction, ultimately organise market phenomena into an intelligible whole whose contradictions can be concretely reproduced in thought. Marx provided the conceptual tools for a theory of the capitalist cycle, but Maksakovsky regards *Capital* as a work yet to be completed. Marx's insight into the concrete came in brilliant flashes of commentary within a theory that had not yet reached the level of concrete totality. The remaining task, according to Maksakovsky, is to go beyond these particular comments in the form of comprehensive theory. By leaving behind certain limiting assumptions in *Capital* and *Theories of Surplus-Value*, Maksakovsky proposes nothing less than to write a concluding chapter to *Capital* as a concrete theory of the capitalist *conjuncture*.

[8] Maksakovsky 1929, p. 6 (p. 4 in this volume).

The conjuncture comprises both the immediacy of economic phenomena and theoretical reflection of their inter-relatedness in the total process of social production. Since the method of reconstructing the totality is Marx's own dialectic, it is important to mention at the outset that Maksakovsky's book is more than an essay in economic theory; like *Capital* itself, it is simultaneously an essay in dialectical logic. As the laws of physics or chemistry 'form' the material world and reveal what is happening beyond the surface of things, so in dialectics the laws of contradiction and transcendence reveal the essential logic that 'governs' and at the same time ideally reflects the total movement of history and society. This means that an introduction to Maksakovsky's work should properly begin by investigating the philosophic origins of his scientific methodology. Hegel's philosophical economics and Marx's economic science provide the necessary context for appreciating Maksakovsky's purpose and his accomplishment.

1. Hegel's dialectical logic

Dialectical political economy is the study of movement and its 'causes' in social history. The theme that prevails throughout Maksakovsky's work is the Enlightenment commitment, shared by Hegel and Marx, to make the world rational. Lenin understood Marx's *Capital* to be an application of 'Hegel's dialectics in its rational form to political economy'.[9] Hegel wrote a *Logic*, but Lenin said that Marx gave dialectics a materialist expression in 'the logic of *Capital*'.[10] 'It is impossible,' Lenin wrote, 'completely to understand Marx's *Capital*, and especially its first chapter, without having thoroughly studied and understood the *whole* of Hegel's *Logic*'.[11]

The fundamental conviction of dialectical thought is as old as Aristotle's *Politics* or Plato's *Republic*: the whole is historically and logically prior to the parts. For Aristotle it was the historically developed ethos of the community that formed the ethical consciousness of individual citizens; for Plato, the universal principle of justice required a social division of labour in which each part made its appropriate functional contribution to a whole ruled by Reason. In the Socratic dialogues, the participants propose successive concepts

---

[9] Lenin 1961, pp. 38, 178; see also p. 361.
[10] Lenin 1961, p. 319.
[11] Lenin 1961, p. 180. See also 'On the Significance of Militant Materialism' in Lenin 1966, pp. 227–36.

aimed at solving a problem. Each concept is then examined until it is found to be inadequate. Nevertheless, the partial truth of each 'solution' is always retained and incorporated into a broader concept. When the broader concept is also found to be inadequate, its own partial truth is incorporated into another, still higher concept. The truth ultimately emerges as the whole, the universal concept that contains, affirms, and is presupposed by all other partial truths found along the way.

In *The Republic*, the division of labour, first considered appropriate because it is merely economically efficient – or, as Socrates says, suited to a city of pigs – ultimately reappears at the highest level of the dialogue in the philosophical principle of justice. Plato concludes that 'When each order – tradesman, Auxiliary, Guardian – keeps to its own proper business in the commonwealth and does its own work, that is justice and what makes a just society'.[12] The unity that transcends this functional division is the rule of Reason through the organising activity of philosophic rulers, who assign each 'soul' to mind only the affairs for which it is best suited. Plato thought a philosopher must enjoy the exclusive prerogative of reasoning dialectically in search of the Good, a universal Idea that transcends all experience and incorporates all partial goods. Since the Good is an Idea, or a concept, it must be pursued conceptually. Dialectics must be an ideal exercise of pure reason. This meant forsaking empiricism in order that thought might advance solely by way of a series of hypotheses that Plato described as

> a flight of steps up which [reason] may mount all the way to something that is not hypothetical, the first principle of all [the Good]; and having grasped this, [reason] may turn back and, holding on to the consequences which depend upon it, descend at last to a conclusion, never making use of any sensible object, but only of Forms, moving through Forms from one to another, and ending with Forms.[13]

Hegel shared this ambition to discover the truth – the whole – and thus to make the world rational. While his philosophy incorporated insight from all previous thinkers, an immediate motivation for his work was the need to respond to Immanuel Kant, his most important predecessor in German idealism. In his critique of empiricism, Kant had insisted on the organising

[12] Plato 1962, p. 129.
[13] Plato 1962, p. 226.

activity of mind as the condition for giving meaning to mere sense impressions. Empiricism expects fact to 'speak' for themselves; nothing can be known beyond what is experienced. Kant replied that we only know the world through *a priori* categories of reason. Mere sense 'data' must be conceptually organised. But, by making a rigid distinction between what is 'out there' and what is 'in here' – in the mind –, Kantian philosophy ended in dualism. If the meaning of everything we know is grasped through categories of thought, Kant said, we could never acquire direct knowledge of the 'thing-in-itself'. Kant's argument led to an insurmountable gap between the knowing subject and the known object. Hegel objected to Kant's conclusion this way:

> On one side there is the Ego. . . . But next to it there is an infinity of sensations and . . . of things in themselves. Once it is abandoned by the categories, this realm [what is 'out there'] cannot be anything but a formless lump. . . . A formal idealism [as distinct from objective idealism] which in this way sets an absolute Ego-point and its intellect on one side, and an absolute manifold, or sensation on the other side, is a dualism.[14]

Hegel transcended this dualism by re-reading Kantian epistemology as ontology: Kant's theory of *how we know* grew over into Hegel's explanation of *what we know*, namely, the rational organisation of being. Hegel thought of his own philosophy as objective idealism. He claimed that concepts are not only in our minds, but are simultaneously the *forms* of all being. Reasoning beings can know the world because it is formed by Reason. If the world is formed by Reason, it must ultimately *conform* to the requirements of Reason. The merely phenomenal is implicitly the ideal; through the labour of thought, it will necessarily become the explicit ideal – a rational world in which reasoning beings will act wholly through the self-determination of their own rational wills.

Hegel argued that it is logically impossible for Being to be merely a 'formless lump'. If Being had no determinate characteristics – if it were pure abstraction – it would be Nothing (no-thing), indicating that there could not possibly be a Kantian thing-in-itself. Being and Nothing are abstract opposites, but their concrete dialectical synthesis is Becoming. Dualism, the *end* of Kant's philosophy, is the *beginning* of Hegel's *Logic*, which later reappears in the first chapter of Marx's *Capital*. Through Becoming, Hegel said, Being acquires

[14] Hegel as quoted in Guyer 1993, p. 191.

determinate *qualities*. To differentiate beings with identical qualities, the concept of *quantity* is required. The synthesis of quality and quantity is *measure*.

Moving from concept to concept, the first part of the *Logic* – the Doctrine of Being – deduces each successive category by overcoming the limitations of its predecessor. The categories of thought then turn out to be the real essence of things. The result is two levels of being: *essence* and *existence*. The Doctrine of Essence deals with paired opposites such as identity and difference, likeness and unlikeness, positive and negative. What holds these contradictions together is the force of thought, articulated in the Doctrine of the Notion and culminating in transcendence of all previous negativity in the Absolute Idea. 'The realized End is thus the overt unity of subjective and objective'.[15]

Hegel believed that *essence* (what ought to be) must become *existence* (what is) when we make the world rational through history. The end (or purpose) of history is the institutionalised, law-governed, self-determination of Reason. Kant claimed that the end-in-itself is a 'good will' that acts on a universal moral law; Hegel replied that the realised unity of the whole, at the level of logic, is the *Idea*. The Idea is a universe *formed* by Reason and a Reason that knows the universe to be formed by its own dialectical logic:

> The Idea may be described in many ways. It may be called reason; subject-object; the unity of the ideal and the real, of the finite and the infinite, of soul and body; the possibility which has its actuality in its own self. . . . All these descriptions apply, because the Idea contains all the relations of understanding, but contains them in their infinite self-return and self-identity.[16]

If self-identity of the whole is established in logic, how does logic, in turn, provide insight into the natural and historical world? In his philosophy of nature, Hegel turned from pure thoughts to existent things. Nature is both rational and irrational, but it is also rational that the irrational exist. This contradiction is what propels nature beyond itself. Reason must surmount contingency to realise what ought to be. Reason requires that reasoning beings make the world into a habitat in which we might consciously exercise our own capacity for rational self-determination. Hegel's major works, including the *Philosophy of History*, the *Phenomenology of Spirit*, and the *Philosophy of*

---

[15] Hegel 1975, §210.
[16] Hegel 1975, §214.

Right, elevate merely natural-empirical history to the level of *logical history*, which in turn culminates in the law-governed state as the realised rule of Reason.

2. Hegel: civil society and ethical life

In terms of understanding Marx's debt to Hegel – and, by implication, Maksakovsky's debt to Hegel and Marx – it is important to recognise that Hegel's *Philosophy of Right* is both a political theory and a theory of political economy. The goal is to restore the rational-ethical *unity* of the Greek polis in a modern world that includes the market economy, universal commodity production, and a *division* of labour extending beyond anything Plato might have imagined. How is it possible to find unity in a world that is functionally divided by the apparent irrationality of universal self-interest in the capitalist market? How is self-determination possible when, in the absence of Plato's philosophic ruler, each individual and each particular will appears on the surface of things to cancel out every other will? Conceiving of dialectic as an historical and conceptual spiral, Hegel responded to these questions by returning to the dialectic of his *Logic* at the more concrete level of political and economic philosophy.

Logic began with Being, an abstraction that was Nothing until it realised its inner potential through acquiring the attributes of quality, quantity, measure, and so forth, ending in the Absolute Idea as a self-generated totality. In *Philosophy of Right* Hegel resumes the same dialectical movement from the abstract to the concrete. He begins with Abstract Right, that is, a hypothetical relation of wills that are abstracted from family, civil society and state – wills that typify the self-interest of bourgeois individualism. The abstract Ego, by analogy with Abstract Being in the *Logic*, is consciousness without form or content and therefore potentially anything – but at this stage still nothing. Ego then determines itself (becomes) through an act of will. If thinking is to raise itself to the level of *existence*, Ego must objectify itself in the thing. Objective idealism entails a continuous dialectic of subjectivity making itself objective and then re-appropriating the object as part of the self.

Self-objectification is a rational expression of inner necessity. The subject forms the object as an outer manifestation of its own inner potential: I work upon myself, work my creative abilities out of myself, through transforming nature in accordance with my own rational projections. In that way, individual will determines itself both as subject and as its own object. It turns out, therefore, that possession of things, at this level of abstraction, has precisely nothing to do with economics: outward possessions are the *logical* condition for inner self-possession. With possession, '. . . I as free will am an object to myself'.[17]

At the level of Abstract Right, each relates to all others exclusively through transfer of things in accordance with contracts. There are, as yet, no ethical bonds. But this means that, while contract posits a common will, every contract is also exposed to 'wrong', and wrong requires affirmation of the Right as what ought to be. Individual awareness of this 'ought' is Morality, but in the absence of ethical ties and lawful duties, Morality is only abstract inwardness: each knows he ought to do good, but good has yet to be objectively determined. This indeterminacy is the fundamental flaw of Abstract Right. Its transcendence necessarily requires movement to progressively more concrete levels of ethical life, in which individuals become law-governed participants of a larger whole, an emerging *community of consciousness.*

Ethical life begins in the family, whose bond is not yet law, but love. In a family, property acquires ethical significance as a 'common possession'[18] and serves the good of the entire family instead of the 'arbitrariness of a single owner's particular needs'.[19] Hegel sees the family as a kind of collective person; individual wills are transcended in the security that supports the well-being of all members. But when the family leads to a plurality of families, unity gives way once again to difference and division in *civil society*, the *system of needs,* in which each relates to all others merely as means to his own ends. Ethical order appears, as a result, to be split once more into the abstraction of 'private persons whose end is their own interest'.[20] Nevertheless, ethical life remains the inner necessity of market relations, and what appears to be merely objective – market exchange – retains implicit ethical purpose.

When he turns directly to economics, Hegel congratulates Adam Smith for detecting, behind the apparent 'mass of accidents' on the market's surface, an inner logic of market *laws.* Market actors are objectively mediated, through division of labour, to serve each other's needs even as they single-mindedly pursue their own interests. Smith's empiricism contributed to 'understanding'

[17] Hegel 1967, §45.
[18] Hegel 1967, §170.
[19] Hegel 1967, §170.
[20] Hegel 1967, §187.

of the market as a law-governed order, but *Understanding* is not yet *Reason*. Reason looks beyond the surface of supply and demand, prices and profits, wages and rents, to find the inner logic that ultimately brings market actors together in ethical communities of consciousness. The truth is the whole, and movement towards the concrete occurs through associations of mutual support. These include classes, each with its own particular shared purpose, and corporations, or particular economic communities based upon skills and shared interests. In what appear to be mere groups of economic interest, Reason finds *esprit de corps*, or spiritual communities. These particular spirits must then be transcended in order to articulate the Spirit of the whole – the laws of the State as the end, or purpose, of Reason.

The State is the purpose of Reason because Reason requires self-determination: '. . . the principle of the modern state requires that the whole of an individual's activity shall be mediated through his will'.[21] Each market actor may appear *immediately* to be driven by economic needs, but the shared higher need is for *mediation* through a system of laws that might simultaneously be 'my' laws and 'our' laws. If, through a system of political representation, every interest takes part in determination of the laws, then law-governed order becomes the supreme articulation of the self-determination of each and all. Freedom, in that sense, becomes objective; it is the ethical objectification of every subjective consciousness. In obeying the laws, each complies with the objective logic of ethical necessity. The objective necessity of freedom is the end of Hegel's *Philosophy of Right*, but it was also implicit from the beginning in the need for self-determination of the abstract Ego, which turned out to presuppose the state and the laws. The whole, in other words, was logically prior to the parts.

In a dialectical spiral, the end is the beginning, and the beginning is the end. The entire movement is a circle of logical necessity in which the part is merely an abstraction until it is rationally included in the whole, which is the *concrete universal* – a universal that has no existence of its own except through the exercise of self-determining freedom by every citizen and every group within a law-governed ethical community. The laws are simultaneously an expression of our own consciousness and the ethical forms that shape our consciousness. In that sense, each citizen is simultaneously subject and object.

---

[21] Hegel 1967, A.177.

The state is the supreme end of history, the end-in-itself that makes all other ends possible. The state is universal because it is not a mere thing, but an expression of Spirit, articulated in laws, which are ideas and therefore universal. The concrete universal is the whole that fulfils and affirms the purpose of every part, which is to make the world rational in order that each may be free. In Plato's terms, Hegel's concrete universal is the Good institutionalised, in 'this time' and 'this place', as the Spirit of a people.

3. Hegel on objectification, mediation, and alienation

Hegel saw his own philosophy as Reason's response to the abstracting consciousness of the French Revolution and the emerging capitalist market. The unity of essence and existence is realised through universal citizenship in the law-governed state. Hegel portrayed the new freedom as an activity of mind that makes the world conform to the requirements of Reason. Having reached Hegel's concrete universal, however, we must now take a moment to reflect more closely upon a problem that ultimately provoked Marx's critique of Hegel's *Philosophy of Right*. The decisive issue in this connection is the activity of *alienation* and its potential to create *poverty*.

We have seen that objectification in the thing, for Hegel, is the first moment of self-determination. But unless I am to become *dependent* upon the thing, Hegel concluded that I must also alienate it. Every addict knows that the first step toward restoring self-determination is to throw away the substance that has become the focus of dependency. Hegel regarded the act of alienation as a universal requirement of Reason. It is the process of alienation that builds relationships of mutual recognition through the logic of contract, which then gives birth to the market. Hegel believed that disposing of the thing is the most concrete way of asserting one's will over it:

> . . . [A]lienation proper is an expression of my will . . . no longer to regard the thing as mine. . . . [A]lienation is seen to be a true mode of taking possession. To take possession of the thing directly is the first moment in property. Use is likewise a way of acquiring property. The third moment then is the unity of these two, taking possession of the thing by alienating it.[22]

[22] Hegel 1967, A.42.

Since alienation of the thing is logically necessary to affirm the independence of personality, it must follow that there are clear limits to what may be alienated. A person may not, lawfully or rationally, alienate personality itself. Reason can tolerate neither slavery nor serfdom. However, since the emerging capitalist market is part of the ethical order, it must also follow that day labourers may freely alienate their products and, for a limited time, their talents. Hegel tells us:

> Single products of my particular physical and mental skill and of my power to act I can alienate to someone else and I can give him the use of my abilities for a restricted period. . . . [But] by alienating the whole of my time, as crystallized in my work, and everything I produced, I would be making into another's property the substance of my being, my universal activity and actuality, my personality.[23]

If I were to alienate everything I produced, I would become mere abstract inwardness with no external existence. Unable to enter into exchange with others, I would negate myself and lose my capacity for citizenship. The state is a universal community of reasoning beings. But, for Hegel, reasoning beings are also, necessarily, property owners: 'The rationale of property is to be found not in the satisfaction of needs but in the supersession of the pure [that is, abstract] subjectivity of personality. In his property a person exists for the first time as reason'.[24] Ideally, Hegel thinks of social means of production as 'the universal permanent capital', a kind of common pool, like the capital of a family, 'which gives each the opportunity, by the exercise of his education and skill, to draw a share from it and so be assured of his livelihood'.[25] If property is a condition of self-determining subjectivity, poverty must also be more than an economic affliction. In a state committed to upholding the Right, poverty is a wrong:

> Against nature man can claim no right, but once society is established, poverty immediately takes the form of a wrong done to one class by another. The important question of how poverty is to be abolished is one of the most disturbing problems which agitate modern society.[26]

---

[23] Hegel 1967, §67.
[24] Hegel 1967, A.24.
[25] Hegel 1967, §199.
[26] Hegel 1967, A.149.

Hegel regarded poverty as an evil – not merely because the poor may be hungry, but because poverty degrades one's *state of mind* and directly violates the universality of the state as an ethical community of consciousness. 'Poverty in itself does not make men into a rabble; a rabble is created only when there is joined to poverty a disposition of mind, an inner indignation against the rich, against society, against the government, etc.'[27] Poverty also logically entails its own opposite and 'brings with it, at the other end of the social scale, conditions which greatly facilitate the concentration of disproportionate wealth in a few hands'.[28]

In the economic doldrums following the Napoleonic wars, Hegel had discovered the evil of poverty and unemployment in emerging capitalist society. To the paradox of unemployment, he had no convincing response. Putting the poor to work, if 'the evil consists precisely in excess of production', could not solve unemployment.[29] Unable to solve the problem, Hegel expelled it from his *Philosophy of Right* by an act of logic. Anticipating later theories of imperialism, he concluded that colonising activity is due 'to the appearance of a number of people who cannot secure the satisfaction of their needs by their own labour once production rises above the requirements of consumers'.[30] Hegel thought civil society is driven to 'colonizing activity . . . by which it supplies to a part of its population a return to life on the family basis in a new land and so also supplies itself with a new demand and field for its industry'.[31] Through imperialism, the evil of poverty appeared to be remedied.

4. Marx on alienation

Once the reality of propertylessness was acknowledged, however, Hegel's elaborate logical circle was broken. Those without property could never be mediated into effective citizenship in the modern state. In his early *Critique of Hegel's Philosophy of Right*, Marx protested that behind Hegel's community of ethical consciousness lay a more mundane reality: 'the political constitution is the constitution of private property'.[32] At the same time, 'the class in need

[27] Hegel 1967, A.149.
[28] Hegel 1967, §244; see also A.149.
[29] Hegel 1967, §245.
[30] Hegel 1967, A.150.
[31] Hegel 1967, §248.
[32] Marx 1970, p. 99; see also p. 109.

of immediate labor, of concrete labor, forms less a class of civil society than the basis upon which the spheres of civil society rest and move'.[33] Marx initially concluded that Hegel's mediated totality must be replaced by the *immediacy* of universal, direct democracy, in which the *political* need for property would disappear and the people themselves would become the state.[34] If political life, as Hegel claimed, is the 'true universal and essential existence',[35] then the political inessentiality of property (in direct democracy) must also imply the inessentiality of property in all other respects. Transcendence of property would entail transcendence of the state itself as the institutionalised *other* that stands over, and dominates, the people.

Criticism of Hegel's political theory also led directly to Marx's first philosophical reappraisal, in the *1844 Manuscripts*, of Hegelian political economy. For Hegel, self-determination involved objectification in the thing, transfer of the thing through contract, and then *re-appropriation of an equivalent thing* in the market, as the system of needs. Marx saw the obvious implication: the propertyless cannot even be persons if the worker objectifies his labour while the 'other', the capitalist, does the appropriating. Marx wrote that when labour is in the service of capital,

> ... the object which labour produces ... confronts it as *something alien*. ... The product of labour is labour which has been congealed in an object ... it is the *objectification* of labour. ... [But] this realization of labour appears as *loss of reality* for the workers; objectification as *loss of the object* and *object-bondage*; appropriation as *estrangement*, as *alienation*.[36]

Marx described production for the market as 'the alienation of activity, the activity of alienation'.[37] Since capital is privately owned, the practice of self-alienation from the thing was also '*estrangement of man* from *man*'.[38] On a universal scale, alienation entailed nothing less than negation of the essential human capacity for 'free, conscious activity'.[39] In terms of universal history, labour was a collective project of the human species involving countless generations in the transformation of primordial material into a human habitat.

[33] Marx 1970, p. 81.
[34] Marx 1970, p. 30; see also pp. 50, 65, 67.
[35] Marx 1970, p. 121.
[36] Tucker 1978, pp. 71–2.
[37] Tucker 1978, p. 74.
[38] Tucker 1978, p. 77.
[39] Tucker 1978, p. 76.

Yet, in this same process, man, as mere worker, had also transformed himself into an animal by selling his essential creative powers to alien others in order to sustain mere biological existence.[40]

By treating political labour as the highest labour accessible to most people – apart from artists, theologians, and philosophers – Hegel had proclaimed the modern state to be a triumph of human Spirit. Marx replied that Hegel had discovered only an '*abstract, logical, speculative* expression for the movement of history',[41] a 'dialectic of pure thought',[42] 'a pure, *restless* revolving within itself',[43] and 'the act of abstraction which revolves in its own circle'.[44] Hegel treated history as a succession of civilizations, or modes of consciousness, in the process of Spirit's becoming. Absent from this entire *speculative* history was the *practical* history of human production and self-production; that is, a concrete understanding of human becoming as a succession of *modes of production*.

Despite its idealistic mystification, however, Hegelian philosophy had implicitly apprehended a profound truth: man makes himself – not through his thoughts, but through his own practical activity of labour.[45] Marx concluded that criticism must now turn from *speculative* philosophy to the *practical* history of production and the means of production as the real, '*open* book of *man's essential powers*'[46] and 'the *comprehended* and *known* process of [man's] *coming-to-be*'.[47] Hegel's dialectical method was formally sound: all that was needed in order to excavate explicit truth was to replace the abstract activity of Reason with a concrete, materialist dialectic of the transformation of human life through 'the medium of industry'.[48]

5. Contradictions of Hegel's philosophical economics

Although Marx attributed to Hegel a 'dialectic of pure thought', Hegel's philosophical economics did anticipate crucial themes that were later incor-

---

[40] Tucker 1978, p. 74.
[41] Tucker 1978, p. 108.
[42] Tucker 1978, p. 112.
[43] Tucker 1978, p. 122.
[44] Tucker 1978, p. 123.
[45] Tucker 1978, p. 112.
[46] Tucker 1978, p. 89.
[47] Tucker 1978, p. 84.
[48] Tucker 1978, p. 90. The first systematic effort in this direction was *The German Ideology*. For a discussion of Marx's journey beyond Hegel, see Day 1989.

porated into Marx's own economic science in *Capital*. In the philosophy of objective idealism, the objective is the embodiment of Reason. One such embodiment, and the instrument of successive acts of the same kind, is the *tool*. Hegel's treatment of tool-making, as the objectification of Reason, will reappear as a central theme in Maksakovsky's work, which will treat technological change as a fundamental force in generating the capitalist cycle. The problem, for both Marx and Maksakovsky, was that tools and technology ultimately debase concrete labour and replace it with an abstraction – labour as a commodity in a reified world of commodities.

Hegel emphasised that man makes *tools* as an act of rational will. The activity of labour is then abstracted in two ways: particular labours are separated from others through division of labour; and in labour with *machines*, physical labour is abstracted from direct contact with natural materials. The more abstract labour becomes, the greater is the possibility of replacing both labour and tools with machines: 'It is only a question of finding . . . a self-differentiating power of nature like the movement of water, wind, steam, etc., and the tool passes over into the *machine* . . .'.[49] Hegel saw that machines can liberate us from toil, but he also worried that machines cause degradation when abstract labour loses the concrete skills of craftsmen. The economic worth of human effort and the wage paid to the worker are then diminished, with poverty as the result:

> . . . this deceit that he practices against nature [appropriation through the mediation of machines] . . . takes its revenge upon him; what he gains from nature, the more he subdues it, the lower he sinks himself. When he lets nature be worked over by a variety of machines, he does not cancel the necessity for his own laboring, but only postpones it, and makes it more distant from nature; . . . the laboring that remains to man becomes itself *more machinelike*; man *diminishes* labor only for the whole [community], not for the single [laborer]; for him it is increased rather; for the more machinelike labor becomes, the less it is worth, and the more one must work in that mode.[50]

Hegel was perfectly aware, especially in his early lectures, that machines deskill labour and correspondingly *devalue* it. Citing Adam Smith's example of division of labour in a pin factory, he noted that the real price of greater

[49] Hegel 1979, pp. 117–18.
[50] Hegel 1979, p. 247.

output is *impoverished human consciousness*: '... in the same ratio that the number [of pins] produced rises, the value of the labor falls; the labor becomes that much deader, it becomes machine work, the skill of the single laborer is infinitely limited, and the consciousness of the factory laborer is impoverished to the last extreme of dullness ...'.[51] In the *1844 Manuscripts*, Marx paraphrased Hegel and made the identical point: industry 'replaces labour by machines – but some of the workers it throws back to a barbarous type of labour, and the other workers it turns into machines. It produces intelligence – but for the worker idiocy, cretinism'.[52]

Hegel saw that, as division of labour widens, individual workers also become distanced through the market, with the result that consciousness of self-determined participation in a whole may be replaced by practical isolation as forced unemployment: '... *the coherence of the singular kind* of labor with the whole infinite mass of needs is quite unsurveyable, and [a matter of] *blind dependence*, so that some far-off operation often suddenly cuts off the labor of a whole class of men who were satisfying their needs by it, and makes it superfluous and useless ...'.[53] When the contribution of each person's labour to the whole becomes incomprehensible, the whole likewise becomes an abstraction, an unconscious totality of needs externally regulated through the power of money. Money becomes 'the form of unity' expressing the coherence of all needs. But if money undertakes to unify in place of the rational bonds of ethical life, the result may be catastrophically dehumanising. Hegel acknowledged that:

> Need and labor, elevated into this [abstract] universality, then form on their own account a monstrous system of community and mutual interdependence in a great people; a life of the dead body [a market 'peopled' by things], that moves itself within itself, one which ebbs and flows in its motion blindly, like the elements, and which requires continual strict dominance and taming like a wild beast.[54]

Since money is the power to transfer wealth, Hegel saw that it also creates the opposites of wealth and poverty, which threaten ultimately to degrade ethical life and dissolve the community into

51 Hegel 1979, p. 248.
52 Tucker 1978, p. 73.
53 Hegel 1979, p. 248.
54 Hegel 1979, p. 249.

> ... the unmitigated extreme of barbarism ... [T]he bestiality of contempt for all higher things enters. The mass of wealth, the pure [abstract] universal, the absence of wisdom, is the heart of the matter [*das Ansich*]. The absolute bond of the people, namely ethical principle, has vanished, and the people is dissolved.[55]

In passages such as these, Hegel's early work denounced the alienating effects of money-worship with the same passion as Marx did in the *1844 Manuscripts*. Marx described money's objective mediation of abstract labour as 'the general overturning of *individualities*'.[56] Recalling Shakespeare, Marx spoke of money as 'the common whore, the common pimp of people and nations'[57] that compels each person literally to sell himself to the other. Money destroys the dignity of labour and replaces it with the animality of universal prostitution. Hegel was not blind to these threats, but by the time he returned to these same issues in *Philosophy of Right*, his philosophical economics had lost its critical sting. Specialised producers now continued to exchange objects of particular utility through the universal medium of money, but behind these exchanges a new dialectic appeared, *a dialectic of value*, which purported to rationalise exchanges within the broader context of ethical life. Hegel's treatment of value led directly to the labour theory of value in the first chapter of Marx's *Capital*.

Hegel saw value as a dialectical unity: particular things have both a *qualitative* aspect, or specific useful properties in relation to a need, and also a *quantitative* aspect, or the generalised ability to be compared with other things that are similarly useful in meeting other needs.[58] Universal commensurability enables the value of things to be abstracted from their specific qualities and *measured* by money.[59] But since Nature, as raw material, is given to us freely, what is being measured may also be regarded as the *labour* required to transform Nature. In that case, value acquires an objective dimension through the expenditure of labour. 'Through work,' Hegel wrote, 'the raw material directly supplied by nature is specifically adapted to ... numerous ends. ... Now this formative change confers value on means and gives them their utility, and

[55] Hegel 1979, p. 171.
[56] Tucker 1978, p. 105.
[57] Tucker 1978, p. 104.
[58] Hegel 1967, §63.
[59] Hegel 1967, A.40.

hence man in what he consumes is mainly concerned with the products of men. It is the product of human effort which man consumes'.[60]

So long as the market combines alienation of particular values with an equivalent re-appropriation of other values in exchange, Hegel could conclude that the standard of justice is upheld: each gives, and each receives his due. This conclusion presupposes, however, that all are *equal participants* in the system of needs, which poverty and the condition of propertylessness gave obvious reasons to doubt, even in the *Philosophy of Right*.

6. The scientific method of economics

Hegel could find neither a philosophical nor an economic solution to the problem of poverty and unemployment. It was precisely the mental and physical impoverishment of the working class that caused Marx to turn from the *philosophy of economics* to *economic science*. Before asking *what* we might know in terms of economic science, however, Marx first had to clarify *how* we know. What is the scientific method for distinguishing surface phenomena from the essential laws regulating the process of social production, distribution, and exchange? What is the concrete, what is the abstract, and where does science begin? In his notebooks for *Capital*, Marx said that, at first glance, it would seem that the concrete is 'population . . . the different branches of production, export and import, annual production and consumption, commodity prices etc.'.[61] But, on closer examination, it turned out that the apparently concrete presupposed many other determinations. Population is an abstraction apart from social classes; class, in turn, is an empty phrase unless specified in terms of categories such as wage-labour and capital, which then presuppose exchange, division of labour, prices, etc. The concrete is only concrete, Marx concluded, 'because it is the concentration of many determinations, hence unity of the diverse'.[62]

It followed that economic science must follow Hegel in assessing the whole dialectically, that is, in terms of the unity of its contradictory relations. Since the whole in question is precisely capitalist society, this presupposition must also determine the logical ordering of economic categories. Marx wrote:

[60] Hegel 1967, §196.
[61] Marx 1973, p. 100.
[62] Marx 1973, p. 101.

'Capital is the all-dominating economic power of bourgeois society. It must form the starting-point as well as the finishing-point . . .'.[63] The distinguishing feature of capitalism is generalised production of commodities for exchange through the transfer of values. Marx concluded that theoretical reproduction of this particular social formation must begin with commodity exchange and the dual nature of value – as use-value and exchange-value – already discussed by Hegel in *Philosophy of Right*.

Marx appropriated the form of Hegel's dialectic but reinterpreted the logical movement in materialist terms. He rejected empiricism, which expects the facts to 'speak' for themselves; he also rejected Hegelian idealism, which said Reason 'works' the whole of existence out of itself. In *Capital*, Marx described the relation between economic science and existence by speaking of the categories of bourgeois economy as 'forms of thought expressing with social validity the conditions and relations of a definite, historically determined mode of production, viz., the production of commodities'.[64] Each category is *an abstraction* insofar as it grasps one particular element of the entire process; each is also *a concrete abstraction* because it apprehends a particular relation as an integral component of the totality.

Marx was aware that empirical history develops unevenly, causing elements of many different economic formations to coexist at any particular time, but his purpose was to determine the law-governed features peculiar to capitalism alone, apart from any external conditions and exogenous disturbances. As a result, the relation of the abstract to the concrete became the relation of capitalism to itself, or the relations *between* all its different elements as a whole. Lenin summarised Marx's method this way:

> In his *Capital*, Marx first analyses the simplest, most ordinary and fundamental, most common and everyday *relation* of bourgeois (commodity) society, a relation encountered billions of times, viz. the exchange of commodities. In this very simple phenomenon (in this 'cell' of bourgeois society) analysis reveals *all* the contradictions (or all the germs of *all* the contradictions) of modern society. The subsequent exposition shows us the development (*both* growth *and* movement) of these contradictions and of this society in the [totality] of its individual parts, from its beginning to its end.[65]

[63] Marx 1973, p. 107.
[64] Marx 1961, p. 76.
[65] Lenin 1961, pp. 360–1; see also Marx 1961, p. 8.

7. The logic of *Capital*

If the commodity is the economic cell-form of capitalism, it must become the whole through self-division and multiplication. Following Hegel, Marx began the first chapter of *Capital* with the fact that 'Every useful thing . . . may be looked at from the two points of view of quality and quantity'.[66] Use-value involves a thing's specific *qualities;* exchange-value refers to a *quantity,* how much of one commodity might exchange for another. But, in the act of exchange, the unity of quality and quantity appears to fall apart. Each owner regards his own commodity exclusively as exchange-value; at the same time, each regards the other's commodity exclusively as use-value. Since exchange requires something in common, these two forms turn out to be surface manifestations of a third term, *value in itself,* or the concept of value.

Value emerges as the common attribute that allows the exchange of commodities. Value, however, is a *concept,* and people in the market do not exchange concepts. Within the division of labour, it is the results of their own labour that they exchange. The *substance* of value must, therefore, be human labour, which means that labour, too, must be a contradictory unity. *Concrete* labour has a specific quality, or a useful skill needed to produce specific use values. But, for each labour to be exchangeable, through commodities, for all others, labour must also be *quantity,* yielding a third term, *abstract human labour.*[67] If value is the *social form* of the product of labour, abstract labour is value's *social substance.* When commodities exchange, each labour transcends its determinate form and appears as social labour. Commodities then exchange in proportion to the social labour they embody. Social value and social labour are abstractions that conceptually replicate the objective everyday relationship of exchanging commodities. To be concrete abstractions, however, they must also point beyond themselves in the direction of totality.

Direct exchange of commodity for commodity is simply barter of one thing for another. Generalised exchange requires the value of all commodities to be registered in a higher form. Money necessarily appears as the mediating link, or the universal equivalent that takes the *measure* of each particular commodity in accordance with a universal standard, the *socially necessary labour time* required for the commodity's production. Money leads to the price

[66] Marx 1961, p. 35.
[67] Marx 1961, p. 46.

form of value. The singular act of barter then becomes two acts that may be separated in space and time. First, a commodity exchanges for money (C-M); subsequently, money exchanges for another commodity (M-C). The division of exchange into these two distinct acts represents the 'cell-form' of fully developed capitalist crises. The essential feature of a crisis is that some commodities lose their exchange-value when M-C fails to accompany C-M; in other words, some commodities will not be sold.

The *law of value* prescribes determination of the magnitude of value by socially necessary labour time. The problem now is that exchange of commodities, through the universal equivalent of money, generates another paradox. Hegel justified the market on the grounds that alienation of a thing ultimately entails re-appropriation of another *equivalent* thing. Yet, in the circulation of commodities, mediated by money, the apparent exchange of equivalents somehow enables the money form of value to *grow*. C-M-C, the formula for commodity circulation mediated by money, develops into M-C-M', the formula for circulation of capital as *self-expanding value*. In this context, capital emerges as the independent substance that expands through successively assuming and then casting off the money and commodity forms.

Since circulation of commodities could not account for *surplus-value* as the origin of new capital, Marx turned to labour-power as the one commodity that simultaneously creates new value in the very act of being consumed. Hegel described the parties to a contract as 'equal to one another whatever the qualitative external difference of the things exchanged. Value is the universal in which the subjects of the contract participate'.[68] Marx replied that the wage contract involves only *formal equality*. The capitalist buys the use-value of labour-power – its ability to create new value – but he pays only the exchange-value, or the cost of physically reproducing a worker fit to work. No capitalist ever enters such a contract without first anticipating that the total value of the new commodities will exceed the wage paid for the labour-power. Capitalism is production for profit and for the self-expansion of value as capital. Marx's economic science replaced economic philosophy when the *alienation* discussed in the *1844 Manuscripts* became *exploitation* in *Capital*.

In the process of exploitation, the worker alienates his essential creative power to another, the capitalist, but the results are now scientifically measurable. The labour process, like the commodity, becomes a unity of opposites: on the

[68] Hegel 1967, §77.

one hand, it involves production of commodities as useful things; on the other, it is capitalist production of commodities as repositories of value and surplus-value.[69] Productive capital likewise comprises a duality of *constant* and *variable* components. Every act of production is expenditure of constant capital (c) and of variable capital (v). The former involves expenditure on machinery, fuel, materials, etc.; the latter, expenditure of capital advanced as wages. The value components of the resulting commodities, individually and in total, can then be designated as c + v + s, with (s) representing the surplus-value. In turn, s/v, the rate of surplus-value (or the rate of exploitation), becomes the initial determinant of the speed with which individual capitals and social capital as a whole accumulate.[70]

The *law of surplus-value,* a particular manifestation of the universal law of value, compels each capitalist to lengthen the working day, increase the intensity of labour, and raise labour productivity through using more advanced means of production. As technology advances, the *law of the rising organic composition of capital* results in a rising ratio c/v, as living labour is replaced by embodied labour. The result is a further contradiction: as capital expands, it appears to require more labour; but, as the organic composition rises, it also appears to require less labour. In Marx's words, 'the greater attraction of labourers by capital is accompanied by their greater repulsion'.[71] The result is 'a law of population peculiar to the capitalist mode of production', which specifies that in cyclical crises labour must periodically become relatively superfluous.

Masses of workers are thrown out of work by an excess of production relative to consumption. At the same time, cyclical 'repulsion' of labour becomes the precondition for its 'attraction' back into a new cycle of production and accumulation. Hegel had thought of unemployment as an inexplicable contingency and an affront to Reason. The logic of *Capital* pointed to a very different conclusion: the peculiar 'social reason' of capitalism objectively requires periodic mass unemployment in order to curtail wages, increase profits, and resume the self-expansion of value. Self-expanding value was the alien subject of the entire economic movement, reducing living labour to its object. As value became more concrete, labour must undergo ever-increasing

[69] Marx 1961, p. 197.
[70] Marx 1961, p. 531.
[71] Marx 1961, p. 631.

abstraction as a commodity to be summoned and dismissed according to value's own requirements.

Marx described the 'reserve army' of surplus population as 'a mass of human material always ready for exploitation' and a 'condition of existence of the capitalist mode of production'.[72] Hegel's universal self-determination of Reason now gave way to the prospect of endlessly repeated business cycles for as long as capitalism might exist:

> As the heavenly bodies, once thrown into a certain definite motion, always repeat this, so it is with social production as soon as it is once thrown into this movement of alternate expansion and contraction. Effects, in their turn, become causes, and the varying accidents of the whole process, which always reproduces its own conditions, take on the form of periodicity. When this periodicity is once consolidated, even Political Economy then sees that the production of a relative surplus-population . . . is a necessary condition of modern industry.[73]

The result is another expression of the universal law of value, namely, the objective *law of concentration and centralisation of capital*. In every crisis, weaker capitalists are consumed by the stronger. Marx says: 'One capitalist always kills many'[74] as 'The battle of competition is fought by cheapening of commodities'.[75] Throughout this cyclical process, the movement of capital appears as the actions of individual capitalists. But when 'a revolution in value' occurs, reducing costs through improved technology, inefficient capitalists also become superfluous. The law of value, as the expression of social reason, acts 'with the elemental force of a natural process'. '. . . [V]alue as capital acquires independent existence' and ultimately produces finance capital, which is disembodied and seems to be completely abstracted from production, where the real self-expansion of value occurs.[76] Even the capitalist turns out to be merely 'capital personified and endowed with consciousness and a will'.[77] The will that drives the process is an alien force that crushes workers and capitalists alike through the nature-like movement of things. Hegel's philosophical projection of the triumph of Reason is replaced by what appears

[72] Marx 1961, p. 632.
[73] Marx 1961, p. 633.
[74] Marx 1961, p. 763.
[75] Marx 1961, p. 626.
[76] Marx 1957, pp. 105–6.
[77] Marx 1961, p. 152.

to be a universe of chaos and contingency. The Rational has reverted to the Natural. The evil of Hegel's 'pauperized rabble' is inevitable.

At the same time as social capital approaches the extremity of abstraction, however, it simultaneously creates its own negation in the revolutionary force of the working class. Marx summarises the logic of *Capital* this way:

> Along with the constantly diminishing number of the magnates of capital, who usurp and monopolise all advantages of this process of transformation, grows the mass of misery, oppression, slavery, degradation, exploitation; but with this too grows the revolt of the working-class, a class always increasing in numbers, and disciplined, united, organised by the very mechanism of the process of capitalist production itself. The monopoly of capital becomes a fetter upon the mode of production. . . . Centralisation of the means of production and socialisation of labour at last reach a point where they become incompatible with their capitalist integument. This integument is burst asunder. The knell of capitalist private property sounds. The expropriators are expropriated.[78]

8. Capital points beyond itself

The internal contradictions of capitalism point beyond capitalism to the higher truth of communism. Capitalism creates within Hegel's system of needs, or what Marx called the *Realm of Necessity*, an objective necessity for expanding the *Realm of Freedom*. At the same time as capitalism creates the ultimate abstraction of social labour, it also creates the objective need for technologically sophisticated producers to manage the new means of production. Capitalism points beyond *abstract labour* and a reified *division of labour* to *universal labour*; that is, the social planning of individual labour that is multitalented. Existence will finally correspond with essence when human creativity is emancipated. In place of cyclical unemployment, communism will universally shorten the working day and bring 'the absolute working out of . . . creative potentialities . . . which makes . . . the development of all human powers as such the end in itself . . .'.[79] With production for use rather than exchange, there will remain no barriers to productivity – no fear of overproduction or

[78] Marx 1961, p. 763.
[79] Marx 1973, p. 488.

falling profits. Embodied labour will increasingly be replaced by embodied reason in the form of advancing technology. Scientific knowledge, objectively the highest form of social knowledge, will replace philosophy at the same time as economic planning will replace political economy:

> . . . to the degree that large industry develops, the creation of real wealth comes to depend less on labour time and on the amount of labour employed than on the power of the agencies set in motion during labour time, whose 'powerful effectiveness' is itself . . . out of all proportion to the direct labour time spent on their production, but depends rather on the general state of science and on the progress of technology, or the application of this science to production . . . Labour no longer appears so much to be included within the production process; rather, the human being comes to relate more as watchman and regulator to the production process itself. . . . He steps to the side of the production process instead of being its chief actor.[80]

Scientific production is positive transcendence of the abstraction of labour. As the need to invest in things diminishes, the possibility will increase for investing in people as the highest form of fixed capital.[81] If freely associated producers are to 'regulate' scientific forces of production, they must move in the direction of universal workers with universal knowledge. A concrete whole will require conscious reintegration of living labour with embodied labour; socialisation of the means of production will be the condition for the self-determined social labour of the associated producers. The result will be 'the human being who has become' – one 'in whose head exists the accumulated knowledge of society'.[82]

All that was previously alien and external will finally be re-appropriated 'in here'. Real wealth will be non-labour time; contrary to the inverted logic of capital, the most valuable production will be that requiring the least expenditure of living labour. Since the capitalist law of value measures price and profit in terms of labour, which alone creates surplus-value, gradual displacement of living labour will bring transcendence of the law of value and all of its particular forms of expression. The logic of *Capital* will culminate in the self-negation of capital as an abstract totality of self-expanding value:

[80] Marx 1973, pp. 704–5.
[81] Marx 1973, p. 712.
[82] Marx 1973, p. 712.

> As soon as labour in the direct form has ceased to be the great well-spring of wealth, labour time ceases and must cease to be its measure, and hence exchange value [must cease to be the measure] of use value. . . . With that, production based on exchange value breaks down, and the direct, material production is stripped of the form of penury and antithesis. The free development of individualities, and . . . the general reduction of the necessary labour of society to a minimum . . . then corresponds to the artistic, scientific, etc. development of the individuals in the time set free, and with the means created, for all of them.[83]

9. Maksakovsky: from the abstract toward the concrete

Hegel's economic philosophy and Marx's economic science represent the 'bookends' for Pavel Maksakovsky's theory of the capitalist cycle. Marx translated Hegelian dialectic into a logic that expresses the inner necessity of capitalism and also points beyond capitalism. The realisation of reason, as human self-determination, requires an economic plan, which is Marx's analogue for the laws of the Hegelian state. When the associated producers rationally lay down their own plan, reason will become transparent in a practical, concrete universal of self-determination. The final truth of capitalism is not what capitalism is, but what it must become. From this perspective, the capitalist cycle, as a process of becoming, ceases to be a matter of contingency and becomes a requirement of reason. Pavel Maksakovsky's *The Capitalist Cycle* is a search for the inner dialectical reason that forms the material contradictions of the capitalist system and, at the same time, points beyond those contradictions to proletarian revolution and communism.

In the first chapter of *The Capitalist Cycle*, Maksakovsky criticises bourgeois economists for attempting to *impose* reason on capitalism by scrutinising it *'from the outside'*. By statistically representing the system's surface movements, economists search for patterns that might lead to predictability. If each capitalist could better anticipate the activities of all others, bourgeois economists hope the implication will be to dampen cyclical fluctuations. Through the coordinating activity of the state and monetary authorities, capitalism will become more 'organised'. Maksakovsky argues that this approach is not only incorrect methodologically – it begins with events on the surface rather than

[83] Marx 1973, pp. 705–6.

inner causes – but is also driven by the false hope that capitalism tends towards general equilibrium, or at least a *moving equilibrium* over time, against which 'deviations' may be measured and then corrected. Maksakovsky replies that capitalism, as *a moving system of contradictions*, does indeed manifest an uninterrupted tendency toward equilibrium, but this tendency repeatedly exhausts itself in continuous struggle with other, opposing, tendencies, which determine the inevitability of cycles and crises. *The Capitalist Cycle* begins and ends with the conviction that bourgeois concepts of equilibrium and organised capitalism are ideological fantasies.

These fantasies present themselves as science insofar as they presuppose measurement and manipulation of data in the form of graphs and equations. But as Hegel commented in his *Logic*, science operates at the level of Understanding, not of Reason: 'Thought, as *Understanding*, sticks to the fixity of characters and their distinctness from one another: every such limited abstract it treats as having a subsistence and being of its own'.[84] Understanding treats things merely in their simplicity, assuming their steady, fixed, and permanent qualities. In economic terms, this means nothing more than the fact that tons of steel may be aggregated in terms of total tonnage on the assumption that steel is steel; it is self-identical in its sameness. Alternatively, tons of steel may be measured in terms of price for a similar reason: so many identical tons of steel will have a determinate total price because each ton has the same price as any other.

Hegel thought Reason, as speculative philosophy, has a different and higher task. Since Understanding deals with things that are fixed, it is pre-dialectical. Reason, in contrast, goes beyond Understanding to apprehend the mediating processes whereby discrete *units* become the concrete *totality*. Reason grasps things in their ideal, or logical, movement, and for precisely this reason it apprehends truths that are universal and supersede the limitations of things. Viewing bourgeois economic science in these terms, Maksakovsky thought that it was inherently contradictory. It looks for totality with a form of thought that is unable, by its very nature, to conceive of totality, only of *separate totals*.

Maksakovsky explains these limitations of empiricism in his chapter on methodology. While acknowledging the secondary usefulness of empirical research, he insists, like Marx, that study of 'real' capitalism must *begin* with

[84] Hegel 1975, §80.

the logical relations that prevail between economic laws and categories in conditions of 'pure' capitalism, abstracted from all 'exogenous' factors and influences emanating from non-capitalist forms of production. In the following chapter on 'real reproduction' he turns, therefore, to the logic of *Capital* as the only rational method for conceiving capitalism in the totality of its contradictory interconnections. At first glance, the flaw of capitalism seems to be that individual capitals – like abstract individual wills at the beginning of Hegel's *Philosophy of Right* – will cancel each other out in a state of chaos. Maksakovsky notes that 'The capitalist economy is split into countless capitals, and the system has no single subject – it is not a consciously established *teleological* whole ...'.[85] But he adds that

> ... despite its apparent incoherence, the capitalist economy, like any other, represents a single whole that is composed of closely connected, interacting parts. The complex of individual capitals manifests from within itself a number of objective moments that oppose each other as the expressions of an irreversible, conditioning law. From the close interaction of these individual capitals arises the movement of social capital *as a whole*, which in turn dissolves into these distinct circuits as its constituent links.[86]

Social capital is objectively a whole, but not subjectively. It periodically dissolves into abstract disarray because the inherent 'reason' of the entire system is foreign to each individual capital. The law of value, articulating social reason as the requirement of proportional production, affirms its 'right' only after contradictions have matured between different branches of production in the form of a cyclical crisis.[87] As Marx said in *Grundrisse*, a universal self-coordinating capital is a 'non-thing'.[88] Each capital confronts other capitals as alien to itself, and in their 'reciprocal repulsion' all of them are held together by the universal law of value, acting through the ultimate force of cyclical crises. Like Marx, Maksakovsky sees the crisis as the one fleeting moment in the entire cycle when the implicit reason of the system explicitly asserts itself and compels elements that have fallen apart to reassemble in order that the cycle of reproduction might resume.

The crisis acts as the logical (and real) force that compels the diverse elements

[85] Maksakovsky 1929, p. 46 (p. 48 in this volume).
[86] Maksakovsky 1929, p. 47 (pp. 49–50 in this volume).
[87] Maksakovsky 1929, p. 97.
[88] Marx 1973, p. 421 (p. 104 in this volume).

of social capital to return to objectively necessary relationships of internal *proportionality*. The condition of proportionality is central to Maksakovsky's theory. It expresses the objectively necessary relationship that must prevail between individual sectors of the economy if they are to interact in expanded reproduction. Marx dealt with the requirement of proportionality throughout *Capital*. In the opening chapter of Volume I, he noted that every society must apportion its labour in relation to its competing needs. Even Robinson Crusoe would have to 'apportion his time accurately between his different kinds of work'.[89] In Volume II of *Capital*, Marx portrayed the necessary proportions of reproduction by dividing the entire economy into two departments: one producing means of production, the other producing consumer goods. Marx used this scheme to illustrate both simple reproduction – an abstract 'model' of capitalist stability – and also stable growth, or a 'model' of the expanded reproduction of value.

The reproduction schemes reflected real relations between the two departments, but Maksakovsky's originality comes in his observation that they were also constructed at a level of abstraction that excluded the possibility of cycles or crises. In specific observations throughout his work, Marx did *comment* on the causes and the inevitability of crises, but in his formal models he omitted, among other things, prices, changes in technology, and the effects of credit and financial markets. The reproduction schemes assumed, in other words, that all commodities exchange according to their values, or on the basis of the socially necessary labour expended in producing them, including both living labour and labour embodied in machinery and materials. Only in Volume III of *Capital* were these assumptions systematically lifted. But, since Volumes II and III were both incomplete works, edited by Engels and published after Marx's death, Maksakovsky undertook to write a final chapter in the Marxist theory of expanded reproduction.

As distinct from Marx's models, concrete capitalist reproduction always involves *disproportionality*, or multiple contradictions between the various elements of the total process. Marx's models treated capitalist laws in their *constitutive* form; they showed how the logic of capital constitutes, or forms, reproduction at a high level of abstraction. But Marx only constructed the models in order to specify more clearly the ways in which real capitalism continuously departs from the conditions of an abstract, moving equilibrium.

[89] Marx 1961, p. 76.

For this more concrete purpose, Marx traced the activity of laws in their *regulative* form, that is, the manner in which they 'cause', set limits to, and ultimately correct disproportions in social production. This is the task that Maksakovsky resumes. It requires 'a transition from the general resolution of the problem of social reproduction to the real pattern of this process'.[90] Maksakovsky does this by systematically lifting, one by one, the limiting assumptions that Marx built into the abstract schemes of reproduction.

The *first step* toward more concrete capitalism is to translate 'pure value relations into the form of the price of production'.[91] If analysis remains at the abstract level of value relations, the effect is to assume that all exchanges take place in accordance with the amounts of socially necessary labour embodied, resulting in what Maksakovsky calls 'equilibrium' of labour. But since only living labour creates surplus-value, this would also mean that branches using relatively more constant capital (machinery and materials) than others would receive a correspondingly lower rate of profit. In real reproduction, surplus-value is redistributed between branches in the form of a tendency toward an average rate of profit. An average profit rate, in turn, implies a change in the rate at which some commodities exchange for others. The result is what Marx called the 'price of production', which emerges as the 'equilibrium' condition for non-cyclical reproduction. Moving one step further toward the concrete, the price of production in turn gives way to market price, reflecting supply and demand. In *Grundrisse,* Marx wrote that value is only a 'law of the motions'[92] for market price. Value does not 'set' price; it is the axis about which prices revolve. The way in which this movement begins is through market competition between capitals. Capitals move from one branch of production to another in search of a higher rate of profit. This means that the *second step* required in making Marx's models more concrete is to introduce capitalist competition.

The *third step* needed in the move toward concrete capitalism is to incorporate technological change as the highest form of capitalist competition. At this stage, a distinction must be made between *fixed* capital and *circulating* capital. The latter, involving elements such as fuel and materials, must be regularly and predictably replaced in each round of production. Fixed capital, in contrast,

---

[90] Maksakovsky 1929, p. 51 (p. 54 in this volume).
[91] Ibid. (p. 55 in this volume).
[92] Marx 1973, p. 137.

refers to more durable capital items such as buildings and machinery. Fixed capital has a lifetime that extends over many rounds of production, and each element of fixed capital also has a lifetime different from the others. If each element of fixed capital were replaced only after its physical exhaustion, this would mean generalised randomness in reproduction as a whole. Since no such randomness occurs in concrete capitalism, the key issue now emerges: How is the reproduction of fixed capital determined in such manner that it repeatedly produces cycles of expansion, crisis, and depression? When Maksakovsky turns to the cyclical movement of concrete capitalism, he provides this brief conceptual roadmap to point the way:

> The cyclical character of capitalist development makes itself felt only . . . when we include the role of fixed capital. The unique circulation of fixed capital, or the inevitability of its massive renovation at a single stroke due to periodic changes in the technology of production – this is the basic condition for the 'manifestation' of a cycle. Specific waves of capitalist competition develop because of a massive renovation of fixed capital, which disrupts both the 'harmony' between market 'demand' and 'supply', and also 'proportionality' in the distribution of capitals. The result is overcapitalisation, with social production growing more rapidly than effective demand. Crashes occur and are repeated periodically. They mature dialectically when the regulating influence of the laws of 'equilibrium' is postponed through a prolonged detachment of prices from the price of production and value.[93]

10. The *irrationality* of prices

One of the most unique features of Maksakovsky's explanation of the capitalist cycle is his treatment of the price system. In bourgeois economics, the price system represents what Adam Smith called the 'invisible hand' of the market. Smith's metaphor has since been elaborated in exhaustive mathematical detail to attribute to the market a capacity to gravitate forever toward equilibrium. Spontaneous price adjustments are said to evoke continuous marginal adjustments between individual actors. Market theory treats prices as a kind of 'shorthand' that compensates for lack of perfect knowledge. In their mutual ignorance and indifference, economic actors objectively 'communicate' through

[93] Maksakovsky 1929, p. 55 (p. 59 in this volume).

spontaneous changes of relative prices. This preoccupation with the 'informative' function of prices occludes even the possibility of cyclical crises.

Marx associated such magical beliefs with the *fetishism* of commodities. Far from being the means of promoting equilibrium, Marx thought of market prices as 'irrational' departures from the price of production, which is the condition of proportionality. Maksakovsky speaks of market prices as being irrational for the same reason. Upward deviations of prices from values are the signal that precipitates overcapitalisation, or excessive investments in fixed capital; irrational price declines, in turn, precipitate premature destruction of capital and mass unemployment. The cyclical movement necessarily arises from the fact that *today's prices*, leaving aside speculation, are merely a 'snapshot' of the consequences of *past actions*. Even more irrational is that fact that today's prices, in determining *today's investments*, also determine *tomorrow's production*. How can tomorrow's production possibly be *rationally* determined by today's prices, which are themselves determined by investment decisions that occurred up to a decade earlier – at the beginning of the previous cycle? For Maksakovsky, the only possible result is a production cycle that manifests as much 'rationality' as a cat chasing its own tail. When all capitalists simultaneously invest in response to rising prices, they must all face the future consequence of their individual actions in recurrent social catastrophes of 'overproduction'. The speculative activity of finance capital only facilitates and amplifies this irrationality already inherent in investment.

Prices may be the means by which capitalists 'communicate', but Maksakovsky treats prices as symbols that simultaneously articulate the contradictions found throughout capitalism as a whole. Prices are always in the *here and now* of market immediacy, whereas growth of production always involves a *time lag* that reflects the gestation period of investments – the time between the beginning of new construction and the eventual expansion of output. This means that the language of market supply and demand must always tend to contradict the language of production – just as the same sentence cannot speak simultaneously in both past and present tenses. The crisis is the singular moment of truth when this linguistic duplicity ends. In the seeming irrationality of the crisis, production superimposes its objective necessity upon transitory market prices. At the cost of destroying 'redundant' productive forces, the law of value re-establishes conditions of proportionality needed to resume the next cycle of growth.

11. Conclusion

With this metaphor of the two contradictory languages, Maksakovsky's analysis of the capitalist cycle has the effect of referring us back to the beginnings of philosophy. *The Capitalist Cycle* is an elaborately conceived and highly technical work in economic theory. Like *Capital* itself, however, the book replays, in the idiom of economics, philosophical themes that stretch as far back as Plato and Aristotle. The surface of the book is economic theory, but its subtext and inner logic is philosophy. At the beginning of philosophy, Aristotle claimed that reason is inseparable from language. Language is the medium of thought, and thought alone – not instinct – can undertake to find ethical truth. Aristotle wrote in the *Politics*: 'language serves to declare . . . what is just and what is unjust. It is the peculiarity of man . . . that he alone possesses a perception of good and evil, of the just and the unjust . . .; and it is association [in a common perception] of these things which makes a family and a polis'.[94]

Hegel's *Philosophy of Right* sought to restore the ethical unity of the Greek polis through overcoming the effects of the modern division of labour and the capitalist market. In face of this new reality, Hegel saw the need for language itself to make the dialectical journey from the abstract to the concrete. Hegel first introduced language as the most abstract mode of appropriating the natural world. Through 'naming' things, we stamp our own spirit upon them. Our first active relationship to nature involves making it a realm of meanings that we ourselves bestow: 'This is the primal creativity exercised by Spirit. Adam gave a name to all things. This is the sovereign right [of Spirit], its primal taking-possession of all nature – or the creation of nature out of Spirit [itself]'.[95]

Spirit takes 'possession' of the world through language, but this cognitive activity must point beyond itself to the practical activity of labour, through which we make the world ours by embodying our own Reason in the thing. The ensuing dialectic of objectification, alienation and re-appropriation – of finding ourselves in the world we make – becomes the common theme both of Hegelian economic philosophy and of Marxist economic science. In Hegel's *Philosophy of Right*, language, as 'the most worthy medium for the expression of our mental ideas',[96] returns from its initial abstraction as the supreme

94 Aristotle 1961, 1253a §11–12.
95 Hegel 1983, p. 89.
96 Hegel 1967, §78.

medium through which universal Ideas of ethical life can be articulated. For Hegel, the language of the laws was the highest expression of social Reason.

When Marx reinterpreted Hegel's philosophical economics, the initial result appeared to be a return to absolute contingency: the 'unnamed' and unknown forces of the market frustrated human reason just like the original, elemental forces of nature. Marx then resumed Hegel's dialectic in material terms: he *named* market forces as economic categories – beginning with the commodity, value, and money – and then he discovered the logic that connected the categories into a whole. Capitalism may be law-governed, but its 'reason' also acts behind our backs and always after the fact. The social necessity of labour is determined only after the commodity enters the market, where its exchange-value – or whether it even has exchange-value – will be judged. Marx said: 'In capitalist society . . . where social reason always asserts itself only *post festum* great disturbances may and must constantly occur'.[97]

Marx believed the unique human attribute was the capacity to posit a future and to make it real. This potential was evident from the first act of human labour, which is always teleological. In the *1844 Manuscripts*, Marx said: 'Man makes his life-activity itself the object of his will and of his consciousness. . . . Conscious life-activity directly distinguishes man from animal life-activity'.[98] In *Capital* the same idea recurs:

> We pre-suppose labour in a form that stamps it as exclusively human. A spider conducts operations that resemble those of a weaver, and a bee puts to shame many an architect. . . . But what distinguishes the worst architect from the best of bees is this, that the architect raises his structure in imagination before he erects it in reality. At the end of every labour-process we get a result that already existed in the imagination of the labourer at its commencement.[99]

Human labour is purposeful 'by nature', but individual labours have the potential to cancel each other out until they are consciously integrated. Marx's economic science led back to Hegel's conclusion that we must lay down the law to ourselves in order to fulfil the requirements of reason. An economic plan is not merely a requirement of efficiency; it is the logical precondition

---

[97] Marx 1957, p. 315.
[98] Tucker 1978, p. 76.
[99] Marx 1961, p. 178.

for humans to become human. Only with a scientific plan of production can human beings fulfil their destiny, which is to be both the 'authors' and 'actors' in their own historical drama.[100]

Pavel Maksakovsky's book follows the logic of *Capital* in pursuing the meaning of reason and the conditions for self-determination. His technical economics leads to the discovery that, in the absence of a plan, the highest expression of social reason comes precisely in the catastrophic destruction of a cyclical crisis. A crisis 'judges' past investments by erasing redundant capitals and restoring, if only for a passing moment, the conditions of proportionality within and between the two departments of the economy. But in a larger context, each crisis also points toward a human future, where abstract labour will finally be replaced by the emancipated activity of freely associated producers. If we think in terms of Maksakovsky's metaphor of the two languages of the capitalist market, we can say that a scientific plan will speak a different language entirely – a new, coherent, and non-contradictory language of social self-determination through purposes that will simultaneously be 'mine' and 'ours'.

Until *socialist revolution* overcomes the dualities and duplicities of capitalism, Maksakovsky concludes that the best that reason can accomplish is a succession of *technological revolutions*, which serve as the defining moments of particular economic crises that will ultimately lead to the crash of the capitalist *system* as a whole. The transformative power of technological change frames Maksakovsky's entire argument: it links his economic science back to the philosophical subtext that Marx took over from Hegel, and simultaneously forward to the rational self-organisation of community in communism. Technological change is not an accident, a merely exogenous and contingent event; instead, the historical advance to a higher level of technology is the essential achievement of each cycle, its 'truth' in Hegelian terms. In the material contradictions that compulsively require each capitalist to reduce production costs in the hope of surviving the crisis, Maksakovsky finds higher rational purpose.

Marx spoke of technology as the power of knowledge objectified. Maksakovsky says the law of value negates old technology through moral-technical (not merely physical) wear; and new technologies incorporate the

[100] Marx 1963, p. 98.

'lessons'[101] of each crisis when the 'spirit' of value abandons and replaces obsolescent fixed capital.[102] Emptied of spirit, old enterprises remain behind as derelict 'scrap metal'.[103] The inner logic of capitalism articulates the requirements of reason when it lays down the decree that 'the only way out [of each cycle] is to pass to the next level of technology'.[104] Mature capitalism only appears to be *'the most developed anarchy of economic growth'*; the reality that lies behind and forms this anarchy is always *'law-governed regularity'*.[105] At work through all the contradictions of capitalism is the ultimate 'right' of human reason to create a higher civilisation. Maksakovsky wrote *The Capitalist Cycle* in the hope that Marxist economic science would give voice to the revolutionary 'spirit of the times'.[106] In an age of imperialism, revolution, and war, he hoped his reinterpretation of Marxist economic theory would confirm the objectively logical necessity of better times to come.

By comparison with Maksakovsky's time, our own seems disenchanted and devoid of 'spiritual' purpose. Soviet-style 'state socialism' has collapsed, and globalised capitalism strives to escape the limitations of physical embodiment by endlessly multiplying what Maksakovsky called 'dancing shadows at the ghostly heights of the money market'.[107] In these circumstances, we cannot expect the laws of capitalism to 'speak' to us just as they did to Maksakovsky in 1928. An economy characterised by 'high technology', an interventionist state bureaucracy, a technocratic monetary authority, a vastly expanded service industry, and electronically mediated finance capital on a global scale, can hardly be expected to conform entirely to the patterns that Maksakovsky saw in an earlier stage of industrial capitalism, which was determined by heavy manufacturing.

Nevertheless, the excesses of the 'dot.com' bubble have reaffirmed the dialectical truth that each 'new economy' reproduces at a higher level the contradictions of the 'old'. In that sense, we might say that Maksakovsky's work still expresses 'the spirit of the times'. As a powerful and provocative work of economic theory, it sustains the philosophical ambition of Hegel and

[101] Maksakovsky 1929, p. 95 (p. 102 in this volume).
[102] Maksakovsky 1929, p. 90 (p. 96 in this volume).
[103] Maksakovsky 1929, p. 96 (p. 102 in this volume).
[104] Maksakovsky 1929, p. 89 (p. 95 in this volume).
[105] Maksakovsky 1929, p. 98 (p. 105 in this volume).
[106] Maksakovsky 1929, p. 132 (p. 144 in this volume).
[107] Maksakovsky 1929, p. 21 (p. 19 in this volume).

Marx to create a world that will ultimately satisfy the requirements of reason. In our own age of postmodern despair, Pavel Maksakovsky encourages us to reach beyond ourselves toward what reason says we must become.

References

Aristotle 1961, *The Politics*, translated with an introduction, notes and appendixes by Ernest Barker, Oxford: Oxford University Press.

Behrendt, Lutz-Dieter 1997, 'Die Institute der Roten Professur: Kaderschmieden der sovjetischen Parteiintelligenz (1921–1938)', *Jahrbücher für Geschichte Ost europas*, 45, 4: 597–621.

David-Fox, Michael 1997, *Revolution of the Mind: Higher Learning Among the Bolsheviks, 1918–1929*, Ithaca: Cornell University Press.

Day, Richard B. 1981, *The 'Crisis' and the 'Crash': Soviet Studies of the West (1917–1939)*, London: NLB.

Day, Richard B. 1989, 'Hegel, Marx, Lukacs: The Dialectic of Freedom and Necessity', *History of European Ideas*, 11: 907–34.

Demin, A.A., N.V. Raskov and L.D. Shirokorad (eds.) 1989, *Istoriya politicheskoi ekonomii kapitalizma*, Leningrad: Izdatel'stvo Leningradskovo Universiteta.

Guyer, Paul 1993, 'Thought and Being: Hegel's Critique of Kant's Theoretical Philosophy', in *Cambridge Companion to Hegel*, edited by Frederick C. Beiser, Cambridge: Cambridge University Press.

Hegel, Georg Wilhelm Friedrich 1967, *Hegel's Philosophy of Right*, translated by T.M. Knox, Oxford: Oxford University Press.

Hegel, Georg Wilhelm Friedrich 1975, *Hegel's Logic*, translated by William Wallace, Oxford: Oxford University Press.

Hegel, Georg Wilhelm Friedrich 1979, *System of Ethical Life (1802/3) and First Philosophy of Spirit (Part III of the System of Speculative Philosophy (1803/4)*, edited and translated by H.S. Harris and T.M. Knox, Albany: State University of New York Press.

Hegel, Georg Wilhelm Friedrich 1983, *Hegel and the Human Spirit: A Translation of the Jena Lectures on the Philosophy of Spirit (1805–6)*, translated with commentary by Leo Rauch, Detroit: Wayne State University Press.

Lenin, Vladimir I. 1961, *Collected Works*, Volume 38, Moscow: Foreign Languages Publishing House.

Lenin, Vladimir I. 1966, *Collected Works*, Volume 33, Moscow: Foreign Languages Publishing House.

Maksakovsky, Pavel V. 1928, 'K teorii tsikla i dinamiki sovetskovo khozyaistva', *Bol'shevik*, 6: 8–28 and 7: 9–19.

Maksakovsky, Pavel V. 1929, *Kapitalisticheskii tsikl: ocherk Marksistskoi teorii tsikla*, Moscow: Izdatel'stvo Kommunisticheskoi Akademii.

Marx, Karl 1957, *Capital*, Volume I, Moscow: Foreign Languages Publishing House.

Marx, Karl 1961, *Capital*, Volume II, Moscow: Foreign Languages Publishing House.

Marx, Karl 1963, *The Poverty of Philosophy*, New York: International Publishers.

Marx, Karl 1970, *Critique of Hegel's 'Philosophy of Right'*, translated by Annette Jolin and Joseph O'Malley with introduction and notes by James O'Malley, Cambridge: Cambridge University Press.

Marx, Karl 1973, *Grundrisse: Foundations of the Critique of Political Economy*, translated with foreword by Martin Nicolaus, New York: Vintage.

Mendel'son, Abram S. 1928, *Problema kon'yunktury: Diskussiya v Kommunisticheskoi Akademii*, Moscow: Izdatel'stvo Kommunisticheskoi Akademii.

Plato 1962, *The Republic*, translated with introduction and notes by Francis Macdonald Cornford, Oxford: Oxford University Press.

Preobrazhensky, Evgeny A. 1965, *The New Economics*, translated by Brian Pearce, Oxford: Clarendon Press.

Preobrazhensky, Evgeny A. and Nikolai I. Bukharin 1969, *The ABC of Communism*, translated by Eden and Cedar Paul, Harmondsworth: Penguin.

Preobrazhensky, Evgeny A. 1973, *From the New Economic Policy to Socialism*, translated by Brian Pearce, London: New Park.

Preobrazhensky, Evgeny A. 1979, *The Crisis of Soviet Industrialization*, translated by Donald Filtzer, Armonk: M.E. Sharpe.

Preobrazhensky, Evgeny A. 1985, *The Decline of* Capitalism, translated with introduction by Richard B. Day, Armonk: M.E. Sharpe.

Rubin, Isaak I. 1982, *Essays on Marx's Theory of Value*, translated by Miloš Samardžija and Fredy Perlman, Montreal: Black Rose.

Tucker, Robert C. (ed) 1978, *The Marx-Engels Reader*, Second Edition, New York: W.W. Norton.

Pavel V. Maksakovsky

The Capitalist Cycle

An Essay on the Marxist Theory of the Cycle

Foreword

The work of comrade Maksakovsky is incomplete. It was presented in the autumn of 1927 as a report to the seminar on the theory of reproduction held at the Institute of Red Professors. I had frequent opportunities to discuss with comrade Maksakovsky both the problems that he dealt with and the proposed solutions. I suggested that he continue his work and prepare it for publication. Death has cut short his young life, and our plans were not fulfilled. But even in its incomplete form, the work is of such interest that Maksakovsky's comrades in the seminar and I myself, as leader of the seminar, decided that it must be published, especially now, when there is such growing interest in problems associated with the general theory of the cycle, that is, with problems of the cycle, the crisis, and the conjuncture.

On the surface, comrade Maksakovsky deals with two themes: the problem of the cycle and the problem of the conjuncture. However, the emphasis is on the first theme, and that is where attention is concentrated. The problem of the conjuncture is taken to be identical to the problem of the cycle; hence, the work frequently uses the term 'conjunctural cycle'. Comrade Maksakovsky's work poses the problem of the capitalist cycle and clearly outlines the contours of its theoretical resolution. Comrade Maksakovsky explored the characteristics of the cycle's distinct phases, but he paid relatively less attention to the crisis, as the cycle's central phase, precisely because so much work has already been done on the theory of the crisis. Attention is focused mainly on the remaining phases of the capitalist cycle and on the mechanism whereby each phase is transformed into the next one.

There are a number of controversial assertions made concerning the connection between the conjuncture and the cycle, the methodological presuppositions of a theory of the conjuncture, and so forth. I do not think it is necessary for me to mention them all or to compare comrade Maksakovsky's viewpoint with other positions that differ from his. Nevertheless, I did think that it was appropriate for me to exercise my prerogative as editor and to correct what I regarded as certain debatable and occasionally even incorrect formulations.

The work is written so clearly, with such talent, and at such a high level of theoretical sophistication that even comrade Maksakovsky's mistakes are interesting and instructive. The book's impressive theoretical vitality, the militant revolutionary spirit that pervades this deeply theoretical work, and its excellent form – all of these attributes cause me to regard *The Capitalist Cycle* as one of the very best works recently written on questions concerning the general theory of reproduction.

In the person of comrade Maksakovsky, who died at such a young age, we have lost a major Marxist theoretical force.

A. Mendel'son

Introduction[1]

Study of the capitalist system's dynamic is attracting extraordinary interest due to the commercial-industrial crises that periodically shake the system's foundations. The harmonious illusions of youthful capitalism have long ago vanished into oblivion. Even the 'spirit' of capitalist exchange and wealth has periodically forsaken its commodity integument, putting the fear of God – not to mention losses – into ordinary capitalists, while simultaneously provoking intense interest on the part of their ideologists.

Bourgeois economic research into these problems can be divided into two periods: first, economists attempted to resolve the problem of crises as such; then they focused attention mainly on questions of capitalism's general dynamic. Bourgeois economics was theoretically incapable of comprehending the crisis. Its theoretical arsenal lacked an appropriate method, the necessary objectivity, and a proper sociological grounding. In these circumstances, bourgeois economics turned all the more readily to study of the total dynamic, lumping together the various processes under one general term – the 'conjuncture'. The theoretically unresolved problem of crises was simply carried over into the new

[1] [*Translator's note*: Except where otherwise indicated, footnotes and textual insertions in square brackets are the translator's. For readers' convenience, I give page references to English-language editions of the sources cited by Maksakovsky whenever possible. Where there are minor differences between the Russian and English translations – for example, of texts such as *Capital* – I give the English-language reference but occasionally follow the Russian text used by Maksakovsky.]

problem of the conjuncture. The crisis came to be regarded as merely a 'minor' component of the commercial-industrial cycle. Its causes were thought to depend directly on even more fundamental causes that give rise to the conjuncture. Cassel writes: 'The focus of the study is not crises, as discrete events, but changes in the conjuncture as a whole, as an integrated and continuous movement of the economy'.[2] From this point of view, investigation focuses not on specific contradictions of the capitalist system that erupt in the form of crises, but rather on 'the causal connection between the different factors that condition the wave-like movement of the economy and that are, at the same time, conditioned by this movement'.[3]

The problem of crises was submerged in the problem of the conjuncture. The effect was to canonise the crisis and treat it as a normal phenomenon of capitalist production due to the way economic factors interact. Bourgeois economics theoretically smoothed over and brushed aside capitalist contradictions of enormous power, as if to restore to the capitalist world its former youthful confidence in the unshakeable stability of its economic foundations. The idea of dissolving the problem of crises into the problem of the conjuncture was formulated clearly by Sombart, one of the most outstanding bourgeois economists, while Röpke provided the most vulgar and simplified formulation of the same idea.[4]

Only one small step remained between this approach and the idea of reforming the capitalist economy from within. Bourgeois economists would not have been fully committed representatives of their own class had they

---

[2] Cassel 1925, p. 3. [The Swedish economist Gustav Cassel is best known for work on international monetary problems after the First World War and for his theories of price and interest. He associated the cycle with a declining share of entrepreneurial income during the expansion, causing slower savings and capital formation at the same time as the share of capital goods in the total social product is increasing. His *Theoretische Sozialökonomie* (Leipzig, 1918) was translated into English by Joseph McCabe and published by T.F. Unwin in 1923 as *The Theory of Social Economy*. Harcourt, Brace published another translation by S.L. Barron in 1932. Cassel's work is briefly summarized in Hutchison 1966, pp. 245–50.]

[3] Cassel 1925, p. 4.

[4] 'Not a single modern author any longer attempts seriously to explain crises apart from the phenomenon of the conjuncture', 'and a theory of crises has no basis apart from the theory of the conjuncture'. See *Kon'yunktura*, 1927, pp. 7 and 26. [Maksakovsky is quoting a Russian translation of Wilhelm Röpke, *Die Konjunktur*, 1922. Röpke was a market fundamentalist of the Austrian school who, until his death in 1966, wrote widely on issues in economic, social, and political theory. He influenced post-war German economic reform and also the growth of American neoconservatism. One of his best-known works is his textbook, *The Economics of the Free Society* (Chicago: Henry Regnery Company, 1963), first published in German in 1937.]

not put forth this notion. Having submerged the problem of the crisis in the problem of the conjuncture, and having minimised capitalist contradictions, they now posed the problem of overcoming those same contradictions in practice. The background of this strategic plan had two dimensions: first, the conviction that crises have become more moderate in recent decades; and second, the developing ideology of finance capitalism. The most recent view of capitalism involves constructing 'an organised society in antagonistic form'.[5] This is the thinking that motivates contemporary study of the capitalist dynamic. The common ambition that coordinates research efforts by different bourgeois schools of thought is to predict the conjuncture by consolidating individual economic indicators into a single system that will project law-governed changes in the economic weather. By developing an economic barometer, bourgeois science hopes to provide each individual capitalist with certain behavioural guidelines that will be appropriate for whatever sphere of the production process in which he is involved. In this way, each capitalist is to be able to avoid errors and excesses by consciously foreseeing the consequences of his economic actions. All the mighty levers of the capitalist system – including the state, trusts, and so forth – are to conduct a deliberate conjunctural policy that will promote national economic interests. The projected effect of these efforts at coordination is to 'smooth out' the conjuncture, moderate its turning points, and eliminate its most specific phenomenon, the crisis, which is considered an eyesore in an otherwise 'well-appointed' system. Just as the springs of an automobile cushion the bumps as it speeds along the road, so economic shocks and abrupt changes are to be replaced by more modest ups and downs.[6] Capitalist society is to emancipate itself and take the driver's seat in determining its own economic process.

This goal determines both the work programme of bourgeois economics and, in large measure, its method. For the moment, we shall not dwell on the utopian character of this programme or the weaknesses of the scientific

[5] [The reference is to Hilferding 1981, pp. 234–5. Hilferding was an eminent Marxist theorist before World War I and an intellectual leader of German Social Democracy. He was Minister of Finance in two German governments during the 1920s. He fled Germany after Hitler came to power, but was ultimately handed over to the Nazis by the French Vichy authorities and died from Gestapo torture in 1941. Both implicit and explicit references to Hilferding's work recur throughout Maksakovsky's book and are noted in the translator's footnotes.]

[6] Paul Mombert 1924, p. 157. [This is a Russian translation of Paul Mombert, *Einfuhrung in das Studium der Konjunktur*, 1921.]

method used by bourgeois researchers and system builders. We shall have more to say on those matters later.

For now, it is important to establish two things: 1) the character and nature of the dynamic economic processes observed in the capitalist economy; and 2) which of these must be included in our investigation and why. In other words, we must accurately specify what is meant by the concept of the conjuncture, and we must also provide a sense (and that is all, for the time being) of which economic processes are, and may be, included in this concept.

Bourgeois economics recognises the following dynamic processes in the capitalist economy: 1) secular trends; 2) long cycles; 3) short (or medium-length) cycles; 4) partial, seasonal fluctuations, and so on. However, not every school accepts the existence of all of these processes, and even more fanciful differences emerge over which of them should be included in the theory of the conjuncture. Some economists expand the concept of the conjuncture to include analysis of every dynamic process in the capitalist economy, including even the social conditions that affect reproduction (Wagner, and to some degree Mombert). Others include all processes except long cycles and secular trends (Röpke). A third group includes short cycles and sectoral conjunctures (Pervushin). And a fourth group, which is the most numerous and widely respected, including in its ranks the most prominent system builders and theorists of the conjuncture, restricts conjuncture theory to studying the nature of short cycles (the Harvard school, Spiethoff, Cassel, Bouniatian, Aftalion and others).

There are two reasons why a Marxist theory of the conjuncture must focus on studying the nature of short cycles. The first is the fact that secular changes, whether or not one accepts their authenticity, extend beyond the historical limits of the capitalist system. A phenomenon that characterises different economic formations is not unique to capitalism and, on these grounds, must be excluded. Secondly, the reality of long cycles is open to scientific debate for a number of important reasons.

The principal watershed in the debate involves such questions as these: Do long cycles have a law-governed cyclical pattern? What is the nature of that pattern, and how is it connected with the main functions of capitalism? Do so-called long cycles really exist, or are they merely a mathematical construction resulting from smoothing out the conjunctural movements of the short cycle? These are important questions, and the answers that one gives will determine how a theory of the conjuncture must be developed. If the existence of long cycles can really be proven, then precisely those cycles must be the foundation for a theory of the conjuncture. In that case, long cycles will include small cycles as specific manifestations of the lawfulness that governs the long cycles. Small cycles will be regarded as fluctuations superimposed on the axis of long cycles. These conclusions lead to one possible methodological approach for analysing the problem. But if long cycles do not exist as an independent phenomenon in the capitalist economy, then the objective of a theory of the conjuncture will be to study only short cycles, which will become the focus through which research will link the fundamental motive forces of the capitalist economy with the specific dynamic of its development. The problem of the physiology of the capitalist economy, of how it is connected to its anatomy and morphology, will be resolved. But, in this case, the result will be a formulation of the problem very different from the first one, with a different way of looking at things and different methods of investigation.

This question cannot be finally resolved in the present work. Here, it is not possible to give an adequate proof that long cycles do not really exist. But a preliminary answer is already implied by how one responds to the question of whether long waves have a law-governed cyclical movement.

Professor N. Kondrat'ev, the most recent proponent of the existence of long cycles, offers the following arguments in support of their cyclical character.[7] First, a change in production technology, discovery of new gold deposits, and inclusion of new countries in the capitalist orbit precede a rising wave. Second, the rising wave is accompanied by more frequent social convulsions and upheavals (wars, revolutions) than the falling wave. Third, a link can be established between the falling wave and prolonged depressions in agriculture.

---

[7] Kondrat'ev 1925, pp. 48, 54, 55, 58. [Kondrat'ev was one of Maksakovsky's most controversial Russian contemporaries. A student of M.I. Tugan-Baranovsky, he became prominent in Soviet economic debates during the 1920s. His work on the theory of 'long cycles' has since resulted in an enormous international literature on the subject. He was denounced by Stalinists for opposing collectivisation of agriculture and later died in a labour camp. Economists in the USSR criticised his work repeatedly on the grounds that the theory of 'long cycles' implied the impossibility of collapse of the capitalist system, whose history Kondrat'ev described in terms of 'moving equilibrium'. In 1922, Kondrat'ev explicitly denied that capitalism's post-war crisis was in any way 'special' or 'extraordinary'. (See Kondrat'ev 1922, p. 209; see also Kondrat'ev 1923, pp. 67–71 *et seq.*) I have discussed Leon Trotsky's response to Kondrat'ev in Day 1976. Trotsky shared Maksakovsky's negative assessment of Kondrat'ev's long cycle, although Mandel, a Marxist, takes a much more positive view. See Mandel 1975; see also Mandel 1978.]

These arguments cannot be considered persuasive. They have a dual character. Is it possible that economic and social conditions exert an influence upon development of the capitalist economy, upon its tone and dynamic? Of course it is possible! To that extent, Professor Kondrat'ev is perfectly correct. But does this mean there is a basis for claiming that these conditions give rise to a cyclical movement, that they repeat themselves cyclically, that they recur within certain intervals of time, that they are so deeply rooted in the capitalist economy that they can be said to generate a law-governed succession of crises? Not even Professor Kondrat'ev goes that far. Such a claim would not be a matter of objective economic analysis but simply of pure mysticism, an empty postulate in place of a well-grounded proof. Long cycles are, at best, a weakly proven hypothesis. They do not have a law-governed cyclical movement, and there is no reason to think they should.

The factors cited by Kondrat'ev affect the capitalist dynamic through their influence on small cycles, on the concrete course of their development (by intensifying the expansion or prolonging the depression). If these cycles are smoothed out mathematically by linking together the points of conjunctural fluctuation, then one can, with a stretch, discern over long periods of time a rising and falling movement that suggests a succession of waves.[8] But what we get as a result is not a real cycle; it is a mathematical pseudo-cycle, whose only cognitive value is to serve as a summary representation of the development of the productive forces within the limits of their capitalist organisation.

It follows that our Marxist conception of the conjuncture includes only those law-governed fluctuations of the system that are known as commercial-industrial, or small, cycles. The essence of the problem of the conjuncture, therefore, is to establish and analyse the action of those forces that impart to the capitalist system its law-governed, fluctuating movements. But fluctuations can be observed in every aspect of capitalist reproduction: in the spheres of production, circulation, and distribution. They are experienced as immutable laws by every capitalist enterprise, regardless of the sphere in which capital is invested. Hence, the theory of the conjuncture studies the *real* production process as it occurs in the capitalist economy, taken as a whole, and reveals the law-governed 'causes' that impart to this process a cyclical form of development. The periods of expansion, crisis, and depression, which comprise the cycle, are essentially distinct stages of reproduction as it emerges from

[8] Bazarov poses the question more or less this way in Bazarov 1926, p. 106.

an intricate complex of interacting economic factors that develop on the basis of the fundamental laws of the capitalist system's movement. The strikingly unique feature of the capitalist economy, distinguishing it from all other formations, is its cyclical dynamic of development. The economic history of capitalism cannot be confined within the limits of a smoothly rising curve. Throughout its long history, capitalism moves in a law-governed manner through shorter stages that are measured by a 7–10 year conjunctural cycle. As the hands of a clock count time through their own movement on the clock-face, so the general history of capitalism consists of law-governed intervals that represent the inner content of that history. There is no reality to the development of capitalism apart from this specific form of movement. Just as each category of the capitalist economy is a real fact only when it assumes an embodied form, so the movement of the entire system becomes a reality only through the unity of its content with its specific form. To eliminate the form would be to abstract from the real expression of the capitalist dynamic and would return us to the original heights of logical abstraction.

The separate phases of the cycle express a determinate condition of the productive forces – rapid growth during an expansion, contraction in a crisis, and stagnation during the depression. Unevenness of development on the part of the productive forces results from their capitalist organisation. It is precisely the economic integument of capitalism that periodically curtails their development. This curtailment becomes objective in the cyclical dynamic of the capitalist economy as it is revealed on the system's surface. Therefore, the cyclical dynamic of capitalism results from interaction of the productive forces with the capitalist integument within which their development occurs. The periodic struggle, which in a law-governed way signifies both repeated 'attacks' by capitalist relations on the progress of material production and the unfailing victory of the productive forces as they pass to the next level of technological development, constitutes the dramatic content of the process and is externally revealed in the cyclical dynamic of the capitalist economy.

Chapter 1

Methodological Foundations of the Theory of the Conjuncture

The problem of the dynamic and of the conjuncture

The first and most important requirement for theoretical clarification of the problem of the conjuncture is a correct methodological approach. The subject under investigation is the unique dynamic of the capitalist economy, which comprises an intricate complex of interconnected phenomena. The dimensions of the problem are far reaching. They include all the economic processes that are felt on the system's surface, both in the market and in production, such as the scale of production, the level of prices, the condition of credit, the money market, and so forth. But study of the conjuncture involves a great deal more than analysis of these processes. The objective is both to discern the connections and interdependence of the aforementioned phenomena in the process of social reproduction and also to disclose the 'causes' that impart to the process its strictly law-governed fluctuations. Periodic waves of expansion make their way through the anarchic confusion on the surface of capitalism and inevitably culminate in a crash. The closer one is to events in the market, the more obvious are the fluctuating movements and the more clearly defined are their turning points.[1]

[1] 'Conjunctural waves manifest themselves soonest and most clearly on the market

The problem of the conjuncture, however, is not limited to observing and systematically analysing its surface expressions. The conjuncture exerts a decisive influence on the relation between social production and consumption. In capitalism, consumption takes on the altered form of effective demand. Together with periodic expansions and contractions of social production, within the limits of capitalist distribution one observes changes in the magnitude of incomes that do not always reflect the direction or the extent of fluctuations occurring in social production. It is a general law that the volume of effective demand lags behind the existing scale of production. Here, we see in clear focus the internal contradiction inherent in capitalism's relations of production; that is, the narrow basis of consumption by comparison with the potential for massive expansion of production.[2] 'Equilibrium' is restored through acute shocks to the entire system together with significant destruction of the productive forces.

The complexity of the problem makes it extremely important to adopt a correct methodological approach. The starting points of the analysis and the method adopted will predetermine the result of any effort to discern the nature of cyclical laws. Bourgeois economics usually begins with empirical phenomena and with things as they appear on the surface – that is to say, inductively. 'We intend to move, as much as possible, from the concrete to the abstract. Thus we look first at changes in material production and at corresponding changes in the means of production. Then we move in succession

(for commodities, for money, for capital and for labour) and are expressed in the periodic rise and fall of prices and, most importantly, in the periodic changes in relative prices, in price dislocations, in so-called price movements that embrace both the prices of commodities and of securities, and finally, in incomes (wages, profits on capital, rent)' (Pervushin 1925, p. 25).

[2] Marx 1962, pp. 239–40. [Marx writes: 'The conditions of direct exploitation, and those of realizing it, are not identical. They diverge not only in place and time, but also logically. The first are only limited by the productive power of society, the latter by the proportional relations of the various branches of production and the consumer power of society. But this last-named is not determined either by the absolute productive power, or by the absolute consumer power, but by the consumer power based on antagonistic conditions of distribution, which reduce the consumption of the bulk of society to a minimum within more or less narrow limits. It is furthermore restricted by the tendency to accumulate, the drive to expand capital and produce surplus-value on an extended scale. This is law for capitalist production, imposed by incessant revolutions in the methods of production themselves, by the depreciation of existing capital always bound up with them, by the general competitive struggle and the need to improve production and expand its scale. . . . But the more productiveness develops, the more it finds itself at variance with the narrow basis on which the conditions of consumption rest.']

to changes in price formation and incomes in order to complete the investigation with changes in the conditions of the capital market'.[3]

This is the 'classical' way in which bourgeois economics formulates its analysis of the problem. While this approach guarantees a valuable result in terms of a precise and systematic investigation of conjunctural processes in their external connections and dependencies, it also rules out any possibility of detecting the fundamental levers that result in the conjuncture's 'movement'. This kind of investigation is extremely one-sided. It is no surprise, therefore, that bourgeois economics usually finds the motivating forces of the conjunctural cycle in the sphere of monetary circulation and credit – areas that superficially appear to exert a decisive influence on the course of the cycle. Despite significant accomplishments in terms of a systematic ordering of conjunctural phenomena, bourgeois economics merely dwells on the surface of things when it comes to determining the principles of movement. What stands in the way of a more penetrating analysis and blunts the research tools of bourgeois economics is, in the first place, failure to understand fully the nature of the capitalist economy, and secondly, a remarkable detachment of the study of the conjuncture from all the other problems of the capitalist economy. Because of its lack of a rigorous system of economic theory, bourgeois economics mistakenly assigns the problem of the conjuncture an independent status in the general study of the capitalist economy. Its subject matter is strictly separated from all the other processes of the capitalist economy. The very approach involves a high degree of mysticism. 'The conjuncture is a term used to describe that elusive something upon which everything else depends . . .'.[4] The attitude of the ordinary capitalist, for whom the conjuncture represents the all-powerful and irrational will of the market, extends its fetishistic pall over both the subject of the analysis and the approach taken by bourgeois economics. Naturally, this does nothing to make the analysis more profound. It is interesting to note in this connection that those bourgeois schools that base their study of capitalism on a monistic principle, value, and undertake from this starting point to construct an economic theory of capitalism, are much more successful in analysing the 'causes' that give rise to capitalism's cyclical development. It is enough to recall Bouniatian and Aftalion, who are adherents of the so-called psychological school.[5]

[3] Cassel 1925, p. 15.

[4] Röpke 1927, p. 15.

[5] [Mentor Bouniatian wrote several books on business cycles, including *Les crises*

The theory of the conjuncture must be constructed mainly deductively. It is necessary, above all, to determine the economic forces that are at the basis of the cyclical dynamic and 'govern' it. Unless this matter is resolved first, it is impossible to give a correct explanation of the more particular laws that become apparent in the conjuncture. But the paramount role of the deductive approach by no means excludes empirical research. On the contrary, the conjuncture itself is a deeply empirical matter; it involves an enormous complexity of interwoven phenomena, and only in that form does it determine the behaviour of any economic subject. Consequently, empirical study of the conjuncture, together with the resulting initial generalisations, is a vitally necessary component of any theoretical clarification of the problem. It would be impossible to comprehend the conjuncture's laws and how it originates without studying its morphology. For that reason, there is no denying the scientific merit of the extensive work done in this area by bourgeois economics. If they can be kept separate from any general conclusions or influences coming from sociology, the results generated by empirical research into the conjuncture will serve as a necessary prelude to constructing a proper theory.

Both types of approach were fully incorporated into the abstract-analytical method adopted by Marx.[6] The latter, being a variant of the dialectical method

économiques, essai de morphologie et théorie des crises économiques périodiques, et de théorie de la conjoncture économique, which was translated from Russian and published in Paris in 1922. Albert Aftalion wrote on monetary economics and business cycles. His major work on cycles was *Les crises périodiques de surproduction*, 2 volumes, 1913.]

[6] [When Marx discusses method, he adopts Hegel's view that the whole is logically prior to the parts: 'In the succession of the economic categories, as in any other historical, social science, it must not be forgotten that their subject – here, modern bourgeois society – is always what is given, in the head as well as in reality, and that these categories therefore express the forms of being, the characteristics of existence, and often only individual sides of this specific society, this subject, and that therefore this society by no means begins only at the point where one can speak of it *as such*; this holds for *science as well*' (Marx 1973, p. 106; see also Marx 1970, p. 212). The concrete is the reproduction in thought of an initially given whole. Thought grasps the whole by determining its fundamental categories and then logically reconstructing the whole as concrete. Marx writes: 'The economists of the seventeenth century, e.g., always begin with the living whole, with population, nation, state, several states, etc.; but they always conclude by discovering through analysis a small number of determinant, abstract, general relations such as division of labour, money, value, etc. As soon as these individual moments had been more or less firmly established and abstracted, there began the economic system, which ascended from the simple relations, such as labour, division of labour, need, exchange-value, to the level of the state, exchange between nations and the world market. The latter is obviously the scientifically correct method. The concrete is concrete because it is the concentration of many determinations, hence unity of the diverse. It appears in the process of thinking, therefore, as a process of concentration, as a result, not as a point of departure, even

as it is applied specifically to the economy of capitalism, must be the foundation for a theory of the conjuncture. The unique feature of this method is that it looks at capitalist phenomena in their pure form, free from any modifying influences. Every part of the capitalist economy is subjected to logical scrutiny. The resulting laws are linked together in a strictly logical system, with the fundamental laws providing a foundation for more concrete laws that are closer to the surface of the capitalist economy. Each law represents either a more general or a more particular 'model' of capitalism, depending on the type of production relations to which it logically refers. The capitalist system emerges in continuous movement, in an insurmountable contradiction between its separate parts. This is how it is 'conceived' by the abstract method. It is not the abstract method that imparts a contradictory character to capitalism's laws; rather, the system's own development, which is accompanied by growing contradictions and their periodic eruptions, corresponds to the dialectical method.

The principal contradictions of the system are disclosed in the construction of its basic categories: value, surplus-value, and the average rate of profit. On these foundations arise more concrete contradictions that periodically erupt on the system's surface. The former determine the activity of the latter. A process occurs whereby the basic forms assume concrete content; the resulting law-governed movement begins with the totality of particular

though it is the point of departure in reality and hence also the point of departure for observation [*Anschauung*] and conception. Along the first path the full conception was evaporated to yield an abstract determination; along the second, the abstract determinations lead towards a reproduction of the concrete by way of thought. . . . [T]he method of rising from the abstract to the concrete is only the way in which thought appropriates the concrete, reproduces it as concrete in the mind' (Marx 1973, pp. 100–101; see also Marx 1970, p. 206). Thought cannot, as Maksakovsky says, move simply on the empirical surface of things. The meaning of the simplest economic categories, such as labour, is determined by the whole of which they are a part: slave labour and feudal labour are not the same as labour dictated by the expanded reproduction of capital. The same applies to money, credit, and other more concrete categories. Marx posits the abstraction of 'pure capitalism' in order to deal directly and exclusively with the economic categories specific to the capitalist mode of production, setting aside precapitalist interactions that may continue to exist because of capitalism's uneven historical development but which contribute nothing to the understanding of capitalism itself as a unique social and economic system. The general point is that neither empirical observation nor abstraction, on their own, can theoretically reproduce capitalism and the dynamic of its movement. Marx's method is to move from the whole to its categories and, through the interaction of the categories, to reconstruct the whole in its law-governed movement. This is the method Maksakovsky will follow throughout this book.]

phenomena and, at the same time, determines both their direction and their final outcome. The result is an intricate complex of mutually interacting fundamental and more particular laws of capitalist economy that together determine its real existence.

A clear distinction must be made between taking laws in isolation in order to study them in principle – in terms of their form and content – and the way in which their activity unfolds through capitalism's real development. For example, the activity of the law of value is not exhausted within the limits of production and exchange between two or three economic subjects, although it can clearly be looked at within this isolating abstraction. While it 'regulates' the exchange of commodities, which is the basic function of capitalism, value at the same time 'regulates' the entire production process, 'gives birth' to all the complex forms of capitalist market relations, and 'grows over' into several new forms of 'life', that is, into economic categories expressing production relations that have arisen historically on the basis of value.

The study of each category as a constituent part of an intricate complex of interactions makes it possible to trace its fully developed activity. In this way, the essentially dynamic character of each category is revealed instead of being paralysed by a high level of abstraction. The logical partitions that distinguish the activity of each category from the others now vanish. All of the categories represent the closely interwoven parts of a single capitalist complex. In place of the distinct levels and compartments of economic theory, with their clearly defined lines of demarcation, what appears before us is a single body of interwoven laws expressing the developed contradictions of the capitalist economy as they are revealed in its real movement and as they determine the specific form of that movement.

Thus the problem of the conjuncture, or the problem of the specific form and movement of capitalism's dynamic, is above all a problem of the fully developed activity of the laws of capitalist economy. Instead of looking at separate aspects of the dynamic of the whole, and analysing those aspects by establishing the nature of individual categories, the object of an analysis of the conjuncture is logical reconstruction of the economic body of capitalism in its entirety. The task of logically working out the particular features of its 'physiology' has already been completed. The fundamental processes by which the system 'inhales' and 'exhales' are already given, together with the principles of its movement. Moreover, the theory of simple and expanded reproduction has already constructed a bridge leading to resolution of the problem of the conjuncture.[7] What is needed now is to look at how the capitalist 'physiology' works as a whole and how its functions are coordinated – not in the hidden depths of its internal processes, but within the real dimensions of space and time, that is, on capitalism's historical surface.

This is the essence of the problem of the conjuncture. When things are viewed in these terms, each category, as we have already indicated, acquires an emphatically dynamic expression. Each is to be regarded as a constituent moment of capitalist reproduction as it emerges in real-historical form, beginning with its depths in production and ending with dancing shadows at the ghostly heights of the money market.

In his theory of simple and expanded reproduction, Marx provided a general solution to the problem of the dynamic of the capitalist whole. But the problem was posed only in its most general outline and was strongly influenced by the isolating force of abstraction. Relations between the separate parts of social production, in their interaction, were set out on the basis of exchange according to value. The assumptions were such as to abstract from the role of credit and to leave out the dynamic of prices, the flow of capitals, and the specific waves of market competition. Marx says: 'Here we need only consider the forms which capital passes through in the various stages of its development. The real conditions within which the actual process of production takes place are therefore not analysed. It is assumed throughout that the commodity is sold at its value. We do not examine the competition of capitals, nor the credit system …'.[8]

Within this framework, the problem of the dynamic was basically solved in ideal-schematic terms. The next step is the theory of the conjuncture. Marx also indicated the main outlines for solving this part of the problem. In his treatment of the problem of crises, he demonstrated the inevitability of capitalism's cyclical development. Nevertheless, Marx's works do not provide a comprehensive theory of the conjuncture.

Our present concern, which fully corresponds with the spirit of Marx's economic theory, is the question of the dynamic arrangement of separate categories and the influence they exert through their complex interaction. The nature of the cycle must be viewed in close connection with the fully

---

7 [Maksakovsky means that Marx has already completed this work in Volume II of *Capital*.]

8 Marx 1975a, pp. 492–3.

developed activity of all the economic categories. This is the initial key to resolving the problem. The conjuncture is a complex, dynamic process. In capitalism there is nothing whatever that is static. The only difference between the conjuncture and other economic categories is one of scale and cognitive points of view in the treatment of a single capitalist process. In both cases, the object being studied is the capitalist mode of production in its contradictory development. But whereas the analysis of categories involves study of capitalism at high levels of abstraction and, as a result, means looking at things through the prism of a single basic law or a few such laws, the theory of the conjuncture involves study of capitalism as it develops through the totality of its relations.

It follows that the conjuncture does not represent a separate economic category of capitalism in the strict sense of the word. It does not express any unique production relation that is a component part of the mode of production. *The conjuncture is the form in which the action of all the categories of the capitalist economy is expressed through their interaction and interpenetration – a movement that is objectified in the cyclical dynamic of the capitalist whole.* The conjuncture incorporates the action both of fundamental categories and of more particular categories as the latter are arranged on the skeleton of the former; and it is precisely the activity of the particular categories that imparts to the conjuncture its empirical 'corporality'.

Hence, the theory of the conjuncture is the final stage of the Marxist economic conception, the 'dynamic' version of Marx's theory of reproduction, its second and final chapter. Its sphere of 'competence' is remarkably broad. At its lowest level it deals with the problem of value, at the other extreme, with the 'ghostly' fluctuations of the money market. But it is especially important to note that the conjuncture embraces only the interaction of categories: it does not include analysis of each of them but takes them in principle as being already given. Otherwise, the theory of the conjuncture would include the whole theory of the capitalist economy, whereas in reality it is only the final stage of that theory. The theory of the conjuncture observes the way in which the fully developed activity of capitalist categories is objectified in the system's cyclical dynamic.

This means that capitalism knows no static conditions. A scientific theory, providing a theoretical depiction of the system's laws (and, simultaneously, of its contradictions), is a theory of the capitalist economy's 'universal' dynamic. The most profound error of bourgeois economics is to divide capitalism into static and dynamic elements and to take this metaphysical distinction as the starting point for analysis of the conjuncture.

'Under the heading "static" we have in mind the theory that treats economic phenomena in essential terms, apart from their change over time. In contrast, under the heading "dynamic" we understand the theory that studies economic phenomena in their process of change over time', says N. Kondrat'ev.[9] The content of static theory is taken to be the analysis of value, profit, and so forth. Analysis of these fundamental elements of capitalism goes into the static section. It is characteristic of Kondrat'ev to apply this metaphysical criterion to his treatment of Marx's economic system, which he also endeavours to divide into two parts: one static, the other dynamic. Static theory includes the problem of value, the price level, and profit; the teaching concerning reproduction, income, and wages is taken to be dynamic.[10]

S. Pervushin's concept of the conjuncture is equally dependent on a distinction between the static and the dynamic. He says: 'The static approach is characterised by the fact that it deals with the national economy outside of time, as a system of timeless, interconnected magnitudes in a state of equilibrium. The dynamic approach means, on the contrary, that the economy is studied as movement, as a process developing through time and involving uninterrupted changes in the relations between the fundamental elements of the economic whole, which is continuously being reconstructed'.[11] With this distinction he goes even further than Kondrat'ev. Whereas the latter sees the

[9] Kondrat'ev 1924, p. 350. [For Kondrat'ev, the point of view of 'static' theory is that of general equilibrium; this kind of theory begins with the concept of equilibrium and shows how temporary departures from equilibrium are overcome. On p. 355 Kondrat'ev says: 'In contrast, the dynamic point of view looks at economic phenomena in terms of *the process of change of economic elements and of their relationships* and looks for regularities in the course of the changes themselves.']

[10] [One reviewer of Maksakovsky's book, B.L. Livshits, noted that some Soviet Marxists made a distinction very similar to Kondrat'ev's by treating the laws of value, distribution and realisation as elements of 'static' theory, while the theories of concentration and centralisation of capital, of the falling profit rate, and of monopolistic decay were treated as elements of a 'dynamic' theory of structural evolution (Livshits 1929, p. 223).]

[11] Pervushin 1925, p. 10. [Pervushin also thought long periods of time in the world economy are 'relatively static' – for example, 1823–51 and 1873–95 – while others are 'relatively dynamic' – such as 1851–73 and 1895–1914. See Pervushin 1925, p. 4. Pervushin taught at Moscow State University during the 1920s and also worked at Gosplan from 1922–30. He was condemned in the 1930s but survived and worked from 1945–62 at the M.I. Kalinin Institute in Moscow.]

conjuncture embracing a certain type of dynamic processes, which he calls '*reversible*',[12] for Pervushin the concept of the conjuncture includes within itself both a static and a dynamic element. 'We take the view,' he writes, 'that the conjuncture can also be described in two ways, that is, it can be seen in a dynamic and a static aspect, and thus one can construct two concepts of the conjuncture, one dynamic and the other static. In the first case, the conjuncture is regarded as a continuously developing process, so that in this respect the conjuncture is movement; in the second case, that is, with the static approach, the conjuncture is regarded as a certain condition of the national economy at a particular moment in time and is compared to a different condition at some other, previous moment in time'.[13]

This dualistic view of the capitalist whole is a metaphysical scheme and contradicts the laws of a capitalist economy's development. We have already indicated the fundamental reasons for objecting to such a distinction. Capitalism knows no static condition. Theoretical analysis of its fundamental laws (the theory of value and profit) by no means implies investigation 'outside of the categories of change over time', as Professor Kondrat'ev believes. What is involved is analysis of the laws of the system's movement and, consequently,

---

[12] Kondrat'ev 1924, pp. 358, 367 [Kondrat'ev distinguished between irreversible and reversible changes. The former involved evolutionary movements in one direction, such as population growth or changes in the level of total production, which are only reversed in the event of social catastrophe; examples of the latter are movements of commodity prices, interest rates, the level of unemployment, or numbers of bankruptcies. On p. 362 Kondrat'ev said study of irreversible changes deals with 'evolution of the economy as a whole . . . from one stage to another'. *This was the kind of movement that Kondrat'ev thought Marx had abstractly demonstrated in the reproduction schemes.* On p. 371 *Kondrat'ev spoke of the schemes as portraying an economy in 'moving equilibrium'. Study of the conjuncture, in contrast, must focus on reversible changes that are associated exclusively with market phenomena and empirical data* (p. 365). For Maksakovsky, these are not two separate studies; they are merely different levels of abstraction within a single Marxist method. By concentrating on cyclical (or reversible) changes, Kondrat'ev also hoped to avoid being drawn into a debate over whether and when the capitalist *system* might finally be overthrown by proletarian revolution (Kondrat'ev 1923).]

[13] Pervushin 1925, pp. 23–4. [Pervushin denied the existence of Kondrat'ev's long cycles on the grounds that they involved no clear periodicity and were merely 'pseudo-cycles'. He regarded Kondrat'ev's methodology as one of comparative statics rather than a truly dynamic approach: On p. 19 he wrote: '. . . it involves only a static characterisation of a given moment of the conjuncture compared with the previous moment, not the uninterrupted development of a process over time. The thread that binds the separate phases together is broken; the single and self-contained fluctuating process that is called the conjuncture is . . . artificially broken into its fragments and viewed statically. . . . This is a static characterisation and nothing more.' For Pervushin's comments on Kondrat'ev's methodology, see Kondrat'ev 1924, pp. 373–5.]

of its change; but change can be discerned only in the irrational forms of price fluctuations and so forth. There is no void between the 'upper' levels of a capitalist economy and the fundamental forces operating at the 'lower' levels and foundations of the system. On the contrary, there are the closest possible interactions and connections between them. Just as development of economic processes on the surface of things is shaped by the activity of fundamental forces, so the activity of the latter is possible only given the reverse influence coming from the former.[14] The law of value is not a law of 'moving equilibrium' on the part of the capitalist system's (static) fundamental elements, with equilibrium, in turn, being periodically disrupted by dynamic processes found on another plane of the capitalist whole – as Professor Kondrat'ev sees it.[15] The law of value is the fundamental law of the system's movement; it manifests itself in the form of an uninterrupted tendency towards 'equilibrium', which, in turn, exhausts itself in continuous struggle with other, opposing tendencies.[16] This law is the pivotal, spontaneous organising force

[14] [In his final chapter, Maksakovsky will look at the interaction between the fundamental and most remote levels of the capitalist economy when he relates financial markets to 'real' activities in production.]

[15] Kondrat'ev 1924, pp. 360–2. [Relating crises to the concept of moving equilibrium, Kondrat'ev said: 'In its most general form the essence of an economic crisis lies in the fact that . . . a moving system of elements loses its equilibrium and experiences an acute, painful process of transition to the condition of a new moving equilibrium. From the economic point of view a crisis is always only an acute and painful process of liquidating the disparities that have arisen in the structure of a national economy and that destroy the equilibrium of its elements. [A crisis] is the process of establishing a new equilibrium in place of the one that has broken down' (Kondrat'ev 1922, p. 191; see also pp. 199, 204 and 208).]

[16] 'Only as an inner law, vis-à-vis the individual agents, as a blind law of Nature, does the law of value exert its influence here and maintain the social equilibrium of production amidst its accidental fluctuations' (Marx 1962, p. 858).

In his book *Mirovoe khozyaistvo i krizisy* [*The World Economy and Crises*], comrade Osinsky argues against N. Kondrat'ev's attributing the metaphysical concept of 'moving equilibrium' to Marx, but he goes too far when he ignores the existence of such a tendency. [See especially pp. 51–6 of Osinsky's book, where he compares Kondrat'ev's view of 'equilibrium' with Marx's.] Although it is true that a 'moving equilibrium' can never become a real fact in the capitalist economy at any moment of its existence, it is also true that such a tendency does operate. It is represented by the 'law of value', which, for this reason, can be regarded as the system's law of 'equilibrium'. Value appears not only in an 'equilibrium' between supply and demand, which is conceivable in ideal terms, but also in the continuous tendency towards establishment of such equilibrium. Osinsky, who, it seems, is frightened by the very concept of 'equilibrium' and simply sweeps it aside, does not adequately clarify this second point. Marx writes: 'The exchange, or sale, of commodities at their value is the rational state of affairs, i.e. the natural law of their equilibrium. It is this law that explains their deviations, and not vice versa, the deviations that explain the law' (Marx 1962, p. 184).

of the system; the condition for its activity is 'unorganised spontaneity', which can never be overcome within the limits of the capitalist economy. If this 'unorganised spontaneity' is broken down into its components, they turn out to be the laws of wages, credit, and other moments of capitalist reproduction. Their activity receives its 'impetus' from value, but value never completely and exactly dictates their 'predestination'. The complex result of their interconnections is revealed in the process of reproduction; they lead the capitalist system far beyond any conceivable 'tracks' of 'equilibrium' and, in precisely that way, acquire the character of 'unorganised spontaneity', against which value struggles to move social reproduction towards equilibrium of its parts without ever really achieving this outcome. The disappearance of 'unorganised spontaneity', which is essentially presupposed by N. Kondrat'ev's theory of 'static' equilibrium, would inevitably be accompanied by disappearance of lawfulness itself, which is simply the other side of this 'spontaneity'. Can this be the result that Professor Kondrat'ev hoped to achieve?

The formulations of Kondrat'ev, Pervushin, and the whole crowd of bourgeois economists who follow their lead in investigating the conjuncture are simply wrong. Capitalism knows no static condition. This means there can be no static 'aspect' and no 'static' conjuncture to parallel the dynamic expression of these concepts. There is only one capitalist 'dynamic', which expresses the contradictory development of the system and its different theoretical levels. The 'deeper' the category, the more generalised is the activity of this dynamic. But when the aggregate activity of all categories is observed in the real course of capitalist reproduction, this dynamic is clearly discernible on the surface of the cyclical movement. The separate parts of the analysis of capitalism are brought together through a single abstract-analytical method, which treats phenomena not in a metaphysical way, not as if they were frozen and still, but in their constant movement, which is continuously reproduced by the internal contradictions of the system itself and, in the final analysis, is

---

One must take into account, of course, the fact that Osinsky is arguing against an incorrect, metaphysical interpretation of Marxist theory on the part of a bourgeois economist.

[N. Osinsky (also known as V.V. Obolensky) occupied several prominent state and party positions in the USSR during the 1920s. At different times he worked in the Supreme Council of National Economy (VSNKh) and was a member of the presidium of Gosplan. From 1922–5 he was Director of the Institute of World Economy and World Politics, which was subsequently headed for several decades by E.S. Varga and is today known as the Institute of World Economy and International Relations (IMEMO).]

determined by the character of the interaction between the productive forces and their capitalist integument.

While we rule out any static point of view, considering it incompatible with Marxist methodology, we do not deny the cognitive usefulness of capturing the conjunctural process in photographic snapshots or as a kind of cinematic topography. The growth of production in particular branches, the more rapid expansion of the so-called capital-goods industries, the changing level of prices, interest rates, and so on – to capture all of these processes at separate stages of the cycle in a way that illustrates both their own changes and their relations to each other is a necessary step in theoretically comprehending the conjuncture. The Harvard School has enjoyed great successes in this regard and has managed to represent the pattern of the cycle with the help of a few fundamental indicators that graphically portray the conjuncture's movement.[17] Nevertheless, while the Harvard School has produced a model for systematically representing conjunctural processes, they have failed to provide any substantive explanation of the conjuncture's motive forces, which means that they have only weakly conceptualised the results of their own work. This is the more or less common fate of all bourgeois conjunctural research. The cognitive importance of a snapshot of the different planes on which the reproductive movement continuously occurs is considerable. These are snapshots of real processes and reflect the direction of movement over specific periods of time, but they also have absolutely nothing in common with so-called 'static' aspects or 'static' cross-sections. In the analysis of developing economic phenomena, they play the same role as elements of formal logic in the dialectical method.

The methodology of analysing the problem of the conjuncture

Now let us turn to the most important question: What must our point of departure be for constructing a theory of the conjuncture – should it be based on so-called 'pure' capitalism, or can the nature of the cycle be established

[17] [The reference is to *The Harvard Index of General Business Conditions; Its Interpretation*, published in 1923 by the Harvard University Committee on Economic Research. The committee's work was highly mathematical with the intention of establishing an 'economic barometer' that would allow forecasts of economic activity. Its three fundamental indicators dealt with speculation, money markets, and business conditions. There was also a single index of trade, covering the period 1903–23, which incorporated changes in trade, transportation, manufacturing activity and industrial employment.]

by beginning with concrete capitalism and with things as they appear on the historical surface?

Bourgeois economics, in the great majority of cases, begins with concrete capitalism. It looks at capitalism in close connection with 'third' parties and agriculture. Starting out with this multifaceted complex, it then endeavours to find a way to explain the cycle. Some researchers attempt to remove influences that emerge specifically from agricultural fluctuations, but this is not the general approach.

No such difficulties can arise from the way Marxists pose the question. Marx provided the general approach to analysis of the conjuncture in his own analysis of social reproduction and of the entire capitalist economic system. Marx dealt with 'pure' capitalism. The theory of the conjuncture must likewise begin with 'pure' capitalism. The reason is clear: the cyclical form of development is unique to a capitalist economy. The economic formations that historically preceded capitalism and those that will follow capitalism, regardless of what type of economic linkages prevail – whether they are of the exchange or natural type – did not and cannot experience this form of development. As a result, they merely introduce 'aggravating' circumstances into a study of the cycle's law-governed pattern, and it is proper to abstract from them. In concrete terms, we must eliminate: 1) all remnants of natural economy; 2) all elements of simple exchange economy (the so-called non-capitalist environment); and 3) the agricultural economy, in both its simple commodity form and its capitalist form.[18]

There are several reasons for eliminating capitalist agriculture. Insofar as capitalist relations prevail here and production involves a certain level of technology, agriculture is simply a component part of a single capitalist

[18] [The issue of whether a 'third-party', or non-capitalist, market is necessary for realisation of the total social product was a contentious one among Marxists. Rosa Luxemburg believed that domestic underconsumption in capitalist societies made such markets imperative, and on this basis she constructed her theory of imperialism in *The Accumulation of Capital*. Once domestic agriculture was itself capitalist, Luxemburg thought surplus-value could only be realised by exporting to 'third-party' markets elsewhere. Lenin, in contrast, denied that 'third-party' markets were necessary. According to Lenin, 'Marx proved in Volume II [of *Capital*] that capitalist production is quite conceivable without foreign markets, with the growing accumulation of wealth and without any "third parties"' (Lenin 1960, pp. 498–9). For a more detailed discussion of 'pure capitalism', 'third parties', and imperialism, see Day 1981, Chapter One. See also Day 1979–80.]

complex and is therefore subordinated to the general laws of capitalism's dynamic. But since the conjunctural waves extend into agriculture, one might also suppose on these grounds that agriculture should not be excluded from analysis of the cycle. At the same time, however, a number of economic relations operating in agriculture are not found anywhere in the industrial system of capitalism (rentier categories and the conditions giving rise to them), and these relations have the effect of modifying both the laws of competition between capitals and, by implication, the entire economic process. These circumstances alone create serious obstacles to the operation of a pure conjunctural wave in agriculture, even though the general effects of its dynamic will undoubtedly be felt. Moreover, relations that are specific to agriculture also depend upon the unique importance of natural conditions and the effect they have on the production process. Not only are the prices of agricultural products formed differently from those in industry, but the general outcome of production also has the character of a 'harvest'; in other words, it is influenced not just by the given level of technology but even more directly by natural circumstances whose effects cannot be eliminated entirely by technology. If we were to include these unique factors that operate in the agricultural economy, we would encounter the problem of waves that are peculiar to that sector and do not (indeed, because of their different origin, cannot) always correspond with the cyclical waves and might even 'swallow them up'. These are the reasons why agriculture must be excluded from an explanation of the cycle even though agriculture's predominantly capitalist character is presupposed in the course of the analysis.

We must also abstract from other 'admixtures' and 'influences' on the capitalist process of reproduction, especially from the influence of the state, for the object of our investigation is capitalism as a single totality, not as it is (still) divided into separate national units. Similarly, we must abstract from monopolistic alliances and other forms of capitalist association whose purpose is to limit free competition and thus to modify the action of capitalism's laws. At this point in the analysis, mention of the existence of such associations must be accompanied by knowledge of the empirical fact that they do not disrupt the cyclical dynamic of capitalism's development.

Consequently, the general theory of the conjunctural cycle presupposes among its basic conditions the following methodological constraints: 1) treatment of the whole of social production as production occurring within a capitalist context, thereby excluding 'third' parties; 2) exclusion of agriculture, as a special sphere of production whose economic process includes both a more complex totality of relations and also the immediate effect of natural conditions on production (the spontaneity of nature as well as economic factors); 3) abstraction from all organising and organisational forces that modify the appearance of competition and, in general, have an influence on the capitalist reproduction process (the state, syndicates, trusts etc.).

What then remains? The answer is 'pure' capitalism in the totality of its relations, for which Marx provided the theory. Accordingly, the theory of the conjuncture must be constructed on the plane of 'pure' capitalism. The theory of the conjuncture represents the final stage of Marx's economic system and the second part of his theory of social reproduction. The flight of investigative reason continues. The object of the study is 'pure' capitalism and its relations. In methodological terms, the theory of the conjuncture is the highest stage in the study of capitalism, which continues to take place within the framework of the abstract-analytical method.[19]

The next stage of analysis – inclusion of 'third' parties and of agricultural production, with all the accompanying conditions and relations – would extend beyond the limits of the abstract method. The initial theoretical premises would include a much more significant and influential role for more concrete methods of investigation that are appropriate to more narrowly defined objectives. Although the entire mechanism of capitalist production is concretely connected in a thousand different ways with the non-capitalist environment, this is by no means an argument against exclusion of the latter through methodological abstraction, which, in turn, is the key to approaching the most concrete problems – 'as long as those using these abstractions are conscious of the fact that between the abstractions and their applications to empirical reality there is a whole series of logical steps, which under no circumstances may be omitted'.[20]

We can now specify the following stages in working out the problem of the conjuncture. First, there is the theory of the conjuncture in the direct sense of the word. Here, one must analyse the nature of the cycle and the laws

[19] One should note that it is characteristic of R. Luxemburg to carry over into the analysis of the conjuncture the same methodological errors that occur in her analysis of reproduction, making it difficult to detect the motive forces of the capitalist dynamic. Although its approaches are almost entirely the opposite of Luxemburg's, 'in practice' almost all bourgeois economics involves a similar flaw.

[20] Luxemburg and Bukharin 1972, p. 241. [The comment is from Bukharin. My translation differs slightly from this source.]

giving rise to it while also investigating theoretically how these fundamental laws, and the more particular laws superimposed upon them, determine the course of the cycle in its specific outlines. Properly speaking, the whole problem is resolved at this stage. Second, there is the matter of how forms of monopolistic capitalism affect the conjuncture. Third, there is analysis of the concrete capitalist conjuncture over specific periods of time but with the exclusion of agriculture, of 'third' parties, of the economic interactions between separate national components of the capitalist whole, of political events, etc. This stage will involve a concrete study of reproduction as it takes place in one or another country during strictly defined periods of historical time. In turn, this study might be subdivided into several separate monographs dealing with more specific questions, for example, the question of why the timing of the cycle is not the same in all countries, why the cycle is more or less acute, the influence of political events, of opening new markets, of discovering new gold deposits, etc.

Unlike the Marxist way of posing these questions, bourgeois economics begins with the concrete conjuncture and then attempts to 'extract' a theory from it. This is a completely incorrect way of doing things. But it is also true that pure capitalism does not and cannot, in the nature of things, exist. And this is all the more true of its dynamic, which emerges in the context of complex economic processes. At first glance, therefore, it might seem that the manner in which bourgeois economics formulates the issues is more logical than the Marxist approach. Bourgeois economics operates with the economic phenomena of concrete capitalism, endeavouring to find there the causes of the cycle; we, on the other hand, construct a theory of the conjuncture out of 'pure' capitalism, yet we derive its manifestation – its morphology – from the concrete. In theory we abstract from non-capitalist agricultural forms and from politics, yet the concrete economic process, on which theory is based and which it must explain, includes all of these moments and all of their activities.

But this only appears to be a contradiction. In the growth of every country one can clearly discern a cyclical dynamic of economic development. None of the moments to which we have been referring is capable of altering this law-governed peculiarity. The fundamental reason is that a concrete capitalist economy is never dualistic: it allows for no 'equal rights' between existing economic forms; the predominance of capitalist relations is necessarily expressed in the form of a dynamic peculiar to capitalism. Besides, there is no sharp contradiction between the elements of a simple commodity economy and capitalism. They have a common nucleus in economic 'anarchy', which, even in a simple commodity economy, contains the cycle in the form of a potentiality. Agriculture, insofar as it is capitalistically organised, is subordinate to the same tendencies; there is only one aspect of this two-faced Janus that contradicts (or may contradict) the laws of cyclical movement. Hence, the theory of the conjuncture can be based upon the empirical data of conjunctural development once they are refined and systematised, even though the fundamental 'causes' of the cycle can only be derived from 'pure' capitalism.

The fact that there appears to be a contradiction has given rise to several theories of the conjuncture based directly on that appearance. It is enough to cite Pervushin, who over-estimated the influence of agriculture and, while regarding technology as an 'exogenous' factor, ended up denying the 'autogenesis' of the cycle; in other words, he denied any 'purely' capitalist conjuncture.[21] On the whole, bourgeois economics is unable to distinguish between two things: the existence of specific *internal* laws of capitalism, which are the cause of the cycle and 'give birth to it', and the existence of 'exogenous' factors, which influence the conjuncture and, in the course of its movement, intensify one or another of its *concrete* characteristics: for example, the latter may contribute to a more acute outbreak of the crisis, a more prolonged depression, etc. 'Exogenous' factors have a *quantitative* significance; they play themselves out on the basis of the previously established *internal* 'causes' of the cyclical movement that operate continuously. If it is analysis of the latter that properly determines the theory of the cycle, then it follows, of course, that analysis of the former – or study of the concrete conjuncture – presupposes the fully developed activity of the fundamental laws.

---

[21] 'Excluding secular movements and long cycles, we also observe cyclical movements of the general conjuncture that are connected with agricultural fluctuations, taking place *in large measure* due to the influences of changes in the *harvest* and occurring more or less periodically' (Pervushin 1925, p. 38). [Rejecting the idea of a self-generating cycle, Pervushin cited A.C. Pigou's view in *The Economics of Welfare* that harvest fluctuations are one of the fundamental causes of rhythmical fluctuations, perhaps 'even the dominant cause' (Pervushin 1925, pp. 4, 46). Pervushin also thought cyclical expansions, once underway, are more or less predictable, but the onset of depression does not necessarily guarantee a recovery. In other words, cycles are not really self-generating (pp. 54–5). He explained general overproduction and crises mainly by reference to monetary and credit conditions (pp. 66–9).] Röpke says essentially the same thing (Röpke 1927, pp. 59 and 66–7). Recognising the harvest as an 'exogenous' factor, he assigns enormous importance to it and does not establish the 'organic' causes of the cycle.

It is exactly this perspective that enables us to clarify Engels's position when he attributed the English crash of 1847 to the harvest failure of 1846, which led to a major outflow of gold from England in order to purchase grain (domestic purchasing power, on which the sale of English commodities depended, fell abruptly as a result of the harvest failure). The outflow of gold caused the interest rate to rise, bringing with it the bankruptcies of a number of first-class firms. In this respect, the harvest failure on the continent was an even more important causal factor. But this is precisely the kind of cause that 'excites' processes already under way, and it could not have had such a decisive influence on the outbreak of the crisis had other issues not previously been fermenting. Conversely, an organically growing problem of overproduction inevitably would have taken the form of a crisis even in the complete absence of any significant 'exogenous' causes. In a general theory of the conjuncture, we can and must abstract from these 'exogenous' causes, even though every concrete capitalist crisis, whether in 1847 or in 1907, can be understood, in all of its specific details, only by taking into account the totality of concrete causes that accelerate and intensify the outbreak of already maturing 'organic' contradictions. Were it otherwise, each crisis would resemble every other, just like identical drops of water. The fundamental task of theory is to demonstrate the typical character of a crisis, whereas in a concrete study this truth is presupposed and does not figure as the main object of the investigation.

Bourgeois economics has done a great deal of interesting and scientifically useful work in sorting out and systematically organising the empirical material. The Harvard School has achieved the greatest successes. Using complex mathematical and other methodological techniques, they have excluded the influence of secular trends and seasonal variations from the 'graphs' depicting prices, cast iron, and other indicators of the conjunctural dynamic (although the question of whether secular trends actually exist is still far from being resolved). What remain are numerical series that represent cyclical fluctuations and are graphed as three 'curves': speculation; the commercial-industrial (or business) indicator, which is based on the index for iron production; and the index of credit and wholesale prices. These curves typically display not only the normal outline of the conjuncture in a clear and precise manner, but also an interesting sequence in its movement. They 'follow one another in a strictly regular order: first comes "speculation", which the "business" indicator then follows with a delay (a "lag") of about six months, and finally, after another delay of half a year, come the corresponding phases in the movement of the interest rate that is being charged for credit'.[22] This is the best demonstration of the fact that even the concrete dynamic of the capitalist complex, once partial disturbances and ripples are excluded, quite clearly reflects changes in the moving forces of the capitalist cycle.

Equally interesting is the attempt by many economists, who stress the close connection between the commercial-industrial cycle and harvests, to exclude the influence of agriculture from the conjuncture. Here is what Pervushin has to say concerning the results of this work: 'Are purely conjunctural fluctuations determined exclusively by fluctuations in the agricultural economy? Or, to be more precise, are purely conjunctural waves swallowed up by the fluctuations that originate in agriculture? The answer must be in the negative. No investigator has succeeded in demonstrating such a conclusion. On the contrary, Moore's study indicates that when these fluctuations are excluded, other waves of one kind or another do still remain, but they become even *less* regular than they were prior to the removal of agricultural fluctuations. *A great deal less* remains of comprehensiveness and strict periodicity, but these characteristics do still remain'.[23] This conclusion totally contradicts the Marxist manner of looking at the question. Essentially, it leads to the claim that the closer the research approaches to 'pure' capitalism, the weaker is the law-governed cyclical movement. According to this theory, it turns out that the cycle is not purely of capitalist origin but represents a type of dynamic that can be found in several economic formations wherever there are harvests and technology.

Concrete capitalism is an intricate economic complex. We have already shown that neither simple commodity economy – since it involves the exchange links that characterise capitalism – nor the capitalist 'half' of agriculture stands in the way of capitalist 'waves'. On the contrary, what Moore's analysis does is 'free us' from the influence of 'harvest' waves in agriculture that obscure the purity of the conjunctural curve. Why is it that '*A great deal less* remains of comprehensiveness and strict periodicity'? Our reply is that one does not find the reproduction process of *pure* capitalism simply by tearing to shreds the living flesh of *concrete* reproduction. When the actual sinews of reproduction

[22] Bazarov 1926, p. 97.

[23] Pervushin, 1925, p. 48. [Pervushin's reference is to Henry Ludwell Moore, *Economic Cycles, their Law and Cause* (1914). Moore thought the economic cycle was driven by eight-year rainfall cycles. Moore's other principal work on the subject was *Generating Economic Cycles* (1923).]

are abruptly severed, the reproduction process, taking into account the relative significance of agriculture (the exclusion of specific waves also implies partially excluding the material-production apparatus), assumes a *distorted* appearance.[24] If 'pure' capitalism were really possible, it would have its own unique way of integrating its parts, and its separate moments of reproduction would be closely interwoven. In this case, there would be none of the gaping holes that result from surgical removal of some of the parts, which in one way or another have grown into the whole and play a determinate role in the course of reproduction. Neglecting to take this into account, Moore and his followers smugly think that they have demolished the theory of pure capitalism. The reality is quite different. It is in 'pure' capitalism, more than anywhere else, that the cyclical form of the dynamic would find its exact and pure expression, and this dynamic would have the very same relation to the cyclical dynamic of concrete capitalism as, let us say, a body that falls in a vacuum would have to a body that falls in natural space.

'If there were no supplementary market, that fact, on its own, would not mean that capitalism would cease to exist. Capitalism would remain fully "conceivable". But if such a market is available, then the concrete development will necessarily follow the line of least resistance. To do otherwise is what would be "inconceivable".'[25] This comment by Bukharin, concerning the possibility of pure capitalist reproduction, is also fully applicable to its cycles; indeed, these are just two sides of one and the same problem. If it were possible for a pure capitalist economy really to exist, then the purity of its cyclical form of development would find its highest expression. We would see the 'concentrated' activity of all its relations and thus, in the clearest possible way, we would also see the actual activity of its laws. Not merely the fundamental laws, but even the more concrete 'causes' of the cycle would act with the utmost clarity. The most rapid tempo of technological change would be accompanied by the massive replacement of worn-out capital on the basis of extensive competition; the reciprocal expansion of these two processes would peak; the role of the 'periphery' – or of 'third parties' – would be played by weaker capitalist countries; speculation and stock-jobbing would reach their extremes, and so forth.

---

[24] [Part of the social material-production apparatus is reproduced for use in agriculture.]

[25] Luxemburg and Bukharin 1972, pp. 243–4. [My translation differs slightly from the one given in this source.]

Finally, one must note the colossal methodological difficulties involved in working with conjunctural processes and organising them systematically. Just how should we fill in and substitute for the many yawning gaps that result from operationally omitting certain groups of phenomena that nevertheless remain part of the capitalist system's concrete reproduction process? Any attempt to address this issue presupposes, at a minimum, starting with a correct methodological approach. Inability, for example, to distinguish concrete from 'pure' capitalism; the tendency to treat these concepts as if they were the same, to ascribe to concrete capitalism a clearer manifestation of certain specific phenomena, while at the same time expecting their activity to be more feeble in 'pure' capitalist conditions – such confusion predetermines the inaccuracy of any conclusions and constructions. Modern economics certainly cannot boast of having a correct methodology for studying the conjuncture. However, it is vitally important to work out methodologically correct modes of analysis, criteria, etc. that are appropriate to the matter under investigation. In economics, one cannot apply the same exact methods as in the natural sciences, at least not on a broad scale. To analyse the living body of economic phenomena demands a special approach.[26]

Even greater care and scepticism is required in dealing with current attempts in Marxist circles to use the method of natural science as an instrument for studying capitalism, especially its dynamic.[27] Consider, for example, the work of V.A. Bazarov.[28] He asks whether it is possible to use the methods of natural science 'for a quantitative analysis of the social dynamic', and he gives a positive response: 'A single unified method – he says – is completely appropriate if the qualitatively different phenomena have the same organisational links, or if materially different processes are *formally* identical and have one and the same structure. Discovery of quantitative relationships that are formally identical but still have the most profound qualitative differences, and construction on this basis of simple schematic "models" of complex processes – this is the method that is always applied in the exact natural sciences, and it

[26] [Marx wrote: 'In the analysis of economic forms . . . neither microscopes nor chemical reagents are of use. The force of abstraction must replace both' (Marx, 1961, p. 8).]

[27] Among non-Marxists in Russia, this applies to N. Kondrat'ev (see Kondrat'ev 1924, pp. 359–60).

[28] [Bazarov was one of the few Marxist writers who spoke favourably of Kondrat'ev's theory of long cycles. See his review of Kondrat'ev's work in the November 1925 issue of the journal *Ekonomicheskoe obozrenie*, pp. 256–8.]

has proven itself by its numerous accomplishments. If it encounters stubborn opposition in the social sciences, that is mainly due to the simple fact that social scientists have not yet adopted the corresponding practices'.[29] Elsewhere he speaks more clearly and attributes the problem to the 'ignorance of social scientists'. As a model of new 'practices' in economic analysis, consider the following discussion, which refers to the identity between the process of 'flooding the market . . . and a chemical reaction going to completion'.[30] Bazarov comments: 'One can say with absolute certainty that if chemical molecules were involved, in a similarly weak solution, there would be no predictable reaction. *Social molecules* (sic) are blessed with conscious intentions and "free" will, and precisely because of this complexity they do not move inertly through the market in response to random blows and collisions, but instead have a certain directionality and move more or less at a constant speed'.[31] This remark is certainly a 'pearl', and all the others are of roughly the same kind.[32]

The scientific-cognitive value of such remarks, or the extent to which they help to clarify the specific nature of economic phenomena in their development, is highly suspect, but the negative consequences of such an approach are perfectly obvious.

---

[29] Bazarov 1926, p. 106. [Kondrat'ev likewise thought the natural and social sciences can, and do, borrow concepts from each other (Kondrat'ev 1924, pp. 359–60).]

[30] [Bazarov's exact statement is: '. . . protsess nasyshcheniya rynka stanovitsya po svoei organizatsionnoi strukture tozhdestvennym s protekaniem reaktsii 'obmennovo razlozheniya', pri uslovii, chto odin iz produktov reaktsii udalyaetsya iz sfery reagiruyushchikh tel.']

[31] Bazarov 1926, pp. 114, 117. [These issues are discussed in more detail in Maksakovsky 1928.]

[32] [Bazarov's example involves adding hydrochloric acid to a solution of soda until all of the soda molecules are converted into molecules of sodium chloride, with the accompanying release of carbonic acid as a gas. The intended analogy is as follows: the molecules of soda (units of a commodity) disappear as they meet with molecules of hydrochloric acid (purchasers of the commodity). The reaction goes to completion when there are no soda molecules left in the solution. The molecules of soda, whatever their speed or direction of movement, can be assumed in the aggregate to have an equal likelihood of encountering molecules of hydrochloric acid, making the reaction statistically predictable. The question is whether the action of consumers, whose movement in the market is governed by autonomous will, is equally predictable. Bazarov answers that despite 'free' will, the sale of commodities appears to follow a pattern that is even more predictable than a chemical reaction. In a chemical reaction involving a very small number of reactant molecules, the process will not be predictable in the same way as would be the case with larger numbers. But, in the market, the actions of consumers, whatever their number or the number of commodities, are conditioned by regulating influences such as the activities of government or the militia, so that predictability applies even to small numbers that in physics or chemistry would imply chaos.]

What is the effect of emphasising a *formal* identity between economic and natural phenomena? The most important result is to exaggerate the *formal* approach, so that its predominance ends up obscuring the essence of the economic phenomena themselves. What happens when people and groups are treated as 'social molecules' and looked upon in same way as 'chemical molecules'? Just what economic laws can be clarified more successfully by beginning with this comparison of 'formally identical but qualitatively different magnitudes'? The answer is none. The only result is to confuse the question, to destroy the unity of economic analysis by focusing on metaphysical questions of similarity and difference while completely forgetting about *qualitative* essentials. For Marx, the construction of 'models' means logically working out the typical, qualitative relationships of the capitalist economy. This approach has enormous cognitive significance because it makes it possible to sort out the component elements of the capitalist complex and to create a theoretical replica of this interactive whole. For Bazarov, on the contrary, a formal analogy predominates. The analogy does not 'work up' economic phenomena with a view to their internal, dialectical connections, but, on the contrary, tears them out of their connective context and attributes to them a hue and colour borrowed from natural phenomena, so that they may be visualised by the enlightened analyst and, in his hands, become instruments for diagnosing the 'hidden' secrets of the economic process. The crude arbitrariness of *formal* analogies replaces an attempt to penetrate the dialectical development of the economic process by working from within that process itself.

The issue of applying natural-scientific methods to economic research must be resolved in general methodological terms before attempting to employ such methods concretely. Every science has it own scientific method and its own working instruments. Just as one cannot shave steel with a plane made for wood, so one cannot explain market phenomena by reference to a process involving 'a chemical reaction going to completion'. In each case there are qualitative laws that determine the external side of events. Logical totalities cannot be reduced to a formal identity. The general laws that underpin the development of the world of social matter and of simple matter – or natural science – require a specific methodological apparatus that depends upon the concrete specificities of the object being investigated. This does not prevent an exchange of concepts between the different sciences. Such conceptual exchanges do occur and have value. But when economics borrows a concept from natural science, or vice versa, the concept acquires a different meaning.

It becomes assimilated into a different science and acquires it own special content, its own specific implication. In all such matters one must observe proper caution and be fully aware of the limits. Bazarov oversteps those limits.

These issues require critical reflection in order to refine the method of analysis. In particular, the so-called symptomatology of the conjuncture – the study of its indicators of movement, how they are formed and integrated in a graph of the conjunctural process – has, until now, been undertaken mainly by bourgeois economics. This means that a Marxist study of the conjuncture must also rely on materials (indicators, graphs, schemes) that have been produced by researchers who neither use nor are capable of using the dialectical method. Marxist economics must critically review the whole range of these research instruments and work out its own models, thereby making it possible to address the problem of the dynamic not only in depth, but also, and to the same degree, concretely.

The fundamental 'causes' of the conjunctural cycle

The connection between the cyclical dynamic and the capitalist mode of production is so obvious that not a single bourgeois economist disputes it. But since they have no deep understanding of the character of this cyclical movement, they extend it equally to the socialist economy, which they take to mean either a real economy of the future or a compilation of views extracted from socialist ideology (this is the approach of Cassel, Bouniatian, Aftalion, Röpke, and others).

A simple commodity economy has no cyclical dynamic.[33] Neither its historical elements, whose origins lie in direct exchange, nor its more developed elements, involving monetary exchanges, lead to a cyclical movement. The principal manifestation of the cycle is periodic general overproduction of commodities. Because of the low level of technology, this cannot happen in a simple

[33] [Simple commodity economy is production for exchange but without the use of wage-labour. Artisans and private farmers produce commodities with their own means of production. Marx writes: 'The process, therefore, that clears the way for the capitalist system, can be none other than the process that transforms, on the one hand, the social means of subsistence and of production into capital, on the other, the immediate producers into wage labourers' (Marx 1961, p. 714).]

commodity economy. Finally, the exchange relations themselves do not assume a universal character, but are more like 'oases' scattered about in the natural economy. In order to clarify the causes of the cycle, however, all that is needed is to introduce one essential difference between the two stages of simple commodity economy.

With exchange through barter, the possibility of general overproduction is ruled out by two circumstances: first, the low level of technology and second, the lack of monetary connections. The low level of technology excludes the very possibility of overproduction, while the paucity of monetary connections makes it impossible for a partial disruption of sales to become universal. To illustrate, let us hypothesise capitalism without monetary exchanges. No matter how extensive or detailed the social division of labour, in these circumstances no disruption of exchange could ever grow into general overproduction. It was exactly this kind of 'vital' capitalism that Say had in his 'mind's eye' when he formulated the dogma of classical economics to the effect that general overproduction was impossible.[34] But, at the next stage of simple exchange economy, one of the obstacles vanishes with the emergence of monetary connections. Moreover, both conditions for overproduction operate at the stage of exchange economy where large-scale commodity production appears and provides an endless stream of commodities circulating on the market. Now commodity exchange creates a complex chain of dependencies that is fantastically 'consecrated' by the network of monetary connections. This level of the productive forces comes when they are capitalistically organised. Thus, it is in the specific conditions of capitalism – when capitalist laws shape the process through monetary connections – that the initial 'causes' of the conjunctural cycle are to be found.

[34] [In *A Treatise on Political Economy*, first published in 1803, Jean-Baptiste Say claimed that total demand in an economy cannot exceed or fall below total supply because supply creates its own demand. As Say put it, 'products are paid for with products' (Say 1803, p. 153); and 'a glut can take place only when there are too many means of production applied to one kind of product and not enough to another' (pp. 178–9). 'It is worth while to remark, that a product is no sooner created, than it, from that instant, affords a market for other products to the full extent of its own value. When the producer has put the finishing hand to his product, he is most anxious to sell it immediately, lest its value should diminish in his hands. Nor is he less anxious to dispose of the money he may get for it; for the value of money is also perishable. But the only way of getting rid of money is in the purchase of some product or other. Thus the mere circumstance of creation of one product immediately opens a vent for other products' (pp. 138–9).]

A simple commodity economy is characterised by the existence of a single law – the law of value – expressing the relationship between independent commodity producers when they are connected through the monetary form. Here, we find the initial element of anarchy, but there is not yet any cycle. The social division of labour is not yet highly developed; inter-branch competition is rudimentary; the branches that produce means of production and semi-fabricates play a modest role; machine production has yet to replace the traditional ways of doing things, so that any dramatic increase in labour productivity is impossible; and finally, the prevailing economic motive is to convert necessary labour into another consumable form. In this state of affairs, there is only a weakly developed price dynamic and an extraordinary level of price stability, with only modest fluctuations over entire decades. It was impossible in these conditions to have general overproduction, much less a cycle.

But even the simple commodity economy had the embryo of a cyclical movement. Marx writes that the crisis is already inherent in 'the contradiction between sale and purchase and the contradiction of money as a means of payment. . . . [T]he nature of crisis appears in its simplest forms, and, in so far as this form is itself the simplest content of crisis, in its simplest content. But the content is not yet *substantiated*'.[35] Thus, the embryo of crisis and the cyclical form of development is initially inherent in the law of value and its monetary form. Nevertheless, the real existence of the crisis only comes with development of industrial capitalism. 'The contradictions inherent in the circulation of commodities, which are further developed in the circulation of money – and thus, also, the possibilities of *crises* – reproduce themselves,

[35] Marx 1975a, p. 512 [Marx responded to the kind of argument associated with J.-B. Say this way: 'Nothing can be more childish than the dogma, that because every sale is a purchase, and every purchase a sale, therefore the circulation of commodities necessarily implies an equilibrium of sales and purchases. If this means that the number of actual sales is equal to the number of purchases, it is mere tautology. But its real import is to prove that every seller brings his buyer to market with him. Nothing of the kind. . . . No one can sell unless some one else purchases. But no one is forthwith bound to purchase, because he has just sold. Circulation bursts through all the restrictions as to time, place, and individuals, imposed by direct barter, and this it effects by splitting up, into the antithesis of sale and purchase, the direct identity that in barter does exist between the alienation of one's own and the acquisition of another man's product. . . . If the interval in time between the two complementary metamorphoses of a commodity becomes too great, if the split between the sale and the purchase become too pronounced, the intimate connexion between them, their oneness, asserts itself by producing – a crisis' (Marx 1961, pp. 113–14).]

automatically, in capital . . .'.[36] The crisis is realised precisely when it arises 'out of the special aspects of capital which are *peculiar* to it as capital, and not merely comprised in its existence as commodity and money'.[37]

Thus, the crisis only becomes real when value, still preserving its original form and significance, also grows over into capital – a new relation of production. But the relation of exploitation, on its own, is still not enough to cause a crisis to become a law-governed *cyclical* movement or a 'normally' functioning conjuncture. For this to happen, what is required is that 'the commodity-money contradiction be complicated by the fact that prices deviate from values; this contradiction assumes extraordinarily complex forms in capitalist market relations, in the specifically capitalist relations of "demand" and "supply". It is only within the sphere of capitalist competition that this contradiction reaches the final and extremely complex form specific to capitalism (while still "preserving" and "returning" to its fundamental form even within the capitalist form)'.[38]

In this passage, Osinsky gave a perfectly correct interpretation of Marx's thesis to the effect that 'the real crisis can only be educed from the real movement of capitalist production, competition and credit'.[39] What is the meaning of this thesis? It means that, while the crisis is implicit in the structure of the capitalist mode of production, the laws governing its *periodicity* only begin to operate at a *certain* level of capitalist development, when capitalist competition *fully* emerges and creates the 'specifically capitalist relations of "demand" and "supply"', whose starting point is pursuit of the average profit. In other words, the crisis only acquires the character of a phenomenon repeating itself in conformity with laws when the immediate 'regulator' of the capitalist economy becomes the price of production – the historic form of value that not only includes within itself the relation of capitalist exploitation but also presupposes developed, inter-branch competition between capitals. Only on the basis of the price of production does the specific dynamic of market prices arise, reflecting in its wave-like fluctuations the movement of capitalist reproduction that resolves itself in a law-governed manner by way of crises.[40]

---

[36] Marx 1975a, p. 512.
[37] Marx 1975a, pp. 512–13.
[38] Osinsky 1925, p. 64.
[39] Marx 1975a, p. 512.
[40] [When different capitals have different organic compositions, the average rate of profit results from reallocations of surplus-value. The 'price' that incorporates the

To summarise: 1) a simple commodity economy with a single fundamental law – that of value – contains the crisis and the cycle as potentialities; 2) the 'emergence' of capitalist production – including the law of value plus the law of surplus-value – brings real crises that appear *sporadically* but without lawful periodicity (an incomplete, historically 'unfinished' cycle); 3) developed capitalist production – with the law of value, the law of surplus-value, and the law of the average profit – brings *periodic* crises and the completed cycle.

Thus, the cyclical dynamic will become the exact form assumed by capitalist reproduction only at a certain stage of capitalism's development, when it reaches *both qualitative and quantitative* maturity in its fundamental relations (the price of production).

This sequence is confirmed by the historical data. England – the leading capitalist country – had no experience of periodic crises before 1825 even though there were separate 'sporadic' crises in its economy much earlier. It is enough to point out that some historians trace the pedigree of crises as far back as the seventeenth century. However, prior to the first half of the eighteenth century, it was generally impossible to speak of crises in the strict sense of the word, that is, of industrial-capitalist crises. By the end of the eighteenth and the beginning of the nineteenth century, when industrial capital became the prevailing form in England, a few 'sporadic' crises still occurred. There is no doubt that these were basically of industrial origin. The activity of 'organic' conditions was already beginning to prevail over 'exogenous' causes, but it was still difficult to discern cyclical lawfulness in these crises. Capitalism had yet to reach the necessary 'quantitative' maturity; the cohesion between movements of individual capitals was not yet sufficiently complex; there were still enormous influences originating from holdovers of simple commodity production; and many functioning capitalist enterprises had yet to achieve a high technological level.

Another condition that must be taken into account is that the law of the average rate of profit was still emerging. The mass of profit realised by capitalists still approximated the mass of surplus-value created in each branch, and capitalist exploitation had not yet taken on the mature integument of profit that becomes detached from the amount of living labour used in each enterprise. The existing tendency towards the average rate of profit had yet

social average rate of profit is the 'price of production', a conceptual axis around which market prices move.]

to become the basic fact in the consciousness of capitalists or the measuring rod they used for assessing their own activities. This was also reflected in the economics of the time – in the problems that Smith and Ricardo experienced in trying to understand this 'new' tendency.

Thus, historical evidence also verifies the view that the cycle develops gradually. Between the *historical* emergence of the price of production, as the immediate regulator of the capitalist system, and the capitalist dynamic in its law-governed *cyclical* form, there are obviously historical and logical connections. The full substantiation of these connections will come in the following chapter, which will deal directly with the theory of the cycle. Here, it is important to emphasise only the decisive moment – the development of these connections in the form of capitalist competition. With one 'hand', inter-branch competition 'creates' the price of production, converting the 'equilibrium' of labour into 'equilibrium of capitals';[41] with the other hand, it 'gives birth' to the specific relations of market demand and supply and thus to the fluctuating movement of market prices, which is the most important feature in the movement of the cycle. But market competition, based upon the price of production, itself depends upon the influence of another factor – the way in which fixed capital is replaced. This particular connection, involving the interaction between capitalist competition and the character of the replacement of fixed capital, is the most outstanding condition of the cycle. Let us give a preliminary sketch of its importance.

'Only when machine industry has sunk such deep roots that it becomes the dominant influence in the national industry; when, thanks to machine industry, foreign trade becomes more important than domestic trade; . . . finally, when many industrial nations enter into *competition* with one another – only *then* do endlessly repeating cycles appear, with phases that last for years and always lead to a general crisis, which is the completion of one cycle and the beginning of a new one'.[42] What does the development of 'machine

[41] [Instead of commodities exchanging 'equally' according to the labour they embody, the price of production redistributes profit to create a different kind of equality and a different 'equilibrium' condition; that is, each capital now receives the same average rate of profit.]

[42] [Maksakovsky's footnote refers to p. 651 of *Capital* but does not specify either the volume or the edition. The excerpt is probably from Volume I, but I cannot locate it in the English-language edition I am using. His Russian-language text may have been a translation of a different edition of *Capital*.]

industry' mean? It means, above all, that the organic composition of capital rises; that constant capital outweighs variable capital; and, as a specific, observable expression of this fact, that fixed capital grows more rapidly than circulating capital. In turn, the rise of the organic composition of capital, as Marx shows, is accompanied by increased capitalist competition. These two moments condition each other; development of the one accelerates the other and vice versa.

Earlier periods in the development of capitalist industry were characterised by a less important role for fixed capital. As a general rule, circulating capital was dominant, with the consequence that conditions were not appropriate for competition to grow.[43] The specific attribute of circulating capital is that it is entirely replaced with each turnover of capital. Any disturbance resulting from its overproduction or underproduction was not drawn out or 'preserved'. It found expression in price fluctuations and, in response to those pressures, any disturbance was overcome in the next stages of reproduction. The market controlled social production more directly. The apparatus of capitalist competition was less complex and operated in a simple, 'transparent' manner. As a result, the laws of 'equilibrium', whose working instrument is capitalist competition, *fully* exercised their regulating activity throughout the 'cycle' of *circulation*. The price of production – value – regulated capitalist production 'without interruption' *as soon as* disturbances appeared. The tendency towards 'equilibrium' manifested itself by overcoming any 'current' obstacles. All of this took place in circumstances where productive capital essentially meant its circulating part. It is only when specifically market competition develops,[44] and when the existing relation of 'demand' and 'supply' ceases to reflect accurately the proportionality of social production, that direct action of the laws of equilibrium on prices is paralysed. Market spontaneity then causes prices to deviate from values and become totally subordinate to the conjuncture – and then the cycle unfolds. This is the *unique and defining* characteristic of capitalist competition, and it results from the growing significance of fixed capital and the way in which it is actually reproduced.

---

[43] [Maksakovsky is referring to the kind of competition that equalises the profit rate. Equalisation is a consequence of the relative immobility of fixed capital as compared with circulating capital. Where there is little fixed capital, this kind of competition is not yet significant.]

[44] [The reference is again to competition involving the redistribution of surplus-value with a tendency to equalise the rate of profit between capitals.]

Thus, the growth of fixed capital and development of 'machine industry', as Marx said in the remark we cited, is the most important moment in the 'maturation' of the cycle. Only with the rising organic composition of capital does the market for means of production become the determining force. Social production escapes day-to-day control by the laws of 'equilibrium'. The polarisation of production and consumption, which originates with the first appearance of capital, now reaches full development. All the contradictions of the capitalist system, on whatever level they operate, become fully mature.

Without going into detail here, we must come to the following conclusion: while the fundamental condition for appearance of the cycle is that capitalism reach such a degree of development that its 'postulate of equilibrium' becomes the price of production, the second and more concrete condition for the cycle, which develops together and in close connection with the first, is that fixed capital become 'sufficiently' important. On the basis of these two conditions the specific, irrational form of *market* competition emerges, that is, a protracted detachment of prices from the price of production, or value, and it is this detachment that drives the social system towards general overproduction.[45]

Let us now attempt to show logically the initial moving principle of the conjuncture, or the most general 'cause' of the conjunctural cycle, which determines how all the other 'causes' and 'conditions' operate. This will be of the utmost importance for a methodologically correct treatment of the theory of the cycle.

We have already mentioned that the activities of all the categories of the capitalist economy are expressed in the conjuncture. Marx says this clearly and concisely: 'The individual factors, which are condensed in these crises, must . . . emerge and must be described in each sphere of the bourgeois economy, and the further we advance in our examination of the latter, the more aspects of this conflict must be traced on the one hand, and on the other hand it must be shown that its more abstract forms are recurring and are contained in the more concrete forms'.[46] Every category 'participates' in the formation of the conjuncture. It is no surprise, therefore, that Marx speaks of the inevitability of capitalist crises with reference to the problem of value, of money, of profit, credit, etc. as he sets out his most elementary 'model'.

---

45 [In Maksakovsky's usage, 'rationality' refers to conditions dictated by the law of value; 'irrationality' refers to detachment of market prices from the price of production.]

46 Marx 1975a, p. 510.

But we must also mention another thought by Marx. He comments that there are both more general ('abstract') forms of crises, and thus of cycles, and also more concrete forms; and while the abstract are dialectically contained in the concrete, they might also occur independently. Translated into the language of 'categories', this means that the crisis and the cycle are inherent in the most basic form of the law of value. It is precisely this law that expresses the fundamental contradiction of the system – the lack of coordination between social production and consumption, between 'demand' and 'supply'. This 'anarchy' is the basis of all the other contradictions and therefore of the cycle. But this fundamental contradiction, which becomes manifest in crises, does not operate in isolation. Under capitalism, the law of value 'gives birth' to many other categories that express the system's more concrete contradictions. Each of these categories is a category of value.[47] Each expresses a particular relationship of the capitalist economy and is a dialectical form of the 'life' of the law of value – a more concrete form, in and through which the initial action of the law of value appears. The logical development of all the other value relations out of the law of value reflects the dialectical process whereby the relations of independent commodity producers grow over into the complex economy of capitalism in real-historical terms.

Every category of capitalism results from the self-reproduction of the first category.[48] It is only through this self-reproducing process that the law of value reaches full maturity. The regulating role of value gathers force in direct proportion to the complexity of the superstructure of value relations. In a simple commodity economy, which is the first stage of unorganised economy, the activity of the law of value is only weakly felt. Under capitalism, with its intricate superstructure of value relations, the law of value acts with incomparably greater force, for it is only here that we encounter fully formed commodity production. Marx says 'developed circulation of commodities and of money . . . only takes place on the basis of capital'.[49] Elsewhere he writes: '. . . the product wholly assumes the form of a commodity only as a result of the fact that the entire product has to be transformed into exchange-value and also that all the ingredients necessary for its production enter it as

[47] [The Hegelian expressive totality is evident here: all the developed categories are already implicit in the simplest category of value. The beginning is the end; the end is also the beginning.]
[48] [A literal translation would be: 'from the asexual reproduction of the first'.]
[49] Marx 1975a, p. 512.

commodities – in other words it wholly becomes a commodity only with the development and on the basis of capitalist production'.[50] Thus, the law of value gathers force in correspondence with the development of capitalism and directs the activity of all other laws, which arise from it historically.

Taken in isolation, the law of value does not generate a cycle. The obvious example is a simple commodity economy where there is anarchy but not a cycle. Since the anarchy is weak, so too is the law of value. Even in a capitalist economy, the law of value is 'weak' if taken in isolation from the other categories. In that context, it cannot 'give birth' to a cycle even though it is the basic contradiction of the system. But the fact is that the activity of the law of value is never isolated in capitalist conditions. We can only conceive of it in isolation through the force of abstraction. As the 'ancestral' law of the system, it lives and acts through its multiple 'life' forms – through the categories of value, which express the concrete contradictions of the system and find in those contradictions their own concrete content. For example: 1) when the law of surplus-value and profit are included, value becomes the price of production; 2) when value assumes the form of fixed and circulating capital, it 'gives birth' to specifically market competition, which entails price fluctuations, etc. 'The conclusion that we reach is not that production, distribution and exchange, and consumption are identical' writes Marx, 'but that they all form the members of a totality, distinctions within a unity. Production predominates not only over itself, in the antithetical definition of production, but over the other moments as well.' Moreover, 'A definite production thus determines a definite consumption, distribution and exchange as well as definite relations between these different moments'.[51] This model of dialectical reason relates directly to the questions at hand. Value, surplus-value, the average profit, money, credit, and so forth are essential parts of a single whole (the capitalist system) – they are differences within a unity. But the fundamental category is value, which, in the contradictoriness of its more particular forms, embraces both itself and all the other categories, which are dialectical

[50] Marx 1975b, p. 74.

[51] [The reference is to *A Contribution to the Critique of Political Economy*. In the 1970 English translation from Progress Publishers, Moscow, the corresponding pages are 204–5. In the English translation from Peking Foreign Languages Press, 1976, which includes the preface and introduction, the pages are 29–30. Since neither of these translations fully captures the dialectic of Marx's formulation, I have taken this excerpt from Martin Nicolaus's version of *Grundrisse* (Marx 1973, p. 99).]

transformations of value. If the totality of these forces, in their interaction and mutual conditioning, determines the cyclical course of capitalism's development, then the moving principle of this dynamic is found in the law of value and in the character of its spontaneous regulatory action. *Therefore, the fundamental factor of the conjuncture, the moving principle of the cycle, is the law of value, whose activity extends throughout all the 'stages' of capitalist reproduction and is 'transmitted' in the form of the price of production, thereby determining both the direction and the interaction of all the levers of reproduction* (prices, money, credit, 'interest rates' etc.). Contradiction is inherent in the character of the law of value's activity (it asserts itself *post factum*) and is the basis of *that specific* apposition of economic forces whose invariable result is periodic eruptions of accumulating contradictions. It is precisely this activity that imparts to capitalist contradictions their periodic intensification and 'attenuation' together with the abrupt turning points that occur along the way.

Therefore, the starting point for the formation and interaction of the economic forces that objectify themselves in the cycle is found in the original impulse for their interaction, that is, in value.

We have, in consequence, established the following: 1) the theory of the conjuncture leads to study of the nature of the commercial-industrial cycle, which expresses the real course of capitalist reproduction over determinate periods of time; 2) the essence of the problem is to establish the 'causes' that condition the cyclical dynamic of capitalist economy; 3) the most universal condition of the conjuncture is the interaction of the productive forces with their capitalist integument – the periodic contraction imposed by the integument on the productive forces and the repeated victories of the latter in this endless struggle; 4) in the most general economic terms, the conjuncture is the developed form in which the interaction of all the categories of capitalist economy occurs; 5) in historical terms, the appearance of cyclical movement is associated with such a high level of capitalist development that the significance of fixed capital has grown and the immediate 'regulator' of proportionality has become the price of production; 6) the fundamental moving principle of the conjuncture, its ultimate 'cause', is the law of value, which determines the character and direction of activity on the part of all the concrete economic forces through their expression in the conjuncture.

With that said, we must now turn directly to analysis of the conjunctural cycle.

Chapter 2

The General Theory of the Cycle

The problem of real reproduction[1]

We have already said that the problem of the conjuncture is directly associated with the problem of social reproduction. The theory of the conjuncture, accordingly, continues the theory of reproduction and represents its final chapter.[2] These are two successive stages in the elaboration of *a single* problem: the movement of the capitalist system as a whole.

In terms of its fundamental *principles*, Marx solved the problem of the movement of the capitalist whole.

First, he demonstrated the close connection of every individual capital with the vast multitude of others that condition its existence. The capitalist economy is split into countless capitals, and the system has no single subject – it is not a consciously established *teleological* whole, although the existence and development of this intricate complex does display the presence and operation of several objective laws. Every category in the Marxist system of economics is [theoretically embraced by laws][3] that are logically derived through abstraction from the real movement of the entire capitalist complex.

---

[1] [Maksakovsky deals in this chapter only with 'real' reproduction, leaving monetary phenomena to the next chapter.]

[2] [The 'theory of reproduction' refers to the reproduction schemes in *Capital*, Volume II; the 'theory of the conjuncture' refers to 'real' reproduction.]

[3] [Maksakovsky's text says 'Every category . . . is a theoretically known law . . .' Since a category cannot *be* a law, I have substituted the formulation in square brackets.]

Having established in Volume I [of *Capital*] the fundamental laws that constitute the system's foundation, and having shown the inevitable connection between capitalist 'atoms' and the principles involved, in Volume II, Marx gave a more concrete picture of how this connection is realised and the interdependence that results.

Every industrial capital exists simultaneously in three parallel stages through which it moves continuously. One part assumes the monetary form and confronts the world of commodities, which becomes the next form of its embodiment. This is the circuit of money capital. Another part of the same capital, consisting of means of production, is subject to the action of living human labour and 'creates the mystery' of growth on the part of value that has been advanced [as wages]. This is the circuit of productive capital. The third part, taking the form of commodities that strive to be transformed into money, represents the circuit of commodity capital. Each of these stages presupposes, as its necessary condition, an intimate connection between all the separate capitals; to be more exact, each stage is a result of this connection.[4] Thus, any individual capital, in all the phases of its circulation, *directly* merges with the movement of other capitals to form the market circuit. It is through a seeming chaos of 'fortuitous' encounters between commodities and money that the real movement of the capitalist economy occurs. Only in the productive phase is capital 'autonomous', but this independence is also deeply conditioned. Insofar as the continuous flow of capitalist production is determined by the 'normal' movement of the whole complex of capitals in their 'circulation' phases, which, in turn, furnish productive capital with its objectified and human elements, the very possibility of growth on the part of advanced value is determined by the coexistence and unique combination of the entire complex of individual capitals. Thus, despite its apparent incoherence, the capitalist economy, like any other, represents a single whole that is composed of closely connected, interacting parts. The complex of individual capitals manifests from within itself a number of objective moments that oppose each other as the expressions of an irreversible, conditioning law. From the close interaction

[4] [In *Capital*, Volume II, Marx writes: 'The actual circuit of industrial capital in its continuity is . . . the unity of all its three circuits. But it can be such a unity only if all the different parts of capital can go through the successive stages of the circuit, can pass from one phase, from one functional form to another, so that the industrial capital, being the whole of all these parts, exists simultaneously in its various phases and functions and thus describes all three circuits at the same time. The succession [*das Nacheinander*] of these parts is here governed by their co-existence [*das Nebeneinander*]' (Marx 1957, p. 103).]

of these individual capitals arises the movement of social capital *as a whole*, which in turn dissolves into these distinct circuits as its constituent links.

Having established the concept of social capital and its circulation, Marx pointed to the existence of a definite coherence in the movement of social capital through all of its phases. Above all, there is a perfectly clear spatial pattern connecting the multitude of enterprises that constitute separate rungs on the ladder of production. However, 'the spatial coexistence that determines continuity of production only exists thanks to the movement of capital's parts as they successively pass through their different stages. *Spatial coexistence is itself merely the result of a sequence in terms of time*'.[5]

It follows that for a 'normal' flow of social circulation to occur, it is not enough for the coal industry to exist together with a metallurgical industry and an enormous number of other industries, all of which are connected by market links between branches. This condition merely guarantees the *formal* possibility of social capital's transition from one phase to the next. It is also necessary for all phases of every individual capital to follow one another sequentially, without interruption or delay. This requirement is no less important, and its disruption represents a phenomenon unique to a capitalist economy. 'The first metamorphosis of one capital must correspond to the second metamorphosis of the other – says Marx – the departure of one capital from the production process must correspond to the return to the production process of another capital'.[6] Any delay disrupts the complex mechanism of social circulation. 'Thus . . . for example, if a commodity cannot be sold and the movement C^1 -M^1 is interrupted for one part, then the circulation of this part is interrupted and it is not replaced by the means of its reproduction; the succeeding parts, which emerge from the process of production in the form of C^1, find the change of their functions blocked by their predecessors. If such a condition lasts for some time, production contracts and the whole process comes to a halt. *Every stoppage in the sequence of movements by the parts leads to disorder in their spatial coexistence;* every stoppage in one stage brings with it interruption of the whole circulation . . .'.[7]

At this stage of the analysis, Marx already establishes the inevitability of interruptions in social reproduction and the ensuing crisis, which, for present

[5] Marx 1957, p. 103.
[6] Marx 1975a, pp. 510–11.
[7] Marx 1957, p. 103.

purposes, arises from discontinuities in the sequence whereby capitals move through their successive phases.[8] This inevitability appears much more clearly in the following stage – the theory of social reproduction. Beginning with the fact of capital's uninterrupted circulation, law-governed relationships make themselves felt between the separate parts of social production. These relationships are conditions for the uninterrupted development of the system, and their disruption is reflected in the inevitable suspension of social circulation.

The problem that had to be resolved is this: 'How is the *capital* that is consumed in production replaced, in terms of value, out of the annual product (out of C¹-P.M.),[9] and how does the movement of this replacement relate to consumption of surplus-value by the capitalists and of wages by the labourers?'[10] This formulation of the problem embraced reproduction of the materially objectified framework of capitalist production, both in its necessary value relationships and in its corresponding natural form (without which capital cannot grow in value); it also included reproduction of capitalist relationships themselves – that is, reproduction of the class of capitalists on the one hand, and of the working class on the other.

Marx solved this problem of the uninterrupted development of the capitalist whole on both a constant and an expanding scale. The key was to subdivide social production under two headings: production of means of production (Department I), and production of means of consumption (Department II). The solution involved ascertaining definite value relations between the separate

---

[8] [It is not clear that Maksakovsky's reference to 'inevitability' is really appropriate at this stage. On the one hand, he speaks of 'social capital', implying fully developed capitalist production; on the other hand, this particular example refers to what Marx called 'the falling apart of purchase and sale', which points only to 'the general possibility of crisis', a point that Maksakovsky himself makes quite clear on the following pages of this chapter. On the 'possibility' of a crisis, Marx wrote as follows: 'The general, abstract possibility of crisis denotes no more than the *most abstract form* of crisis, without content, without a compelling motivating factor. Sale and purchase may fall apart. They thus represent potential *crisis* and their coincidence always remains a critical factor for the commodity. The transition from one to the other may, however, proceed smoothly. The *most abstract form of crisis* (and therefore the formal possibility of crisis) is thus the *metamorphosis of the commodity* itself; the contradiction of exchange-value and use-value, and furthermore of money and commodity, comprised within the unity of the commodity, exists in metamorphosis only as an involved movement. The factors which turn this possibility of crisis into [an actual] crisis are not contained in this form itself; it only implies that *the framework* for a crisis exists' (Marx 1975a, p. 509; also pp. 513–14).]

[9] [When the initials P.M. occur in the translation they indicate insertions by Maksakovsky. Any insertions in square brackets are provided by the Translator.]

[10] Marx 1957, p. 393.

functional components of both Departments. For simple reproduction, this basic 'proportionality' was expressed in the formula $v_1 + s_1 = c_2$; for expanded reproduction, it was $v_1 + s_1 > c_2$. In the first case [simple reproduction], if the newly created value in Department I were less than the constant capital of Department II, then the latter could not fully assume the natural form needed in order for it to function productively; in the opposite circumstance, a certain portion of the income of Department I could not be consumed. In the second case (expanded reproduction), 'all the new variable capital of Department I, and that Department's portion of surplus-value subject to non-productive consumption, must be equal to the new constant capital of Department II'.[11] Disruption of these conditions would inevitably cause overproduction, an interruption in circulation and a crisis.

Together with these basic relations, in the course of his analysis Marx also unveiled a number of more particular 'proportionalities'. To begin with, there must be a certain relationship between the scale of production of life's necessities and of luxury items: 'the v that is laid out in the production of luxuries is equal in value (assuming simple reproduction – P.M.) to a corresponding portion of s, produced in the form of necessities of life, and hence must be smaller than the whole of this s . . .'.[12] For analysis of the conjuncture, enormous importance attaches to a second particular proportionality revealed by Marx – *between the fixed capital that wears out each year and the newly applied fixed capital*. In simple reproduction, 'a fixed component part of constant capital II, which is reconverted into money to the full extent of its value and therefore must be renewed each year *in natura* (section 1), should be equal to the annual depreciation of the other component part of constant capital II, which continues to function in its old natural form'.[13]

These 'proportionalities' further subdivide into more particular ones between

[11] Luxemburg and Bukharin 1972, p. 159. [For the Russian edition see Bukharin 1928, p. 10.]

[12] Marx 1957, p. 408.

[13] Marx 1957, p. 464. [Marx is noting that different elements of fixed capital have different life spans and that fixed capital depreciates over an extended period. This means that some capitalists are continuously setting aside a portion of *current* revenues in depreciation accounts, anticipating the time when *future* physical replacement becomes necessary. If some capitalists take money capital out of circulation, and these *savings* are not offset by other capitalists' *investments* of previously accumulated money capital, 'There would be a crisis – a crisis in production – in spite of reproduction on an unchanging scale.' See also Marx 1957, p. 467 and the analysis of expanded reproduction in Chapter 21 of *Capital*, Volume II. For a discussion, see Day 1979–80.]

separate branches of production. In their totality, they determine the possibility of uninterrupted movement of the capitalist system, or its 'moving equilibrium', when the scale of production is either constant or expanding. But such a state of 'moving equilibrium' is merely a theoretically conceivable state of affairs, not only for capitalist production as a whole, but also for each of its individual branches at any particular time. Hence, the analysis of simple and expanded reproduction provided by Marx is not adequate for representing the *real* course of capitalist reproduction as it occurs at any given moment.[14] In both value and physical terms, Marx established a network of lawful relations that permeate the moving system and determine the very possibility of this complex movement. Nevertheless, at this stage of the analysis, he abstracted from the inevitable disruptions of these 'proportionalities'. He based his analysis on the following postulates: 1) exchange of commodities according to their value; 2) unchanging values for the component parts of productive capital; 3) absence of growth in the organic composition of capital; 4) exclusion of the influence of credit (both on the reproduction process and on monetary circulation); 5) exclusion of foreign trade. These postulates by no means imply, however, that Marx operated with an 'imponderable' quantity, that he 'poked his cane in the mist' – to use Rosa Luxemburg's phrase – as someone else might do in similar circumstances. The subject of Marx's analysis was *real* capitalism. In his theory of social reproduction, he provided a general 'model' of the movement of the capitalist whole – but it remained a 'model'. He discovered the laws that represent the foundation of the movement of *real* reproduction, but he described the activities of these laws and relations in their *pure*, constitutive form. This is the real basis of the 'moving equilibrium' of the capitalist system and its turbulent changes. However, at this stage, the real mechanism of realising these changes, which required that a number of complicating moments be included, was not yet provided. Marx conducted the entire analysis of real reproduction at a certain level of abstraction. He resolved the problem in terms of its principles and its content. Such an

[14] [Like Marx, Maksakovsky will use the *theoretical* concept of equilibrium to explain *real* disequilibrium, or disproportionality. For Marx, real 'equilibrium' is a fleeting moment in the immediate wake of a crisis (Marx 1962, p. 244). Although Marx used the schemes of proportionate reproduction to demonstrate the abstract theory of non-cyclical growth, he said that in real reproduction 'the proportionality of the individual branches of production springs as a general process from disproportionality' (Marx 1962, p. 251). A similar comment occurs in Marx 1973, p. 414.]

approach is both the specific achievement of Marxism and the fundamental condition that enables Marxist analysis to penetrate the secret depths of the laws of the capitalist system.[15]

General resolution of the problem, however, is not the same as a comprehensive analysis of the *real course* of capitalist reproduction. It is not possible to depict capitalism's pattern of development within the limitations of a smoothly rising curve.[16] When the problem of reproduction is posed that abstractly, the cyclical pattern of capitalist reproduction cannot be revealed. For that purpose, one needs to advance to the next and final stage of a more concrete analysis, while remaining within the context of the abstract method. Thus, a transition must occur from general resolution of the problem of social reproduction to the real pattern of this process. Above all, this transition must include: 1) extensive action of the law of value and the resulting prices; 2) growth of the organic composition of capital, which is connected with the fully developed activity of capitalist competition; 3) the role of credit. The 'cause' of cyclical movement must be found precisely in the fully developed activity of the mechanism of real reproduction, which is revealed by including the foregoing factors that Marx left out of his general theory of reproduction. As Marx says elsewhere, the cyclical movement can be understood 'only in the real movement of capitalist production, competition, and credit'.

This real movement is inseparable from continuous rupturing of all the 'proportionalities' of social reproduction. In reality, the latter only exist in the form of a law-governed tendency and manifest themselves continuously through a system of obstacles. However, the disruptions to which these proportionalities are subject also have limits. Were it otherwise, the association of capitalists would dissolve into its constituent elements, and the social circulation would become impossible. The real path of capitalist production

---

[15] It is characteristic of bourgeois economists to try to make their investigations more productive in the area of the conjuncture by means of a Marxist approach to solving the problem. 'If we are building a theory of conjunctural fluctuations, it is clear that an abstractly constructed scheme of the national economy in conditions of dynamic equilibrium helps us greatly to discover the mechanism and causes of conjunctural fluctuations, as well as the mechanism and causes of deviations from the path of smooth evolution of the economy, in order that we might thus create an abstract theory of the conjuncture' (Kondrat'ev 1924, p. 372).

[16] [The reference is to Kondrat'ev's graph of capitalism's long-term trend line, which was intended to represent the system's 'moving equilibrium' in real reproduction. This and other graphs are reproduced in Day 1976. See also the Appendix in Day 1981.]

lies between these extremes. It excludes any final equilibrium of mutually adjusted elements of production, for this condition is incompatible with the real development of capitalism; at the same time, it also excludes any minute-to-minute threat of the system's collapse. To be precise, the pattern of the capitalist system's development is characterised by a cyclical dynamic, involving successive intervals of 'peaceful prosperity' and periodic crisis.

Thus, the cyclical movement of capitalist reproduction entails continuous disruptions of all the 'proportions' of reproduction: $v_1 + s_1$ is not equal to c_2, if we look at this lawful requirement within the context of simple reproduction; and the new v of Department I, together with that portion of s going to non-productive consumption, is not equal to the new c of Department II in conditions of expanded reproduction. For these reasons, the proportion is disrupted between the wearing out of fixed capital and its annual renovation; the relation between production of necessities and production of luxuries is also disrupted, and so forth.

There are several logical steps in the transition from the general theory of reproduction to the theory of the conjuncture and the real course of reproduction. The *first* step is translation of pure value relations into the form of the price of production. Because Marx studied social reproduction at a level of abstraction that did not yet include the fully developed activity of capitalist competition, surplus-value was not yet transformed into the average profit.[17] Distribution of productive forces between branches was taken to mean distribution of labour, while 'equilibrium' between the separate branches of production was achieved through exchange according to values. Hence,

---

[17] [When different capitals have different organic compositions, the average rate of profit results from reallocations of surplus-value. The 'price' that incorporates the social average rate of profit is the 'price of production', a conceptual axis around which market prices move: '*Price* is therefore distinguished from *value* . . . because the latter appears as the law of the motions which the former runs through. But the two are constantly different and never balance out, or balance only coincidentally and exceptionally. The price of a commodity constantly stands above or below the value of the commodity, and the value of the commodity exists only in this up-and-down movement of commodity prices. Supply and demand constantly determine the prices of commodities; [they] never balance, or only coincidentally . . .' (Marx 1973, pp. 137–8). See also p. 140: 'Because labour time as the measure of value exists only as an ideal, it cannot serve as the matter of price-comparisons . . . Price as distinct from value is necessarily money price.' Marx also discusses price of production and equalisation of profit rates in *Capital*, Volume III, pp. 176–7 *et seq*. This distinction between market price and value (in the form of the price of production) will play the central role in Maksakovsky's exposition of the cyclical dynamic of 'real' capitalism and its relation to the 'abstract' conditions of equilibrium.]

the first modification to be introduced is the establishment of 'pure' capitalist 'equilibrium', defined by 'proportionality' in the distribution of capitals. Because 'equilibrium' of capitals, when their organic compositions differ, means disruption of the 'equilibrium' of labour, it follows that the quantitative relations between Departments I and II, together with the relations between their separate parts, must be changed. If we take the formula of expanded reproduction,[18] the price of production in Department I will be higher than value (approximately 125 and 120), while in Department II it will be lower (approximately 125 and 133);[19] to achieve a new 'equilibrium' will require a correspondingly larger magnitude of value in Department II by comparison with I. With the original relationships, Department I would make an excessive demand upon the products of II, and underproduction would be revealed – or a disruption of reproduction. This is the first modification in the analysis.

Let us proceed. By means of a purely mathematical operation, we have introduced 'equilibrium' of capitals in place of the 'equilibrium' of labour. In reality, this process occurs through the far-reaching activity of capitalist competition, which, at a certain stage of capitalism's history, transforms surplus-value into the average profit and, correspondingly, value into the price of production.[20] Having completed this 'historical' act, capitalist competition remains as the irreplaceable instrument of its endless 'repetition'. Adjustment of the separate parts of social production to one another, and the tendency to re-establish the 'proportions' that are continuously being disrupted, takes place through the mechanism of capitalist competition. There does not exist any average condition of production under capitalism; no 'moving equilibrium' ever is, or ever will be, achieved in reality. Not only in the expansion, but even in the period of depression there is no such 'average' state of affairs. At each stage of reproduction, development inevitably involves overcoming constant disproportions. The tendency towards equilibrium is never one hundred per cent realised: it cannot be expressed exactly in fixed proportions of production, nor can it appear in reality 'except through the

[18] I $4000c + 1000v + 1000s = 6000$
II $1500c + 750v + 750s = 3000$

[19] These conclusions are approximately correct for the totals of Departments I and II because, in Department I, as a rule, the organic composition of capital is higher than in Department II.

[20] 'The price of production is . . . the external . . . form of commodity values, the form that the commodity takes *in the process of competition*' (Marx 1962, p. 194).

constant neutralisation of a constant disharmony'.[21] The instrument for restoring the disrupted relationship is capitalist competition in all of its various manifestations. Thus, the second step in the transition from the general theory of reproduction to the theory of the conjuncture is inclusion of the mechanism of capitalist competition.

We shall examine the movement of capitalist competition from two perspectives: 1) by equating the whole of social capital with its circulating part; 2) by including the role of fixed capital. This is exactly the methodological approach that Marx took in analysing the nature of circulating capital in the general analysis of reproduction. This approach helps us to discover the specific 'conditions' that lie at the basis of cycles.

In the first case, the object of the analysis is real capitalism, but with significantly reduced anarchy. Curtailment of anarchy results from the fact that we omit fixed capital along with differences in the organic composition. In turn, this presupposes significant levelling of labour productivity in the various branches and enterprises so that, for the sake of clarity, we can abstract completely from such productivity differences. The result is that 'proportionalities' of production are disrupted not so much by changes in the magnitude of values – the prices of production – as through 'errors' in the market adjustment between separate units of capitalist production. Accordingly, the activity of capitalist competition will also be weakened, for it depends directly upon the quantity and complexity of the factors that determine the reproduction process.

In these conditions – that is, when we equate social capital with its circulating part – no cycle can arise. The obvious reason is the lack of any corresponding 'range' of disruption in the 'proportions' of reproduction. The peculiarity of circulating capital – and this is why it is a special category – is that the value it represents 'is entirely transferred to the product, passes with it through the two metamorphoses in the sphere of circulation, and, by virtue of this continuous renewal, *always remains incorporated in the process of production*'.[22] Its total magnitude is renewed with each turnover of capital and reappears, with no change, both in the production process and as commodity capital.

---

[21] Marx 1975a, p. 529.

[22] Marx 1957, p. 165. ['Circulating capital' refers to elements that must be replaced in each period of production. 'Fixed capital' refers to elements that are amortised over their entire lifetime and, apart from technological renovation imposed by a crisis, are physically replaced only after several periods of production.]

Hence, there is no possibility of protracted, long drawn-out disruptions. Each branch of production experiences complete and thorough control of the market with *each* turnover of capital and even during each of its phases. Any deviation from 'proportionality' makes itself known *immediately* in the form of a deviation of market prices from prices of production, or from values. The mechanism of competition is then immediately activated, leading to a flow of capital into the given branch when prices rise, or, conversely, to an outflow of capital and a refusal to accumulate in other branches, where market prices fall below the instrument by which they are measured [the price of production]. The laws of 'equilibrium' (value and the price of production), which are at the basis of all reproduction 'proportions', 'regulate' social production in *every* phase of the circulation of its component parts.

In these conditions, a serious, *prolonged* disruption of social reproduction is impossible. The law of value rules social production 'with an iron hand'. Market value (the market price of production) determines the relation of 'demand' and 'supply' on the market. The same factors that give birth to capitalist competition are strictly 'ruled' by it, as demand and supply are themselves altered through the pressure of prices on the corresponding flow of capitals.[23] In this way, when we equate social capital with its circulating part, general overproduction and a cycle are impossible. Waves of expansion and contraction, if one might speak in such terms, can develop into nothing more than *fleeting* disruptions that are easily surmounted. Accordingly, the internal antagonisms of the system's relations of distribution cannot adequately come to the surface. The internal 'organic' conditions for a cycle and a crisis are not present.

Thus, having taken a second step away from the general theory of reproduction (our starting point), we still have not encountered a cycle. 'Circulating' capitalism – if such a system could really exist – would not know of any cyclical pattern in the reproduction process. An historical illustration can be found by reference to early capitalism, which was characterised by the quantitative preponderance of circulating capital and, for that reason, never knew any 'organic' crises.

[23] In a typical short excerpt, Marx considers competition in *Capital*. 'Supply and demand determine the market price, and so does the market price, and the market value in the further analysis, determine supply and demand.' 'For instance, if the demand, and consequently the market price, fall, capital will be withdrawn from this branch, thus causing supply to shrink' (Marx 1962, p. 187).

The cyclical character of capitalist development makes itself felt only at a *third* stage of transition to real reproduction – when we include the role of fixed capital. The unique circulation of fixed capital, or the inevitability of its massive renovation at a single stroke due to periodic changes in the technology of production – this is the basic condition for the 'manifestation' of a cycle. Specific waves of capitalist competition develop because of a massive renovation of fixed capital, which disrupts both the 'harmony' between market 'demand' and 'supply' and also 'proportionality' in the distribution of capitals. The result is overcapitalisation, with social production growing more rapidly than effective demand. Crashes occur and are repeated periodically. They mature dialectically when the regulating influence of the laws of 'equilibrium' is postponed through a prolonged detachment of prices from the price of production and value. Let us now turn to a detailed examination of this process.

The theory of cyclical expansion. The maturing of overproduction

'Developed capitalism is characterised by the ever-growing role of fixed capital. Fixed capital is the axis around which the production process revolves. The magnitude of the value of circulating capital is determined by the scale of production, and the scale of production is determined by the magnitude of fixed capital', says Marx.[24] Fixed capital becomes an ever-growing part of productive capital. Thus, the character of the turnover of fixed capital must be of decisive importance for the dynamic of a capitalist economy.

The peculiarity of fixed capital, which distinguishes it as a separate part of productive capital, is the fact that if 'the transformation of its value into money keeps pace with the conversion into money of the commodity which is the carrier of its value,' then 'its reconversion from the money form into a use-form proceeds separately from the reconversion of the commodities into other elements of their production and is determined by its own period of reproduction, that is, by the time during which the instruments of labour wear out and must be replaced by others of the same kind'.[25]

[24] [Maksakovsky's reference is to p. 138 of the 1923 Russian translation of *Capital*, II. The passage does not occur in the English translation that I am using.]

[25] Marx 1957, p. 163.

Does this peculiarity, on its own, explain the existence of a cycle that is connected with disruption of the 'proportions' of social reproduction? By no means. Replacement of fixed capital is the most important of the moments that constitute social 'proportionality'. Marx formulated this 'proportionality' as an equality between the annually renewed part of fixed capital and the annual wear of its functioning part. The significance of this 'proportionality' for social 'equilibrium' is enormous. It is only, let us say, in circumstances where one group of capitalists of Department II are converting the accumulated value of wear of fixed capital into the natural form of fixed capital, while another group, thanks to Department I, are acquiring it as their amortisation fund, that the 'proportionality' of $v_1 + s_1$ and c_2 is possible in accordance with the formulae: $v_1 + {}^1/_2\, s = c_2$; $v_1 + {}^1/_2\, s > c_2$; and $v_1 + {}^1/_2\, s < c_2$.

Thus, after including the division of productive capital into its fixed and circulating parts, and having at the same time presupposed its 'normal' annual replacement, we still shall not have general overproduction, much less a cycle. In reality, however, such smooth replacement will not occur. In its pure form, the 'proportionality' that we are discussing represents a postulate of the abstract theory of social reproduction. It is disrupted by technological revolutions in production, which are the initial preconditions for a massive replacement of fixed capital all at once; otherwise, a significant part of the capitalists would be deprived of the opportunity to fulfil their capitalist function. The evenly progressing development of a capitalist economy is replaced by its cyclical development. Here is what Marx has to say in this regard: 'As the value and the durability of the applied fixed capital grow with the development of the capitalist mode of production, so the lifetime of industry and of industrial capital lengthens in each particular field of investment to a period of many years, say ten years on an average. Whereas the development of fixed capital extends the length of this life on the one hand, *it is shortened on the other by continuous revolutions in the means of production,* which likewise incessantly gain momentum with the development of the capitalist mode of production. This involves a change in the means of production and their constant replacement, because *they are subject to moral depreciation long before they expire physically*. . . . The cycle of interconnected turnovers, embracing a number of years in which capital is held fast by its fixed constituent part, furnishes a material basis for the periodic crises. During this cycle, business undergoes successive periods of *depression, medium activity, precipitancy, crisis*. True, periods in which capital is invested differ greatly and far from coincide in time. But *a crisis always forms the starting point of large new investments of capital.* Therefore, from the point of view of society as a whole, they more or less provide a new material basis for the next turnover cycle'.[26] Here, Marx provided a comprehensive answer to the question of the causes of the premature wearing out of fixed capital – its moral wear.[27] This involves continuous revolutions in the means of production. In developed capitalism, the impulse for applying new, more advanced methods of production is usually provided by a crisis. In the accompanying circumstance of falling prices, moral wear becomes an exceptional force and is 'the starting point of large new investments of capital' and of a change in the existing technological structure. Despite the fact that physical wear is, in large measure, an essential precondition of moral wear, it is precisely the *latter* that determines, above all, the need for a massive replacement of fixed capital. Insofar as technological growth is a direct condition for, and a consequence of, the development of capitalist production, the more developed is the latter, the greater is the possible scale of moral wear, and the greater too is the importance that it assumes as the initial condition for the cycle.

Therefore, the rupture of 'proportionality' – between the fixed capital that is wearing out each year and the part that is being replaced – represents the visible cause of disturbance in the smooth course of capitalist reproduction and is also the force that determines its cyclical pattern. Let us examine the concrete development of this process.

The period that directly follows a crisis is characterised by a low utilisation rate for fixed capital. Elements of fixed capital depart from the productive sphere more rapidly than corresponding new units replace them. Thus, despite the presence of expanded reproduction, the scale of production steadily declines.[28] In the closing years of the ensuing depression, the opposite tendency begins to grow. Capitalism has within its grasp – because of concentration

---

[26] Marx 1957, pp. 185–6.

[27] ['Moral wear' refers to technological obsolescence: with moral wear, the 'reason' embodied in existing fixed capital gives way to a higher objectification in more advanced forms of machinery. The emphasis on technological change as the advance of 'reason' is an important expression of the Hegelian influence in Maksakovsky's work.]

[28] [Some investments in new fixed capital continue – there are elements of expanded reproduction in particular firms and branches – but they are outweighed by current accumulations of money capital.]

and centralisation – sufficient resources to replace morally (and physically) depleted equipment with new units that are more technologically advanced. This process usually involves additional capital investments. The absorptive capacity of the market grows through an expansion of productive demand and through a certain increase in personal consumption.

Depression passes over into expansion from the moment when the growing production reaches the 'maximum' point of the previous rising wave. Cassel writes: 'As soon as production regains the peak of the previous high conjuncture, then, experience suggests, every depression is fully overcome and the national economy enters a new period of high conjuncture'.[29] The coefficient of growth and the application of new fixed capital in production begin to surpass the rate of wear and tear.[30] The increased output of fixed capital is able not only to plug the gaping hole of moral-physical wear, but also to achieve a progressive increase of social production. We can take this increase of production, beyond the previously established record, to be the beginning of a new expansion, whose way is prepared by a preceding interval of recovery that corresponds to the unfolding process of fixed-capital renewal.

The pattern of the conjunctural cycle corresponds more closely to a four-phase than to a three-phase scheme: 1) *depression* (the first period), characterised by a prevailing tendency towards contraction of production rather than expansion; 2) *recovery*, characterised by prevalence of the opposite tendencies and by a smooth process of reproduction (this phase comes closest to the theoretical concept of equilibrium between the component elements of production as a whole); 3) *prosperity* – the maximal expansion of production, together with the highest level of prices, but also bringing the first signs of emerging overproduction in the form of a slowdown in the turnover of capital and a tightening of credit (disruption of the fundamental 'proportions', or growth of disproportions); 4) *crisis*, representing a many-sided form of the outbreak of contradictions and, at the same time, the lever with which to overcome them.

The mechanism of expansion and the way in which it occurs present a complicated picture. It involves a process of rapid growth in the separate branches of social production, which also affect each other. The peculiar feature

---

[29] Cassel 1925, p. 65.

[30] [New expenditures on fixed capital exceed current depreciation in the form of money capital.]

of expanded reproduction in this period, as we have seen, is that it entails gradual rupture of all the proportions of reproduction, which are connected with the rapid development of production. The starting point of the expansion, its concrete and defining condition, is the massive renovation of physically and morally exhausted fixed capital as a direct result of the crisis. The massive character of this process is explained by the unfavourable relationship between demand and supply during the depression. Supply, as a rule, exceeds demand. Therefore, market prices are lower than the prices of production – or values. The capitals that have been advanced can yield a profit only if production costs are significantly reduced. Leaving aside the case of monopoly, this is possible only through improvement of the technical composition of the capital in use. Application of new technologies occurs by means of competition and is the normal response of those capitalists who have the ability to survive. The remaining capitals, which are not capable of such 'renovation', either die out or are 'held in reserve' over a period of years until the next expansion.[31]

Once it has begun, the process of renewing fixed capital signifies the 'birth' of rising demand for Department I's production. This demand comes both from within Department I and from II. The branches of Department I begin to recover. The recovery and ensuing expansion embrace production of both materials and elements of fixed capital. Growth of fixed capital is reflected in the increased production of circulating capital, whose magnitude is determined by the volume of fixed capital in use and by the fact that, in the subsequent production links of Departments I and II, it often takes the form of fixed capital. Thus, all the branches that produce means of production undergo expansion.

However, because of the high organic composition of the capital it uses, Department I is not immediately able to expand in accordance with the rapidly increasing tempo of demand. As long as expansion occurs through restoring the existing equipment to full utilisation, things go more or less well. However, the steadily growing demand quickly exceeds these limits. Then the recovery passes over into a high conjuncture. Demand begins to exceed supply. The market conjuncture is expressed in rising market prices. The effort to overcome

[31] [Technologically outmoded capitals might return to production when higher market prices restore their ability to yield a profit. Until then, they represent a 'reserve' of unused production capacity. Emphasis upon the role of 'reserve' production capacity led E.A. Preobrazhensky to a very different theory of the cycle in conditions of monopoly capitalism (Preobrazhensky 1985, especially Chapter 7.)]

the unfavourable effect of low market prices on profits during the post-crisis period, by raising the organic composition of capital, is now objectified in a rising price level for the products of Department I. Rising market prices break out of the regulating zone of values. 'When additional capital – writes Marx – is produced at a very rapid rate, and its reconversion into productive capital increases the demand for all the elements of the latter to such an extent that actual production cannot keep pace with it, this brings about *a rise in the prices of all commodities that enter into the formation of capital.*'[32] Prices rise for steel, lumber, cement, and other materials for fixed capital. This rise in prices is not a result of speculation – it expresses the underproduction of products and the impossibility, at any particular moment, of fully satisfying the growing demand of the direct consumers.

Expanded production of means of production, in turn, cannot but be reflected in the growth of branches in Department II. The connecting link between them is the rise of personal consumption. 'The limits of consumption are extended by the exertions of the reproduction process itself,' says Marx. 'On the one hand this increases the consumption of revenue on the part of labourers and capitalists; on the other hand, tension in the process of reproduction corresponds with an exertion of productive consumption'.[33] Therefore, growth of productive consumption during the expansion is normally accompanied by increasing consumer demand on the part of both workers and industrial capitalists. The incomes of these two main classes depend directly on the conjuncture.[34] The incomes of money capitalists are considerably less dependent; and the incomes of 'intermediate classes' – of free professionals, the intelligentsia who are not involved in production, bureaucrats, etc. – show almost no dependence at all.[35] The dynamic of wages is of central importance for the

[32] Marx 1975a, p. 494.

[33] Marx 1962, p. 471.

[34] [Influenced by Rosa Luxemburg's *The Accumulation of Capital*, many Soviet economists believed that capitalism entails a tendency toward *chronic* underconsumption. Others, influenced by Rudolf Hilferding's *Finance Capital*, saw consumption as a function of the reproduction of capital. Maksakovsky considered Luxemburg's view to be a non-dialectical simplification of *Capital*. I examine these issues at length in Day 1981.]

[35] See the indices provided in Cassel 1925, pp. 75–80. See also Marx 1962, p. 479: 'The incomes of the unproductive classes and of those who live on fixed incomes remain in the main stationary during the inflation of prices which goes hand in hand with over-production and over-speculation. Hence their consuming capacity diminishes relatively, and with it their ability to replace that portion of the total reproduction

increase of production in Department II. Statistical data on the movement of wages establish a regular pattern of increase in a period of expansion and decline in a depression. This applies to all branches, even including agriculture (one part of which reflects the general conjunctural movement). The basic cause for the increase is the growing shortage of labour-power that occurs with the expansion of Departments I and II, despite the fact that the reserve army is recruited back into production. Labour-power experiences the 'fate' of all commodities during the period of expansion – it sells at a price higher than its value. However, the nominal indices do not reflect the real level. Because of the rising general price index for consumption, the real content of wages grows much more slowly than their monetary expression. All economists are aware of this. Together with the relative rise of wages, their total also grows absolutely. The limits of the consumer market grow not only due to the relative increase of consuming capacity on the part of every worker, but also because of the number of workers who are participating in production.

The increase of consumer demand, resulting from the expansion of production, in turn finds expression in the growth of branches in Department II. Here too, the pressure of demand has a significant effect on prices, which begin to rise. New enterprises are erected, and old ones are expanded. This is the source of still more new demand for means of production and, above all, for the materials needed for fixed capital. Hence, the rising wave spreads by way of an increase of consumer demand in the branches of Department II and returns to Department I in the form of still more demand for equipment. Being reflected once again in rising production and in the associated increase of the number of employed workers and their wages, the expanding wave is objectified in a further expansion of Department II, and so on. In this way, there takes place a feverish growth of production during the stage of expansion, and social production races ahead – until it encounters a shortage of effective demand.

How does this shortage of effective demand arise? At first glance, such a possibility seems to be excluded because the increase of social production, being reflected in the growth of incomes, itself appears to create the necessary

which would normally enter into their consumption. Even when their demand remains nominally the same, it decreases in reality.' [If Maksakovsky were dealing with modern capitalist economies, he would have to pay a great deal more attention to the possible counter-cyclical effects of incomes generated in the service sector. At the time, services were of minor importance.]

base of effective demand. Increased opportunities for additional capitalisation are matched by a rise in the total volume and level of wages. But the whole 'secret' lies in the fact that, *first*, the increased capitalisation during the expansion can easily become detached from the base of effective demand, for the volume of profits, realised by capitalists during the expansion, has no direct dependence on the growth of working-class incomes. Whereas the latter are strictly limited by the customary standard of living – by the law of value of labour-power, which cannot be infringed within the limits of capitalist economy – the only limits to the former are competition and the level of technological development. Both of these influential moments have a positive effect in the period of expansion, and the mass of realised surplus-value far exceeds the limits associated with the average profit. This creates a potential for the base of personal effective demand to lag behind. 'Disharmony' appears in the form of increased capitalisation that inevitably outpaces demand. *Second*, the massive upsurge of social production rests not only upon capitalisation of newly realised surplus-value, but also upon consolidation of all the financial resources of society, which are redistributed through credit and thus assume a productive form. The result is to amplify still further the threat of a rupture. *Third*, the remarkable rise of wages begins in the second half of the expansion, during the so-called high conjuncture, when there is already evidence of a decline in the share of the capitalists (or of entrepreneurial income), due to difficulties on the part of capital in passing through its 'circulation' phases, and also due to the rising costs of production associated with higher wages and higher prices for materials.

The *fourth* important moment determining a lag in the base of consumer demand is 'inadequate' growth of consumption on the part of the capitalist class itself. Kautsky's example shows that in order to preserve social 'equilibrium', with an unchanging organic composition of capital, consumption by the working class must grow by 44% over five years, that of the capitalists by 71%.[36] Therefore, the rate of increase of capitalist consumption must be higher than that of the workers. This cannot occur in reality. There are objective obstacles to expansion of non-productive demand by the capitalists such as the need for greater capitalisation, which is dictated not only by the attempt to maximise profits but also by the objective laws of capitalist competition.

[36] Kautsky 1924, p. 445.

Here we have the *fourth* item in the list of 'causes' that lead to rupture of the 'equilibrium' between production and consumption.

The *fifth* important condition for a 'rupture' is a rise in the organic composition of capital. Increase of production is accompanied during the expansion not only by extensive growth, but also, as part of the effort to maximise profits, by a rising organic composition of capital. Although this rise is slower than during the pre-expansion period, it does contribute to a decline of the working-class share in the values being produced. This is a specific expression of the growth of labour productivity in circumstances where labour is organised by capital. Productivity growth, in turn, brings about a fall in the value of labour-power and a relative increase in the commodities available for mass consumption. A relative narrowing of the consumption base takes place during the expansion; moreover, taking into account the elevated level of market prices (in Department II), this narrowing occurs at a faster pace than would be required by the changing conditions for 'moving equilibrium'. Consumption by capitalists, as we have seen, shows the same tendency towards relative contraction. As a result, in the *concrete* conditions of a rise in the organic composition of capital during the expansion, we find one of the 'conditions' for the rupture of 'equilibrium' between production and consumption.

However, decline of the working-class share in the aggregate product does not entail a *necessary* rupture between production and consumption. If that were the case, capitalism would be in a condition of *permanent* crisis, for in all stages of the cycle the organic composition grows at one tempo or another. For this reason, Marxist economics rejects the view of Rodbertus, who attributed the cause of a capitalist crisis to this perfectly normal fact. The whole issue has to do with the *concrete* conditions that prevail during the period of expansion, when: 1) narrowing of the consumption base is accompanied by the massive character of expanded production; 2) this expansion is 'oriented' not upon the price of production and value, which would ensure receipt of a 'proper' average profit, but rather upon the *elevated* market price, which, instead of expressing the 'proportions' of social production, is associated with a unique phenomenon – that is, the impossibility of production growing at the same rate as demand when the latter is amplified by a massive renovation of capital. If we were to presuppose exchange in terms of values, that is, if we were to exclude these 'abnormal' conditions, then the rise of the organic composition of capital would not disrupt the elements of social 'equilibrium'.

At any given moment, the volume of effective demand would 'harmoniously' correspond to the volume of social production.

Contrary to the assertion of Tugan, a more rapid growth of the productive market, as an expression of spontaneous capitalist industrialisation, does not at all imply that consumer demand diminishes in importance.[37] The consumer market, both before and during industrialisation, is the final condition for 'realisation' of all the processes of reproduction. As consumer demand falls in terms of value, the effectiveness of each of its units grows in direct proportion to the relative decline of consumption's share in the total value.[38] If, for example, the relation of social c to v were 5:1, then, looking at the matter schematically, one could say that each consumption unit would support the weight of five production units and would serve as the final condition for their economic realisation. Production of means of consumption has developed on the basis of consumer demand, insofar as the product passes through a number of stages while being worked up. Thus, Department II divides into a number of branches that are more or less closely connected with each other. The presence of consumer demand is further objectified in an even larger scale of production in Department I. A broadly developed production apparatus, for the supply of means of production, depends upon the consumer goods branches, which, in turn, receive equipment from other specialised capital-producing branches. As a result of the complexity of materials and types of fixed capital, which correspond to the existing technological practices and methods of production, and thanks also to the massive character of this production, which occurs for the same reasons, Department I comprises an enormous number of branches of production with a complex technical division of labour, a greater number of preliminary production stages, and a much closer association and interdependence of the separate links of the production process than is the case in Department II.

---

[37] [The reference is to the Russian economist Mikhail Tugan-Baranovsky, one of the most prominent pre-revolutionary 'legal Marxists'. He argued that investment expands until all available capital funds are exhausted, at which time disproportions emerge between different branches and between production and consumption, causing a new period of stagnation and depression. See *Promyshlennye krizisy v sovremennoi Anglii*, republished in French as *Les Crises industrielles en Angleterre*, Paris, 1913. Rosa Luxemburg comments on Tugan's relation to Marxism in Chapter 23 of *The Accumulation of Capital*. A brief summary of Tugan's work can be found in Hutchinson 1966, pp. 377–9.]

[38] [Maksakovsky is not referring to Keynesian 'effective demand' but to the relation between demand for consumer goods and the growing fixed capital that it presupposes because of the advance of technology.]

The connection of social production with the consumer market makes itself felt directly through the branches of Department II. This Department can only expand when the consumption base grows. Hence, when we speak of a fall in the share of personal consumption, we must not forget that it still grows *absolutely*. Moreover, its absolute growth during the expansion is a *direct* 'cause' of the rising wave in the branches of Department II. Here it is objectified in an increase of production, and the latter is only possible when there is supplementary demand for the production of Department I, which also expands in turn. It must not be forgotten, of course, that the *general* impetus for the entire expansionary process comes from the massive renovation of fixed capital, which itself results from the crisis. However, the scale of production in the branches of Department II is not *absolutely* dependent on the existing volume of consumer demand. These branches can increase demand by reducing the value of commodities through raising labour productivity. Then the price level declines and, provided there is no corresponding drop in wages, there will be an *increase* of consumer demand, which then will also support production of means of consumption on a broader scale. However, this kind of phenomenon does not characterise the entire period of expansion. The prices of all products, taken together, rise rather than fall. Orienting itself upon these high prices, which do not represent social 'equilibrium', Department II, just like I, expands at a faster tempo than is the case with consumer demand over the course of the expansion as a whole. The result is that disproportions mature and erupt in the market.

The rise of the organic composition of capital in Department II, which accompanies the general growth of production, increases demand from that Department for the production of Department I. On this basis, the branches that produce means of production are able to expand rapidly, indeed, at a much more rapid tempo than is the case in Department II. The growth of consumer demand can be compared to throwing a stone into the water, causing ripples to spread continuously outward. The further the ripples spread, the further removed from consumption are the production branches that are affected. Hence, the greatest growth during the phase of expansion is in branches that produce means of production, and among them, in the branches producing materials that go into fixed capital. As we have seen, this occurs in the first place because the production process in the branches of Department I involves a greater number of interconnected branches and enterprises than in Department II. The rising wave, whose source is the growth of consumer demand, flows at each sector of the consumption front through one or two enterprises that are closely connected by production dependencies. For instance, to satisfy the worker's need for clothing first involves demand for finished garments and then for more textile production. The suppliers who serve the needs of the worker are numerous, but they do not move in a body. They do not respond like a vast number of production links in a single chain; instead, they resemble separate, loosely associated production circles.

Things are different in Department I, which serves as the preparatory stage for consumer goods production. Here, production is organised like a complex, self-contained column, with a great number of enterprises being interconnected both *horizontally* and *vertically*. Thus, the expansionary wave of consumer demand, already extending outwards as it reaches this point, dictates the need for a distinctly larger scale of production growth. Being expressed concretely in the demand for machines, it not only embraces the machinery front *horizontally*, but is also transmitted *vertically* to the raw material bases of the machinery industry: to steel, coal, ore, lumber, cement, and a whole number of other branches that are connected with, and cannot be separated from, the machinery industry. Typically, the greatest expansion occurs not in the machinery industry itself, which is 'responding' to the directive from Department II (and through it, to consumer demand), but rather in iron and steel, the main materials for production of fixed capital. This occurs because demand for one or another type of machine calls forth not just the demand of the machine-producing industry for steel, but also expansion of fixed capital in general; for instance, construction of a new railway network, of railway equipment, etc. This particular feature of growth in Department I is also the basic condition that explains why the widening wave of expansion is most apparent in a sharp leap of the production index in Department I.

Moreover, since the rate of growth of the organic composition of capital is higher here than the social average, an enormous pressure of productive demand develops within Department I, for which consumer demand and even the productive demand of II serve merely as the first impulse. These interdependent branches of Department I become each other's best customers. The rippling sound of personal consumption grows into a dramatically intensifying rumble in the branches that produce fixed capital and the necessary materials. Here, there are no norms of expansion to give direct 'instructions', for the control of consumer demand is far away and there are much greater profits being realised. Thus, the rising wave, which originates in the growth of consumer demand, 'gives birth' within the limits of Department I to an internal, 'autonomous' *self-expanding* wave, which, in conditions of high prices, high profits, and a constantly unsatisfied market, will inevitably lead to massive overproduction. The social system increasingly resembles an inverted, truncated cone, with a relatively shrinking base in the form of consumer demand to support a rapidly expanding production of the elements of fixed capital.

In the course of this analysis, we have abstracted from the sequence of interaction between the elements that give birth to the expansion. The initial moment, we know, is the massive renovation of fixed capital that drives Department I to recovery and expansion, thus leading to the increase of consumer demand and output in Department II. The growth of consumer demand appears as a function, or a consequence, of expanding production. However, this does not alter in any way the objective fact that consumer demand is the principal foundation that 'supports' capitalist production. Such a role for consumer demand is determined by the fact that: 1) production of means of production is a complex and far-reaching preparatory process for production of means of consumption; 2) the consumer demand of most people fluctuates very little, being determined by the strict laws of capitalism's relations of distribution – while, at the same time, there are no such restrictive conditions on the expanding scale of production. Starting from this fact, it is perfectly correct, in methodological terms, to specify the moment of consumption as the ultimate condition in determining the 'equilibrium' of the social system, and then to conduct the analysis in terms of disturbances in the sequence of activities on the part of the concrete factors involved in capitalist expansion.[39]

Let us now return to the concrete course of the cycle. We have seen that the expansionary wave, spreading through the branches of Departments I and II, leads to a massive increase of production. This increase depends upon two moments: 1) the fact that 'normally' functioning capitalists receive not only the average profit, but also super-profits; 2) the fact that effective demand grows more rapidly than the possibilities for satisfying it. As a result, market

[39] [When Maksakovsky's book appeared, these remarks would have indirectly lent support to Bukharin's criticism of Stalinist industrialisation. See Bukharin 1982, pp. 301–30.]

prices for the social product are higher than prices of production. Here, we have the primary source of super-profits. Although production costs are rising, most market prices rise even more quickly. Every capitalist puts more into expanding production. This explains the massive capitalisations, which at a certain point lead to general overproduction. The level of market prices rises especially quickly in the branches of Department I. The reason is, first, that the pressure of demand is greatest here, and the same is true of the super-profit received as the difference between the market price and the price of production. Secondly, the organic composition of capital rises more quickly here, being connected with receipt of a large, differential super-profit, representing the difference between social average costs and the individual costs of production. These are the moments that support the massive tempo of supplementary capitalisations, leaving far behind the corresponding phenomena in Department II. However, the possibilities for expansion of production in branches producing means of production are not limited by the mass of profit being realised. Capitalist competition also diverts in this direction a large part of the newly formed capitals that are flowing from all the spheres of social production and circulation. Then – and this is an important moment – most of the monetary accumulation of society also flows here, as it is redistributed through credit and takes the form of means of production. Existing branches of production grow, and new ones are created. Construction of railway networks led this process in the nineteenth century. In the twentieth century, the electrical industry has moved to the forefront along with the branches that serve it.[40]

Thus, the process of disrupting the 'proportionality' of social reproduction takes place because of prices that become detached from prices of production – or values. The disharmony intensifies both in the relation between social production and consumer demand, and in terms of the scale of production in Departments I and II. More rapid growth of the production apparatus in Department I, as compared with II, must inevitably find expression in overproduction of means of production, which then makes the initial disproportionality even more acute. It follows that *the period of expansion is also the period in which overproduction matures and becomes apparent in the market.* In the *real* course of capitalist reproduction, the expansion can lead to no other outcome than a crisis.

---

[40] Cassel 1925, p. 116.

Marx formulates the inevitability of overproduction this way: overproduction can occur because the market and production are two separate moments, creating the possibility 'that the expansion of one does *not* correspond with the expansion of the other; that the limits of the market are not extended rapidly enough for production, or that new markets – new extensions of the market – may be rapidly outpaced by production, so that the expanded market becomes just as much a barrier as the narrower market was formerly'.[41]

Referring to the maturation of this process, Spiethoff divides the expansion into four stages. The *first* stage involves the use of existing equipment. The *second* occurs when the catalyst of high profits creates new enterprises because market demand exceeds supply. In this connection, there develops a widespread demand within production itself. Productive consumption grows at a rapid tempo, but 'initially the products of this expansionary process of reproduction do not appear as a counter-balance . . . to demand. This happens in the *third* stage, when new production establishments appear *not only* as bearers of *demand, but also* as bearers of *supply;* at the same time, a period begins when high prices must soon come under threat. The final period is the complete *opposite* of the second. The products of feverishly expanded production are thrown onto the market when the corresponding volume of demand is *lacking*. The onset of this condition has decisive significance'.[42] Here, we have a perfectly correct division of the expansion into a series of stages. Decisive importance belongs to the third stage, when newly created capitalist enterprises come forth as *'bearers of supply'*. The massive character of this supply, which is conditioned by high profits and by the conditions that create those profits, intensifies due to other circumstances. Not being subject to direct control by the consumer market, this Department develops enormous demand from within production in response to its own *'local'* conditions. 'Thanks, on the one hand, to lack of direct contact with the final consumer, and, on the other hand, to close mutual ties between toolmakers – writes Bouniatian – there emerges an *artificial* mutual stimulus for branches of industry that are

[41] Marx 1975a, p. 525.

[42] Spiethoff, excerpt from an article in the collection *Problema rynka i krizisov* [The Problem of the Market and Crises], pp. 258–89. [Arthur Spiethoff, like Tugan, borrowed from Marx. His theory was similar to Maksakovsky's insofar as he located the origins of overproduction in the difficulty of foreseeing the cumulative effect of decisions taken by individual capitalists in response to market and cartel prices. For a summary of Spiethoff's contribution, see Hutchison 1966, pp. 379–83.]

interconnected through productive consumption of each other's products: expansion of one branch not only promotes development of other branches that depend upon it, but also frequently creates among them consumers of its own products. What occurs in these branches is . . . something analogous to the *mutual drafting* of friendly promissory notes in a credit economy, when in both cases *there is absolutely no real economic foundation'*.[43]

This system of mutual orders, which ensures excellent sales by enterprises while construction is underway, leaves them face to face with a sharp contraction of market demand as soon as they have finished equipping one another. On the one hand, existing enterprises no longer pose a demand for equipment – thus narrowing the market – while on the other hand, they also become new suppliers themselves, thus overburdening the already contracting market. This 'local' tendency becomes particularly widespread during the rise of the organic composition of capital – which expands the basis of productive consumption – and with the development of joint-stock companies. The higher the organic composition of capital, the more intensive is mutual servicing in production, and the longer is the interval of time required for new enterprises to move from their 'confirmation' to their role as agents of supply. Joint-stock companies also create a more flexible form of mutual supply, organising 'daughter' and 'granddaughter' firms, one of whose objectives is to ensure an extensive market for the joint-stock company that fathered these offspring. Thus, the more developed capitalism becomes, the more obvious and imposing must overproduction also become.[44]

Let us now look more closely at the emergence of overproduction. For the sake of a more concrete analysis, we shall divide Department I into three groups: the *first* produces raw materials (mining, the branches of ferrous metallurgy, and so forth); the *second* produces fixed capital for Department I; the *third* produces fixed capital for Department II.

Growth of demand from Department II calls forth expansion in the third

[43] Bouniatian, *Ekonomicheskie krizisy*, p. 65. See also Mombert 1924, p. 135: 'Certain factories, in the last decades of the 19th century, expanded and conducted their affairs on the basis of credits provided to them by machine-building plants.' [Mentor Bouniatian wrote several books on business cycles, including *Les crises économiques, essai de morphologie et théorie des crises économiques périodiques, et de théorie de la conjoncture économique*, translated from Russian and published in Paris in 1922. I do not have the Russian text used by Maksakovsky.]

[44] This is obscured by the action of other factors, which will be discussed in the following chapter. [The reference is to credit and financial markets.]

group. However, this is possible only if there is growth in the second group, which, in turn, requires growth of production in the first group. Here, we have a basic node of dependencies and mutual conditioning in production. Insofar as the organic composition rises as we move from the third group to the first, and because the first group is the supplier of basic materials, without which no process of expansion is conceivable elsewhere, it follows that the greatest strain of demand will be felt precisely in the first group, where it cannot possibly be satisfied quickly. This is what explains the step-like pattern of price increases. While rising insignificantly in Department II, they grow all the more rapidly as we move from the third group to the first group in Department I. Therefore, the further a branch is removed from direct consumer demand, the greater are both the demands it faces and its corresponding scale of new capitalisations.[45] Consequently, the main lever of social overproduction is found in the branches that supply materials for production of fixed capital.[46]

Because of their chain-like connections, overproduction in these branches includes overproduction in the other branches of Department I. If there is overproduction of iron, it includes overproduction of iron ore and coal; it also presupposes overproduction of machines, for the increasing overproduction of iron would not be possible without its growing consumption. 'There cannot, therefore, be any question of the [underproduction] of those articles whose overproduction is already implied because they enter as an element, raw material, auxiliary material or means of production, into those articles . . . whose positive overproduction is precisely the fact to be explained'.[47] It follows that 'universal' overproduction, in turn, is fundamentally 'partial' overproduction.[48] There cannot exist a state of affairs in which overproduction

[45] In the present context, this issue can only be presented schematically.

[46] [Maksakovsky is looking backward into the production process. Markets also look forward, but he leaves speculation to the following chapter.]

[47] Marx 1975, p. 530. [There is a type-setting error in Maksakovsky's quotation. His text refers to 'overproduction', whereas Marx speaks of 'underproduction'. I have made the change to correspond with Marx's comment.]

[48] [Marx was disputing the view that only partial overproduction is possible, not a general glut of markets: 'The *relativity* of over-production . . . is expressed in this way: There is no *universal* over-production, because if over-production were universal, all spheres of production would retain the same relation to one another . . ." (Marx 1975a, p. 530). 'This explanation of over-production in one field by under-production in another field therefore means merely that if production were proportionate, there would be no over-production. . . . Or, in even more abstract form: There would be no over-production in one place, if over-production took place to the same extent everywhere' (Marx 1975a, p. 532). Marx replies that this argument abstracts from

(or underproduction) embraces *all branches*. It is also true that not all partial overproduction becomes 'general'; otherwise, capitalism would never escape from a condition of permanent crisis. The general character of overproduction emerges only when partial overproduction finds its ultimate expression in an outbreak of contradictions between social production and consumption. It affects particular branches and involves, say, overproduction of iron and woven cloth. However, overproduction of woven cloth already entails overproduction of machinery, and the latter already presupposes overproduction of iron. Therefore, social overproduction occurs, above all, in the overproduction of iron and steel – the most basic materials of fixed capital – upon which both Departments 'labour' as they accommodate and influence each other in the process of reproduction.

Thus, it is not at all necessary that there be *differential* overproduction of every branch in relation to all the others.[49] A capitalist crisis is prepared by *partial* overproduction; this is the fundamental cause, and it includes overproduction at the earlier stages, which is transmitted, through the linkages of production, to the branches that depend on production of basic materials. Hence, there is overproduction in the branches of Department II. These branches are the agents that ferment and hasten overproduction in the main

money and assumes that every sale is simultaneously a purchase, as in barter. But capitalist exchanges are not barter exchanges: 'This whole subterfuge then rests on abstracting from *money* and from the fact that we are not concerned with an exchange of products, but with the circulation of commodities, an essential part of which is the separation of purchase and sale' (Marx 1975, pp. 532–3). The mediation of exchange by money creates the *possibility* of crises, but Maksakovsky is here dealing with the *necessity* of crises, which he associates with overproduction of means of production. This kind of overproduction is both caused by, and is the cause of, a high level of demand for fixed capital from Department II, which entails the upward deviation of market prices from values and promotes overcapitalisation in Department I. For Maksakovsky, partial disproportions of physical production are the material counterpart of the contradictory movement of prices and values, and it is the spontaneously uneven movement of the whole reproduction of social capital that is objectified in the disproportionalities of the parts.]

[49] In concrete conditions, this often does occur. Overproduction of coal is included in overproduction of iron, but this does not exclude *differential* overproduction of coal in relation to iron when its production exceeds the demand coming from ferrous metallurgy and other branches. [Maksakovsky is paraphrasing Marx: 'For example, although sufficient coal must have been produced in order to keep going all those industries into which coal enters as a necessary condition of production, and therefore the *over-production* of coal is implied in the *over-production* of iron, yarn, etc. (even if coal was produced only in proportion to the production of iron and yarn [etc.]) it is *also* possible that more coal was produced than was required even for the over-production of iron, yarn, etc. This is not only possible, but very probable' (Marx 1975a, p. 531).]

branches of Department I insofar as they consume more means of production and are themselves dependent in their overproduction on the overproduction of means of production. Emergence of their overproduction is also connected with more workers being employed, who thus pose additional demand for means of consumption. What we have here is a dialectical interaction.

It follows that Cassel and a number of other economists are mistaken when they regard a crisis as the result of overproduction of means of production, as distinct from the smooth flow of production of means of consumption. This smooth flow is possible only based on exchange according to values (prices of production). During the period of expansion, this condition does not apply either in Department I or in II. The resulting process, whereby prices rise differentially and become detached from values, is the general precondition for overcapitalisation in both Departments. Existence of 'overcapitalisation' in II is most clearly revealed when it turns out to be impossible for Department I to sell all of its output, a condition which then results in a reduction of the number of employed workers and a corresponding drop in consumer demand. But this moment is *quantitative* in character; it only deepens the already existing disharmony between Department II and its market – a disharmony that develops *parallel* to the growth of disguised overproduction in Department I – all on the general basis of prices that are temporarily detached from values. In the forefront of overproduction stands Department I, or more precisely, those branches of I that constitute the central axes of the entire social production apparatus. They represent the peak of the 'overproduction' pyramid because here the fundamental 'cause' of overproduction – the detachment of market prices from values – is expressed most forcefully both in quantitative terms and by virtue of the special central position that these branches hold in production. The overproduction that is revealed in the market essentially signifies an excess of industrial capital in strictly determined forms. A part of the social production apparatus and of commodity capital turns out to be redundant. 'As a result of delayed returns (in the form of money, P.M.), glutted markets, or fallen prices,' writes Marx, 'a superabundance of industrial capital becomes available, but in a form in which it cannot perform its functions. There are huge quantities of commodity capital, but they cannot be sold. There are huge quantities of fixed capital, but they are largely idle due to stagnant reproduction.'[50] 'Overproduction of capital is

[50] Marx 1962, p. 471.

never anything more than overproduction of means of production – of means of labour and necessities of life – which may serve as capital.'[51] Social 'equilibrium' is restored through massive destruction of industrial capital in the two forms of productive and commodity capital. An excess of industrial capital in the third form, money, cannot be represented here because every expression of this excess is connected with a transition out of its industrial status and into the form of loan capital.[52]

The next question of interest is whether the whole assortment of the social product becomes equally impossible to sell at the moment when the crisis erupts.

The clearest expression of overproduction occurs in production of means of production. Here its character is *absolute*. At the instant when overproduction breaks out, no reduction in prices can bring any perceptible increase of sales. The reason lies in the very nature of productive consumption. The absorptive capacity of the consumer market, in contrast, is determined by two factors: the size of incomes, and the price level for consumer goods. This absorptive capacity is enormously elastic and expands in inverse proportion to the level of prices. 'If the means of subsistence were cheaper, or money wages higher, the labourers would buy more of them, and a greater "social need" would arise for the given assortment of commodities . . .'.[53] Here, we have one of the reasons why overproduction in Department II is less pervasive. However, productive consumption cannot increase during this period. Once commodities cannot be sold, enterprises stop expanding, and demand falls for means of production. The reduction of prices to the level of values has no apparent influence on the sale of means of production. At the moment when the crisis appears, the overproduction of many means of production will be *absolute*. 'After the end of a period of expansion that has lasted for several years, demand for them (items of productive consumption, P.M.) is satisfied – both the demand that was unfulfilled after the period of depression and that which subsequently grew up. From this point on there is no need to fill any gaps, only to compensate for the wearing out of such goods and gradually to increase their quantity in correspondence with the growth of the economy.'[54] In reality, exactly the opposite occurs. The initial plugging of 'gaps' is in-

---

[51] Marx 1962, p. 250.
[52] [This issue is dealt with in the next chapter, 'The Role of Credit in the Conjuncture'.]
[53] Marx 1962, p. 185.
[54] Spiethoff in *Problemy rynka i krizisov*, p. 260.

separable from a steady increase of production that is now being thrown onto the market. The consequence is that overproduction appears all the more forcefully in the market for means of production.

The market expression of overproduction is a decisive excess of supply over demand at the given price level. Insofar as the price level has risen in all branches of production, the final result is to arrest sales of all commodities. Because 'crises are usually preceded by a general inflation in prices of all articles of capitalist production,' 'all of them therefore cause a glut in the market at the prices they had prior to the crash. The market can absorb a larger volume of commodities at falling prices, at prices that have fallen below their price of production, than it could absorb at their former market prices'.[55] Thus, overproduction prevails not only with high market prices, but even with prices of production. Capitalism is incapable of forestalling the crisis through a corresponding reduction in the prices of all products.[56] Such a measure contradicts the very nature of the self-expansion of values, yet the general glut in social reproduction makes it unavoidable. Whatever the reduction in prices, however, the redundant means of production still cannot be used. When the turnover of all capitals has been impeded, nothing can raise productive demand. On the contrary, each capital already has excessive means of production on hand, which in turn are responsible for the excess of commodities now being thrown onto the market.

At this point, we have to answer an important theoretical question: What is the origin of the total sum of surplus-value that all capitalists realise in the form of super-profits during the expansion? At first sight, this phenomenon seems to contradict the law of value and surplus-value. Given the law of average profit, receipt of super-profit by one capitalist implies less than the average rate for others. Society's fund of surplus-value is strictly determined. The very formation of an average profit excludes any one-sided (upward) deviation from the norm. Yet, during the period of expansion, we have to deal with just such an irrational event. This means that we must totally rule out any possibility of saying that the super-profit of one capitalist is a redistribution to his advantage from the profit of another capitalist, who operates with a below-average rate. Whence comes this excess of surplus-value? Obviously, the source of this surplus cannot be found in the period

[55] Marx 1975a, p. 505.
[56] [Capitalists will not voluntarily accept prices below the price of production.]

of high conjuncture, when the bias of profits is uniformly in one direction. Nor can it be located outside the capitalist system – Marx's method excludes that possibility.[57] There is no way to solve the problem if one looks at capitalist production solely in the period of expansion. But the complete capitalist 'history' is a full cycle, which includes all of its stages. High profits during the expansion are essentially nothing more than the realisation of surplus-value that was created, but not fully realised, at the time of the depression, for, in that period, as a general rule, prices fall below the price of production due to the unfavourable relation between demand and supply. The downward deviation of market prices during the period of depression is compensated by an upward deviation during the expansion. Over the course of the cycle, the average corresponds to values, if we abstract from possible changes of the latter. 'In this way, the market prices that have deviated from market values adjust themselves and yield an average that corresponds to market values, as deviations from the latter cancel each other as plus and minus'.[58] Therefore, the surplus profit received during the expansion is surplus-value that was created, but not fully realised, during the depression.[59]

Let us now draw some conclusions. We have examined concretely the mechanism of expansion as it occurs through a complex interaction of a number of economic factors. The axis about which the activities of these factors are distributed was the massive renovation of fixed capital, which is associated with reproduction as it proceeds *concretely*. It was precisely this

[57] [The implied reference is to Rosa Luxemburg's theory of imperialism and the importance of 'third parties' in Luxemburg 1963.]

[58] Marx 1962, p. 186. [Marx makes the further comment that 'If supply and demand coincide, the market-price of commodities corresponds to their price of production, i.e. their price then appears to be regulated by the immanent laws of capitalist production, independently of competition, since the fluctuations of supply and demand explain nothing but deviations of market-prices from prices of production. These deviations mutually balance one another, so that in the course of certain longer periods the average market-prices equal the prices of production' (Marx 1962, p. 349). Maksakovsky will now argue that the deviations mentioned by Marx are not random; they are uniquely determined by the different phases in the cycle of capital's reproduction. The total sum of prices corresponds to the total of values, but only in the course of an entire cycle, never at any particular moment.]

[59] [In a review of Maksakovsky's book, B.L. Livshits claimed that the upward movement in prices during an expansion was partly due to a simultaneous rise in the *value* of commodities caused by increased use of older equipment pending completion of new construction and the installation of new technology. When the difference between the lowest and the highest price of a commodity might vary from 50–100% over the course of a cycle, Livshits doubted that the entire variation could be attributed to a discrepancy between price and value (Livshits 1929, pp. 225–6.)]

massive renovation that gave birth at once, because of the crisis, to a rising tendency in the course of reproduction. During the expansion, the growing character of social production was clear. However, this growth of the entire social system ended at a certain stage in a crash. Consequently, in the activities resulting from expansionary forces, there were moments that organically *disrupted* the 'moving equilibrium' of the growing social system.

What were these moments? When we equated productive capital with its circulating part, we ruled out any possibility of general overproduction. If we include fixed capital, but presuppose its smooth replacement from year to year according to the formula of 'equilibrium' between the parts that are wearing out and those that are being replaced, we still do not encounter any general overproduction.[60] It is only when we introduce the moment of disruption of this 'proportionality', by taking into account the sudden massive renewal of fixed capital, that we disclose the cyclical character of capitalist reproduction. In the first case, we have no 'condition' that would explain a prolonged departure of the system from 'equilibrium'; in the second case, that condition is obvious.

The distinguishing outward sign of a 'non-cyclical' condition was the absence of *one specific* condition of market competition. Market 'demand' and 'supply' did not long deviate from each other. Any excess of 'demand' over 'supply', being accompanied by rising market prices, brought with it a rapid inflow of new capital into the given branch. The tendency to restore the disturbed 'equilibrium' set in without any *particular* delay. Nevertheless, things change quite abruptly as soon as we include the sudden, large-scale renovation of fixed capital. In circumstances of progressively growing demand, 'equilibrium' can be preserved only with a speedy and massive expansion of production. However, that possibility is excluded. Whatever capitalism's capacity for significant expansion might be, it is not able 'suddenly' to satisfy the massive demand that results from moral wear of existing equipment. As a result, the available supply of commodities lags behind the growing demand, and the tendency towards 'equilibrium' comes to a halt. It is not possible to 'rectify' production speedily as the disruptions occur. On the contrary, the further the expansion develops, the more aggregate supply lags behind demand, and the greater is the detachment of market prices from values, or

[60] [Total new investments in fixed capital would equal total current depreciation in the form of money capital.]

from the prices of production. The ongoing process of redistributing capitals is unable to eliminate these disruptions because society, at this *particular* moment, does not possess sufficient productive forces with which to satisfy the current demand. Despite the significant growth of its technical-production apparatus, capitalist society proves unable, in timely fashion, to satisfy its own need for elements of productive capital and for means of consumption. The system as a whole becomes exhausted under the burden of *underproduction*. However, this does not mean that individual capitalist 'atoms' face any strict limitations. On the contrary, they all realise super-profits as they 'toil' vigorously to expand the system. Prices for finished products manage to rise more rapidly than those for the materials and semi-fabricates that enter into the costs of production. The increase of market prices exceeds the increase in costs of production. As time passes, capitalist society eventually finds within itself sufficient forces to satisfy fully the existing demand. However, this very process is also inescapably connected with the maturation of a crisis.

A strange phenomenon occurs. Demand, being the other dimension of expanding production, *permanently* exceeds supply over the whole period of the expansion. When, after the most strenuous production efforts, capitalism completely satisfies its own demand for items of productive and personal consumption, a periodic crash must unavoidably follow. This fact requires us to reflect upon the nature of market competition and the extent to which the market relation of 'demand' and 'supply', which *directly* determines the scale of expanding production, is an accurate expression of the system's conditions of 'equilibrium'. With a *smoothly* advancing replacement of fixed capital, the *market* 'equilibrium' of demand and supply would correspond to the fundamental 'equilibrium' of individual branches and of the entire social system as a whole. In concrete terms, if 'supply and demand never equal one another *in any* given case, their deviations from the condition of equality follow one another in such a way – the result of a deviation in one direction is that it calls forth a deviation in the opposite direction – that there is a *complete equilibrium* between supply and demand when the whole is viewed over a long enough period, but only as an average of past fluctuations, and only as the continuous movement of their contradiction. In this way market prices, which have deviated from market values, equalise themselves and yield an average that conforms to market value.'[61] Thus, market divergences

[61] Marx 1962, p. 186.

of demand and supply have a short-term and sporadic character. Market relations do not enter into long-term contradiction with the 'proportionality' of social production. Their theoretically conceivable 'equilibrium' corresponds to the 'equilibrium' of the fundamental elements of the social system.

Things are quite different, however, in the context of the *real* relations that prevail during the expansion. Here, market 'equilibrium' irrationally fails to answer the needs of 'equilibrium' of the social system. The very nature of market equilibrium changes dramatically. At the beginning of the expansion, the continuous excess of demand over supply more or less correctly reflected the need for a corresponding reallocation of capitals. The price increase on products from Department I, exceeding that in II, expressed the need for an intensive production effort in I in order to preserve the 'equilibrium' of the growing system. However, capitalist production is unable to satisfy fully both its own productive requirements and personal demand *immediately* upon their appearance. The 'deficit' of production in relation to consumption steadily increases. This fact is expressed in *market* terms by further deviations of demand from supply, accompanied by a further rise in prices. In the language of the market, the 'disproportion' grows. However, production has already 'laboured' long to fill the breach, rapidly expanding existing enterprises and branches and building new ones. In turn, inter-branch competition – the lever of 'equilibrium' between the component parts of the system – is at work 'everywhere'. Capital flows into production from other spheres together with a steady stream of surplus-value. Nevertheless, during the first and the second parts of the expansion, the condition of *underproduction* not only persists but also steadily intensifies.[62]

Capitalist society has sufficient potential capital at its disposal, but it is not able quickly to give it the *productive* form of functioning means of production. On the contrary, the flow of this capital into production initially signifies a *multiplication* of social purchasing power and thus a growing impossibility of fully satisfying it at this particular moment.[63] The high technical composition, which every capital must adopt at the given stage of development as it 'craves'

[62] The reference is to Spiethoff's stages of the expansion.

[63] [Note the anticipation of the Keynesian 'multiplier'. Much of the Keynesian analysis of savings and investment is already apparent in Maksakovsky's exposition and in Marx's *Capital*. The major difference is that Maksakovsky sees today's crisis being determined by *past* investments, whereas Keynes emphasises expectations of the *future* as the determinant of today's investment activity and thus of current aggregate demand.]

to function productively, is the principal obstacle to speedy satisfaction of demand. Consequently, it is no surprise that it is not a shortage of M or a delay in the movement C^1–M^1 that determines the prolonged rupture of 'equilibrium' during the expansion, but rather the difficulties that stand in the way of a timely conversion of M into C, or the lack of identity between the available money capital (and surplus-value) and its ability to function productively. From the point of view of the 'normal' transformation of capital values, what we have here is an *irrational* contradiction between the distinct forms that capital assumes. The productive form assumes overwhelming importance, and the whole period of the expansion is a unique expression of its *predominance* over the money form. The partners in this '*salto mortale*'[64] exchange places. The symbol of capitalist wealth becomes functioning means of production.

Such a state of affairs cannot long endure. The difficulties of converting M into C are gradually overcome, and the system moves toward restoration of its disrupted *production* 'equilibrium'. The greater is the divergence of 'demand' from 'supply' in a particular branch, the more intensive is the process of capitalisation. The scale of *newly created* enterprises also anticipates further growth of market demand. At a certain stage in the development of this process, the *production* 'equilibrium' of the system is restored. Society has at its disposal a production apparatus that is able to satisfy the existing productive and consumer demand. However, only an *insignificant* part of that apparatus has completed the final stage of construction and been transformed from a 'bearer of demand' into a 'subject of supply'. The larger part still represents productive capital that is 'asleep' – that is, it exists in the form of a 'consumer' but not yet as a 'producer'. For this reason, *market* competition is unable to reflect the current growth of productive capital that is in the *preparatory* stage on its way to becoming *functional*. Demand still exceeds supply, and the level of prices remains higher than the prices of production. If, in the language of production (including its preparatory stages), 'equilibrium' is 'almost' established, in the language of the market, *underproduction* continues to grow. *The market mirror* ('demand' and 'supply') *ceases to reflect what is happening in production.*

Until the newly created production apparatus actually begins to operate,

[64] ['Deadly leap' or 'dangerous undertaking'.]

the market links of capitalist competition cannot reflect the results of inter-branch competition of capitals, which rebalances the system. One might provisionally speak of a developing contradiction between branches, which could not exist if there were a smooth process of replacing fixed capital. The concept of market 'equilibrium' enters into contradiction with the concept of the system's 'equilibrium'. That which, in the language of the market, signifies *underproduction*, in the language of production-represents near completion of the process of establishing 'equilibrium'. That which, in the language of the market, becomes 'equilibrium' – that is to say, when supply catches up with demand – in the language of the system, will signify fully developed 'overproduction'. Supply catches up with demand in the market only when the newly built factories and plants become 'subjects of supply' – when they throw their production onto the market. However, this will inevitably mean overproduction. The scale of capitalisation, being oriented on market *indicators*, will inevitably exceed the required norm of expansion in production. Overproduction becomes even more apparent when the massive delivery of commodities to the market coincides, at the end of the preparatory work, with a reduction of demand for elements of equipment on the part of the newly 'finished' enterprises.

As we said previously, the protracted lack of correspondence between supply and demand is associated with an equally protracted conflict between market prices and prices of production. In this latter conflict, market prices prevail up to the end of the expansion. They are the actual regulator that 'manages' the movement of capitals. The market mechanism, which envelops the wealth of the capitalist, escapes from its 'subordination' to value and develops its own internal momentum. By guaranteeing super-profits, it creates pressures for massive additional capitalisations up to the very end of the expansion. As construction of the necessary production enterprises approaches completion, this 'super-capitalisation' then results in the production of 'overproduction'. High prices are transformed at a certain stage of the expansion into a false and *irrational* indicator. The emerging overproduction achieves a 'balance' of 'demand' and 'supply', but only 'for an instant'. This 'balancing' does not become a market expression of the 'proportionality' of social production; instead, it is merely a brief moment (an 'instant') in a sharp decline of market prices, as they pass through the regulating zone of value in their downward movement and express a dialectically maturing overproduction that is breaking through to the system's surface.

Therefore: 1) the massive renovation of fixed capital 'gives birth' to the expansion phase of capitalist reproduction; 2) insofar as growth of social demand exceeds the possibilities for a correspondingly rapid increase of production, the entire period of expansion unfolds in the context of, and in response to, a rising level of prices and thus of profits; 3) the impossibility of a rapid expansion (corresponding to demand) is determined not by a shortage of money capital or a low level of technology, but rather, on the one hand, by the high level of capital's technical composition – which represents a further addition to productive demand – and, on the other hand, by the lengthening period required for capital construction; 4) at a certain stage in development of the expansion, when the process of equipping new enterprises draws to a close, the market indicators (prices, profits) cease to express the elements of production 'equilibrium' and acquire an irrational character, so that the emerging 'equilibrium' of the social system does not and cannot find expression in a declining tendency on the part of prices, or their return to the 'bosom' of value in the prices of production; 5) the volume of additional capitalisation, which is connected with these events, crosses through the stage of 'equilibrium' and at once leads social production out of the condition of 'underproduction' and into that of 'overproduction' in the main branches, which then grows over into a crisis.

In the growth of the expansion – which is also the growth of overproduction – the *character* of the law of value's activity in the capitalist epoch is reflected as if in a mirror. In a simple commodity economy (and also in a capitalist economy, if we assume that fixed capital is evenly replaced), value 'regulates' production and, with each deviation of prices, manages to 'cope' with the task. However, the capitalist tendency toward restoration of the disturbed 'equilibrium' is different: value can win out only after a prolonged interval of time following the moment of 'disruption', an interval that embraces several years of expansion. The activity of the law of value – or prices of production – is expressed in a *pronounced* change of the conjuncture and in the *succession of its distinct phases*. The actually occurring production process is subordinated like never before to the law of value – *in the final analysis*. Never before was its subordination to this law, which constitutes the basis of the social system, so complete. The defining pattern of capitalist development is the clearest expression of this 'subordination'. It is the result of interaction between the law of value and the principal factor in the disruption of 'equilibrium' – namely, the sudden, massive renewal of fixed capital and the ensuing excess of social production over market demand. It is on this basis that there arise such specific market phenomena as the high level of prices during the stage of expansion. The whole reproduction process actually takes place around an axis of rising market prices that neither reflect nor correspond to changing value magnitudes. On the contrary, market prices can even move in a direction opposite to changes in the prices of production. The magnitude of value (prices of production) can decline in branches where technologically advanced capital is widely used, yet prices continue to rise. The result is that the various production 'proportionalities' of the system are disrupted. Department I grows, in disguised forms, more quickly than II. The slower development of c in Department II inevitably leads to the impossibility of $v_1 + s_1$ *fully* exchanging its natural form for the money form. Hence, there is overproduction of means of production. A prolonged disruption of exchange according to values – or prices of production – is identical with a greater or lesser disruption of all reproduction proportions in general. This means overproduction of means of production, the inevitable overproduction of items that workers consume, etc. The appearance of disparities in the assortment of commodities being produced causes the overproduction to become still more acute.

On its own, disruption of any one of these value relationships would interrupt the 'normal' course of reproduction in one way or another and, in certain circumstances, lead the system into a crisis. That kind of disruption, however, would have only a sporadic character. The 'pace-setter' of periodic disturbances, which inevitably end in a crisis, is disproportionality between the part of fixed capital that wears out each year and the part being replaced. In the real conditions of reproduction, this is the fundamental proportionality. Its disturbance, originating with the results of a crisis (or with technological change), typically becomes the starting point for disruption of all other proportionalities. If the causes of disturbance in this fundamental 'proportionality' were to disappear, capitalist anarchy would be deprived of its highest form of expression – the cycle. But that would also require sociological preconditions that could never appear in a capitalist economy. *'An organised society within an antagonistic form' – or ultra-imperialism* – would no longer have a cycle.[65] In that case, the reproduction process would essentially proceed

[65] [Karl Kautsky used the term 'ultra-imperialism' to anticipate international coordination of capitals in avoidance of imperialist wars. Rudolf Hilferding spoke of 'organised capitalism' to theorise a phase of capitalist development involving elimination

in conformity with the abstract schemes of simple and expanded reproduction.

It is not value relations that determine the growth of individual branches during the expansion, but market prices. At first sight, this would seem to imply a process of disruptions that would affect capitalism even more than a periodic crisis. This would certainly be true if prices deviated *randomly* in individual branches. In that case, exceptionally acute disproportions would arise because expansion of production in some branches would be accompanied by contraction in others. However, that kind of situation does not occur in reality; during an expansion, prices deviate *in one direction* – upwards. In these circumstances, much of the growth of society's production apparatus actually does correspond to the 'proportionalities' of expanded reproduction. However, this by no means mitigates the severity of overproduction. The degree of overproduction is determined not by the absolute expansion of production, but rather by the *evenness* of the expansion and the extent to which it is coordinated with consumer demand. Relatively minor overproduction can lead to a crisis if there is not sufficient absorptive capacity in the consumer market, whereas a much larger expansion – when growth of all the moments of reproduction is properly coordinated – will only mean 'prosperity'.

Nevertheless, the consumer market generally grows less during an expansion than total production (and begins to contract at the first sign of difficulty in sales), while in terms of production relations the main branches of Department I also grow much more quickly than Department II. It is perfectly clear, therefore, that the crisis reveals both a full-fledged disproportion between Departments I and II and a more general disproportion between social production and consumer demand, which finds expression through overproduction in Department II. The direct cause of this 'inflated' growth is the greater departure of prices from the price of production for the output of Department I than is the case in II.

However, even in the case of a uniform departure of market prices from the price of production, social production still could not maintain the

---

of cyclical crises through universal cartelisation (Hilferding 1981, p. 234). Hilferding regarded this outcome as theoretically conceivable, but practically and politically impossible (pp. 296–7). The issue of 'organised capitalism' played a central role in Soviet debates during the 1920s over Nikolai Bukharin's theory of 'state capitalism' and post-war capitalist 'stabilisation'. For Hilferding's views and their reinterpretation by Bukharin, see Day 1981, pp. 21–39.]

'equilibrium' of its parts, contrary to the claim of Hilferding. 'If the prices of all commodities were to rise by 10 per cent or 100 per cent,' he writes, 'their exchange relationship would remain unchanged. The rise in prices would then have no effect upon production; there would be no redistribution of capital among the various branches of production and *no change in the proportional relations*. If production is carried on in the proper proportions (as was shown in the schema presented earlier) these relations need not change and no disruption need occur'.[66]

Hilferding would be correct only it we assume that a uniform rise in prices *reflects* a corresponding change in values and the price of production. In that case, reproduction proportions would remain undisturbed. However, he is referring to the period of expansion, when prices rise above values, and in that context he is mistaken. Leaving aside the question of whether 'relative exchange relations' are preserved between branches when prices rise by the same percentage, let us note that Hilferding's fundamental *methodological* error is that he conceives of the 'proportionality' of the system in terms of an 'equilibrium' within production that leaves out the role of consumer demand. With this starting point, it is easy to come to the superficial conclusion that a uniform rise of the prices of commodities in Departments I and II will not disrupt the 'proportions' of reproduction. However, a 'local' equilibrium of Departments I and II, detached from consumer demand, *does not exist* in reality. Consumption of income by workers and capitalists is the most important condition for social realisation; that is, for the different parts of the production whole to assume the forms necessary for them to function productively. If the rate of growth of incomes does not keep pace with the scale of social production, overproduction inevitably results.

'Harmony' between production and consumer demand exists only so long as commodities exchange according to prices of production, or values. Any upward deviation of market prices from prices of production, even if it occurs uniformly, means a dislocation of these conditions. Despite the fact that a general price rise includes labour-power, the rate of increase of working-class incomes and of non-productive consumption of surplus-value *lags behind* the potential for capitalist production to expand. That potential is 'created' by a favourable market conjuncture. The productive body of capitalism avoids

[66] Hilferding 1981, p. 261. [The 'schema' to which Hilferding refers are Marx's models of reproduction.]

becoming distended only when the 'iron rod' of the law of value exerts direct pressure on the 'proportions' of its parts. A uniform upward deviation of prices, which (let us assume) did not create a disproportion between Departments I and II, would inevitably provide the impulse for *such* an expansion of production as would *outstrip* the rise in working-class income, for the latter is strictly limited in capitalism's antagonistic conditions of distribution and in the presence of the reserve army. At the current stage of technology, capitalist production is literally 'bursting' with overproduction. It is pointless even to raise the issue of whether overproduction, in the aforementioned circumstances, would be sufficient to grow over into a cyclical crisis, for absolutely artificial conditions are being assumed; for instance, that there is neither any disproportion between Departments I and II nor the related issue of the massive renovation of fixed capital. The contradiction between capitalism's production capacity and its relations of distribution exists as a fact and is revealed in the form of partial or universal overproduction. For that reason, Hilferding, with his theory of a 'local' equilibrium occurring within production, is incorrect. He has not considered all the moments in the transition from the abstract theory of social reproduction to the analysis of the real process. When analysing *real* reproduction, Hilferding and Tugan both treat personal consumption as a simple function of production with no independent significance, either qualitatively or *quantitatively.* They do not understand that the law of value, which is the foundation of proportionality in social reproduction, is, at the same time, the law of 'proportionality' between social production and consumer demand. A lag in the regulating activity of value, expressed in a prolonged upward deviation of the market price from the price of production, prepares the way for an outbreak of contradictions between capitalism's relations of distribution and its capacity for rapid expansion on the basis of capitalisation of surplus-value. The concrete expression of this contradiction is the way in which consumer demand grows more slowly than the development of production. We have already examined how this process occurs. This is the central moment of overproduction and thus of the cycle. It would be impossible to provide a theoretical explanation of the real course of capitalist reproduction without considering this contradiction. Hilferding's fundamental error is *methodological*; it involves his failure to clarify fully the activity of the law of value within the comprehensive linkages of capitalist reproduction.

Direct involvement of the law of value, in its role as 'regulator', is associated with a contradiction between production and consumption that has already erupted in the market. Through the fall in prices, value works towards 'equilibrium' of all the elements of production on a new basis. The crisis is a *deformed* expression of the *victory* of the tendency toward 'equilibrium' over the 'self-repelling' forces of capitalist anarchy. The battlefield for their struggle is the social turnover process, including the unity of its phases of production and circulation. 'If they (the phases of production and circulation, P.M.) were only separate, without being a unity – writes Marx – then their unity could not be established by force and there could be no crisis. If they were only a unity, without being separate, then no violent separation would be possible without implying a crisis. *Crisis represents the forcible establishment of unity between moments that have become independent, and the enforced separation from one another of moments that are essentially a unity.*'[67]

Here, Marx brilliantly characterised the essence of a crisis. He revealed its dialectical nature. The process of production and circulation represents the unity of the turnover of capital. Nevertheless, this unity is not monolithic – it is an anarchic sum of the autonomous parts of the social whole. *The crisis expresses mutual alienation* of these moments, the familiar struggle of individual and separate capitals against the social conditions of their turnover. However, if the crisis were merely a condensed expression of this struggle and *nothing more*, continued existence of a social whole would be impossible. The already existing 'autonomous' and 'anti-social' tendencies of individual capitals would be reinforced; and, because every phase of each capital's turnover depends directly upon the passage of other capitals through their own successive phases, if these tendencies prevailed even briefly, they would cause the social system's deformation and disintegration into its most basic elements, which cannot exist unless they are closely interconnected. The reason why mature contradictions erupt into a crisis is precisely so that they may be overcome. The presence of forces that overcome contradictions is demonstrated by the fact that the system continues to exist. The crisis *forcibly* creates a unity 'between moments that have become independent', thus guaranteeing a new stage of development. This aspect of the crisis expresses the activity of the laws of equilibrium – *of the law of value, which, through a sharp drop in prices, strictly curtails both the redundant production apparatus and the excess of commodity capital that has been created by extraordinary capitalisation on the basis of high*

[67] Marx 1975a, p. 513.

prices that are detached from value, or from the price of production. By performing this surgical operation, value drives the social system toward 'equilibrium' of its parts, without *ever* achieving 'final perfection' in its work.

The drop in production is accompanied by a further reduction in demand, which then must be expressed in further production cuts. Taking its general impetus from the moment of crisis, the process of establishing 'equilibrium' now embraces a whole period of reproduction known as the *depression*. Here, the 'philosophy of the epoch' is not to promote growth of the productive forces, but rather to work out new *quantitative* foundations for a social 'equilibrium' based on changing technology, which is entering the next stage of its development. Initially taking the form of a downward spiral of production, the depression prepares all the elements for new record-breaking growth, which is realised during the ensuing stage of expansion.

Thus, the cyclical 'figure' of capitalist reproduction – R. Luxemburg's term – expresses the characteristic activity of the law of value ('transmitted' through prices of production) in the capitalist epoch. The specifically capitalist expression of this activity involves loss of the ability to manage the system directly through the dynamic of prices, except in the *final* instance. The more protracted is the action of factors that cause price to deviate from value – or from the price of production – the more serious is the disruption and the more *urgent* the form of overcoming those deviations. Instead of prices frequently moving up and down about their resultant norm, as in the period of *'non-cyclical'* capitalism, in developed capitalism we find long-term movements of prices (and profits) that are the natural precondition for 'super-capitalisations'. Short-term fluctuations in the scale of production, around the resultant average in each branch, are replaced by catastrophic movement of the entire social system, which, over long periods, races far 'ahead' of the 'moving equilibrium' of its own overall growth. Partial deviations, the ripples of capitalist anarchy, are replaced by sharply defined conjunctural waves. Having lost the ability to overcome the system's current difficulties, the law of value now asserts itself through acute, periodic ruptures of the high conjuncture. Growth of capitalist anarchy, reaching its culmination in the cycle, coincides with an increase of the force with which the fundamental laws of the system must act. Were this not the case, flourishing anarchy would long ago have devoured the foundations of 'equilibrium', the economic ligaments would have been severed, the production apparatus would have disintegrated into a heap of materially objectified wreckage, and the system would have ceased to exist.

The urgency with which the laws of 'equilibrium' operate is obvious and is manifested in the crisis. However, the actual activity of these laws – and their forcefulness – is due to factors that disrupt exchange according to value, or prices of production. The greater is the pressure exerted by those factors, the greater is the activity of the forces that hold things together. Were the forces of alienation not present, there would also be no forces of spontaneous organisation. These are two sides of the same coin. Thus, whatever the determining importance of the massive renovation of fixed capital in generating the cycle, this factor – being the basic disintegrative force – is merely a condition and circumstance of the activity of the law of value. The cyclical dynamic of capitalism, like the simple fluctuating movements of its less developed elements in an earlier historical period, is a *result of the characteristic activity of the law of value, which draws from the disruptions of price formation, whether they be long or short in duration, the immanent strength needed to transcend those same disruptions.* Insofar as transcendence at one 'moment' is connected with inevitable rupture at the next 'moment', the conditions that evoke the activity of the law of value are continuously reproduced. We see this clearly in the course of the depression, which concretely expresses the law of value's 'levelling' effect on capitalist production when it jumps its rails. The depression, in turn, inevitably grows over into a new periodic disruption.

The theory of depression. The self-development of the cycle

The fact that the law of value comes onto the scene and begins to operate during the crisis by no means implies that the system will rapidly move to a condition of 'equilibrium'. Just as the disproportionality of social production takes time to emerge, so it takes time to overcome that disproportionality. These are two aspects of a single process, which, taken together, are the principal content of the cycle. The time required to complete them is measured by the cycle's length. Expansion and overproduction develop in stages, and the same is true, during the depression, of the fall in social production towards the condition of 'equilibrium'. Decline from the previous height, which occurs in the crisis, 'then gives way to a slow but steady reverse movement in the form of interaction between the different economic spheres. The fall in the rate of profit and in the compensation for labour puts pressure on consumption, which contracts and causes prices to fall, while the continuing fall in prices curtails output. Limitations on production further decrease both compensation for labour and the rate of profit, etc., etc. The result is a "vicious circle" in which interaction between different areas of economic life sustains and intensifies the tendency towards depression'.[68]

This is an excellent characterisation of the course of the depression. The moving principle of the depressive tendency is the same as in the expansion – the contradiction between production and consumption and their dialectical interaction. Whereas the period of expansion sees these moments interacting on a widening basis, determined by the upward movement of prices for all commodities, including labour-power, the depression involves the same process in reverse and is determined by the downward movement of prices. However, the result of the interaction between these two factors is different in the two periods. During the expansion, the productive forces surged forward as they 'took the bit in their teeth' and temporarily escaped supervision by value, whereas the depression presents a more 'peaceful' picture in which the system gradually returns to the 'stall' of equilibrium between its parts and experiences significant atrophy of the productive forces.

The defining characteristic of depression is the contraction of output. 'Depression is a period in which the need for material means of production is less than in the preceding period of high conjuncture,' says Cassel.[69] The fall in output, dictated by low prices and profits, is associated with reduction in the number of employed workers and the wages they receive. This condition provokes continuous cuts in production, and so on. Theoretically, one might imagine this process going on endlessly, right up to the full destruction of capitalism's production apparatus, but this would only seem to be the case at first glance. The fall of social production creates other tendencies that bring the process to a halt. *First*, the drop in total wages simultaneously means a rise in the purchasing power of each wage unit as the consumer price index falls. The fall in the index (from prices above value to the other extreme of prices below value) exceeds the reduction in the payment for labour because the latter is subject to a strict norm imposed by the value of labour-power. Consequently, consumer demand 'stabilises' at a certain stage and (if we abstract from further partial drops in production) can begin to show a rising trend.[70] At a certain stage, this trend brings the 'retreat' in Department II to

---

[68] Spiethoff in *Problema rynka i krizisov*, p. 269.
[69] Cassel 1925, p. 63.
[70] [Writing his review of Maksakovsky's book at the end of 1929, Livshits denied

a halt. A *second* factor involves annual population growth, increased buying power on the part of those with 'fixed' incomes, which do not depend on the conjuncture, etc. Generally speaking, the disproportionality between Department II and consumer demand is less acute than between Departments I and II. The 'scissors' in II can be closed more easily and more quickly.

Things are much more complex when it comes to the branches of Department I. Because of acute overproduction at the moment of crisis, on the one hand, and the almost complete collapse of productive demand at the *beginning* of the depression, on the other hand, a sharply declining index of production prevails in I, especially in iron and steel production. The circulation of capital values contracts, and the whole process slows. A significant portion of fixed capital stands idle. With the low prices that prevail on the productive market, the only way out is to reduce costs of production either by raising the productivity of labour or through the concentration of capital. In these conditions, the effectiveness of existing demand can *grow*, and demand can even increase absolutely. We have already mentioned that an unchanged volume of consumer demand can entail a significantly greater scale of social production in proportion to the rise in the organic composition of capital.

Thus, the *only* way out is to pass to the next level of technology. This process occurs during the depression and involves two characteristic phases. Because reduced demand means that it is not possible for the whole production apparatus to operate, the laws of competition drive backward enterprises, which can only produce commodities at high prices, out of business. Only select facilities remain in operation, which are able to recoup their costs of production and acquire a profit even when prices have fallen. This means that the volume of socially necessary labour changes, costs of production decline, and the possibility emerges for realisation of profit despite the low price level. Existing social demand is satisfied by the enterprises that operate with the most up-to-date technology, and the measure of value (market value) falls significantly.

Declining market value is accompanied by a change in the relation between market demand and supply. Consider an example: previously, with a market value of 15 roubles, supply sharply exceeded demand, the market was overflowing, the actual price was 12 roubles, there was too much produced, sales

that consumer demand could be a stabilising factor at a time when millions of workers faced 'chronic' unemployment (Livshits 1929, p. 227).]

were difficult, and it was impossible to realise profit. With a fall of market value (or the market price of production) by 3 roubles to 12, the functioning capital receives a 'legitimate' profit. Abstracting for the moment from any increase of supply, which is another expression of rising labour productivity, we would have an *established* 'equilibrium' of social production.

Thus: 1) a sudden reduction of demand, resulting from the turn in the cycle, leads to a curtailment of the fixed capital in productive use; 2) production's centre of gravity moves to the best-equipped enterprises, whose technical conditions begin to determine the magnitude of value; 3) the reduced value (price of production) ensures an average profit and, given the lower price level, now 'takes control' of market competition, altering the relation of demand to supply and pushing it toward 'equilibrium'. The specific phenomenon of detachment of market indicators from the 'equilibrium' conditions of the system, a state of affairs that arose in the period of prosperity, is now provisionally overcome. This first phase in the transition of social production to the next level of technology results from the intensifying struggle for survival within the production apparatus as it faces the harsh context of sharply reduced demand.

Liquidating social 'disproportionality', this phase immediately sets in motion the fundamental catalysts for a new *quantitative* 'equilibrium'. The equipment that is taken out of use ceases to be a material embodiment of capital. At any given moment, capitalist relations are only compatible with a material-technical environment that is capable of supporting them, that is, of guaranteeing their expanded reproduction. The 'spirit' of value, which penetrates these relations, temporarily or even permanently abandons those elements of production that cannot yield profits when prices have fallen. 'Insofar as the reproduction process is checked and the labour process is restricted or in some instances is completely stopped, *real* capital is *destroyed*,' writes Marx. '*Machinery that is not used is not capital*. . . . Use-values, including newly produced machines, which lie idle or are not completed – all of these are destruction of capital. . . . Their use-value and their exchange-value go to the devil'.[71] This is what accounts for the enormous moral wear of capital in the period of depression.

When the leading capitalist enterprises replace their entire production apparatus, this does not yet signify return of the system to its 'normal'

[71] Marx 1975a, pp. 495–6.

condition. Through great losses it has liquidated the acute disproportionality of its parts, but the scale of production has also been curtailed; consumer demand, as the guarantee of renewed expansion, grows only weakly; prices continue to show a falling tendency; the rate of profit is modest. Accordingly, during the first stage of the technological renovation of society, or in the *first* part of the depression, we still do not have a 'normal' condition of reproduction, only rough 'elements' of equilibrium without any external indications of the system's growth. Up to this point, further development is still inconceivable.

The first stage of technological advance then 'gives birth' to the second. The law of value, by changing its evaluations, has inflicted *moral* wear on a large part of the functioning fixed capital. A number of capitalist enterprises perish, while others, which are more viable, change the technical design of their capital. Gaining strength from the concentration and centralisation of existing money capital, they generate *additional* demand for elements of productive capital. This demand is objectified through expansion of production in Department I, which, through a number of links, passes along demand for the entire social product. 'The existing stagnation in production has prepared the way for its further expansion within capitalistic limits,' writes Marx.[72] Depression dialectically *grows over* into expansion – which is connected with emergence of overproduction, which, in turn, will pass through a crisis into depression, and so on, until reaching capitalist 'infinity'.[73] 'The same *vicious* circle will be described once more under expanded conditions of production (the stage of cyclical expansion, P.M.), with an expanded market and increased productive forces'.[74] A high conjuncture owes its existence to depression in the same way as the latter is the inevitable consequence of a high conjuncture. Thus, it is perfectly clear that there is no point to the kind of analysis that takes as its starting point merely external indicators of the development of the conjunctural process and, beginning with these superficial phenomena, attempts to 'extract' a theory. In this case, formalism and schematism substitute for an understanding of the dialectical complexity of a process that cannot be squeezed into schemes, however 'subtle' they may be.

The very fact of an acute drop in prices creates in itself the basic conditions

---

72 Marx 1962, p. 250.

73 [The reference is to Hegel's 'bad infinity', meaning a perpetual cycle resulting from capital's inability to function as a self-determining social whole.]

74 Marx 1962, p. 250.

for depression to grow over into expansion. 'A large part of the nominal capital of society, i.e., of the exchange-value of the existing capital, is once and for all destroyed,' writes Marx, 'although this very destruction, since it does not *affect* the use-value, may very much *expedite* the new reproduction'.[75] Through its work of demolition, capital reduces the scale of production in terms of value. However, not all use-value perishes. The unsold commodity, losing a significant part of its exchange-value in present conditions, does not lose, to the same degree, its use-value. A unit of exchange-value, given the general reduction of prices, now generally represents a larger quantity of use-values. This process is most evident in branches of Department I, whose output has met with sharply reduced demand. As soon as the system approaches a general 'equilibrium' of its parts, the tendency towards 'renovation' of fixed capital becomes evident. Acceleration of this tendency is strongly encouraged by the fact that enterprises, with their reduced profits or with the additional cash funds at their disposal, can purchase sharply discounted means of production.[76]

The capitalists lost some of the exchange-value of their capitals, but the magnitude of their effective demand also significantly increased. Naturally, because prices have fallen unevenly, not all capitalists are equally able to exploit this circumstance. Nevertheless, cheap means of production and cheap labour, in one way or another, promote the recovery of enterprises. In the face of the moral and physical wear dictated by capitalist competition, it is easier for enterprises to adjust to the changed technological conditions when they operate in a market where prices for means of production have declined. The *dialectical contradiction* that is lodged in the commodity, its dual nature, together with moral and physical wear, is the most important cause of the *growing over* of depression into the stage of expansion.

Consequently, the fundamental moments of the transition from depression to expansion may be described as follows: 'In the condition of depres-

[75] Marx 1975a, p. 496.

[76] 'Low prices for the instruments of labour facilitate the opening of new enterprises, and the low rate of profit makes it necessary to regard as profitable even those branches of production that did not merit any attention during the period of prosperity. Thus, new enterprises grow up, and with them new market demand. A further increase of demand for these products is added to the demand already caused by the "technical" and "moral" wear of the instruments of labour that were installed when industry was flourishing. Ultimately, this means that a new industrial expansion begins' (O. Bauer in *Problema rynka i krizisov*, p. 89).

sion almost the entire existing equipment suddenly turns out to be morally depleted. . . . The way to a new, prolonged recovery can only be found on the basis of a major increase of labour productivity. The latter is not only posited, but is also made technically possible by the mechanism of the capitalist crisis. The least powerful capitalists are bankrupt, or nearly bankrupt; their enterprises can be bought up for a song by the magnates who dominate their particular branch of production. . . . Backward factories are liquidated, the better ones are quickly reconstructed according to the latest word in science . . . the organisation of production is rationalised with the utmost thoroughness. As a result, the productivity of labour grows so much that it turns out to be possible to run production profitably not only without raising prices, but even with the reduced prices that were established at the outset of the depression'.[77]

What is the character of reproduction in the period of depression? The author of the preceding quotation, V.A. Bazarov, holds that depression is characterised by simple reproduction: 'Depression is a system of *static equilibrium*, which stabilises a capitalist economy temporarily at the existing level and within the limits of an *unchanging* volume of physical production'.[78] Closely connected with this statement is Bazarov's next contention: if, 'at the crest of the (rising – P.M.) wave, overproduction develops,' then depression can also be regarded as relative *underproduction*, which is overcome at the beginning of the 'recovery'.[79]

These two related assertions are completely incorrect. Depression is not 'a system of static equilibrium', for capitalism knows neither any such stationary condition nor its attribute of *simple* reproduction. Not one of the stages of the cycle can be conceived in terms of the laws of simple reproduction; in the period both of expansion and of depression, the capitalist system experiences a condition of *expanded* reproduction.[80]

Marx established two kinds of indicators to characterise *the type* of reproduction: 1) *value* relations between the separate parts of the social whole;

77 Bazarov 1926, p. 95.
78 Bazarov 1926, p. 96.
79 Bazarov 1926, p. 113.
80 [Several Soviet writers agreed with Bazarov that depression should be interpreted in terms of Marx's scheme of simple reproduction. According to Bazarov, crises are precipitated by monetary phenomena, and depression might become chronic because recovery depends on technological changes that are never automatic (Bazarov 1927).]

2) the *physical* volume of production. However, this by no means implies that there is a necessary correspondence between these two indicators at *every* stage of the cycle's movement. They correspond only in the stage of expansion. A smoothly rising curve, with no sharp breaks or zigzags, is the ideal type of capitalist development that underpins the Marxist theory of expanded reproduction. In reality, no such capitalism exists. Nevertheless, growth does occur during the period of expansion, both in the scale of production and in terms of the value relations characterising expanded reproduction: $v_1 + s_1 > c_2$, even though there are deviations from the 'norm'. All the economic processes develop around the axis of expanded reproduction and are accompanied by massive capitalisation of surplus-value.

The period of depression preserves this fundamental characteristic. Here, too, $v_1 + s_1$ is not equal to c_2, the realised surplus-value that is being partially capitalised. Even if the majority of enterprises do not participate in this ongoing capitalisation, it still occurs in the social system as a whole. In any other circumstances, production of means of production would have to be cut back to an extraordinary degree.

Marx says that the scale of simple reproduction in I is such that it presupposes expanded reproduction in II: given the level of development of production of means of production, if there were no increasing sales, Department I would more than satisfy the needs of social production in terms of repairs and 'normal' amortisation.[81] Where can these surpluses be sold? There is some growth on the part of new enterprises set up during the depression, but *most*

[81] Marx 1975a, pp. 480–1. [Maksakovsky is referring to the following passage: 'Even if the total capital employed in machine-building were only large enough to replace the annual wear and tear of machinery, it would produce much more machinery each year than required, since in part the wear and tear exists nominally [as depreciation accounts], and in reality it only has to be replaced in kind after a certain number of years. The capital thus employed, therefore yields annually a mass of machinery which is available for new capital investments and anticipates these new capital investments. For example, the factory of the machine-builder begins production, say, this year. He supplies £12,000 worth of machinery during the year. If he were merely to replace the machinery produced by him [assuming it lasts for twelve years], he would only have to produce machinery worth £1,000 in each of the eleven following years and even this annual production would not be annually consumed. An even smaller part of his production would be used if he invested the whole of his capital. A continuous expansion of production in the branches of industry which use these machines is required in order to keep his capital employed and merely to reproduce it annually. (An even greater expansion is required if he himself accumulates.) Thus *even the mere reproduction of the capital invested in this sphere* requires continuous accumulation in the remaining spheres of production.']

important is the technological reconstruction of existing enterprises. During the period of depression, there is virtually no normal amortisation. Replacement of worn-out equipment involves massive new expenditures of money capital, whose general sum far exceeds the amortisation fund. Normal replacement is inseparable from additional purchases of equipment because of the higher technical design of new fixed capital and the rising technical composition of output. Circulation of fixed-capital values continuously merges with circulation of newly 'attracted' money capital, which is trying for the first time to assume the form of productive capital. However, the result of this joint circulation is not yet reflected in any 'physical expansion of production'. On the contrary, in the first period of depression, moral-technical wear proceeded much more quickly than the amortisation process plus supplementary capitalisation, meaning that the scale of actual production contracted. Even so, the fact remains that new capitalisations – expanded reproduction, or a certain value relationship of $v_1 + s_1$ to c_2 – did occur.

The second period of the depression is characterised by the fact that the amortisation-expansion process outweighs moral-technical wear. Even in this period, however, the process of expanded reproduction could not result in significant growth of the resulting commodities as compared with the previous period (of the depression). The reason is that growing purchases of means of production do not yet entail a rapid increase of production. During the expansion, the contradiction between the time when new fixed capital was purchased and the time when it began to function had the effect of aggravating overproduction.[82] During the depression, the same contradiction makes it impossible for the current processes of supplementary capitalisation to result in a rapid increase of the mass of circulating commodities available for personal and productive consumption. When this disguised process becomes sufficiently apparent on the market, bringing with it a new wave of expansion, then we shall have the *growing over* of depression into the phase of expansion. The forces that mature in the period of depression, involving the concealed processes of supplementary capitalisations, are connected with the transition of social production to a new technological level. At a certain stage, those forces begin to negate the very existence of the depression.

[82] [Maksakovsky's text says 'aggravating *production*', but there appears to be a typographical error, which I have corrected to render the statement consistent with his arguments in this chapter.]

It follows that depression represents a *special* condition of capitalist reproduction, distinguished by the social system's transition to the *next* level of *technological* development. For depression, as for the period of expansion, the characteristic state of affairs remains expanded reproduction. Were it otherwise, it would be impossible to explain the *transformation* of depression into expansion. But since the 'main' task was, above all, to replace instruments of labour that were worn out in the moral-technical sense with new instruments of a higher technical construction, the continuing process of expanded reproduction could not immediately take the form of a massive growth of the productive and the consumer markets. Insofar as expanded reproduction completed the task of transferring the social system onto a new technical path, one might say that it had an *intensive* character and could not simultaneously result in massive expansion of the physical scale of production. By contrast, once the expansion unfolds *mainly* on the basis of a new level of technology, incorporating the 'lessons' of the depression, then reproduction assumes an *extensive* character and finds expression, above all, in growth of society's production apparatus. Since it is not generally possible to draw a clear line between the periods of expansion and depression, the proposed distinctions are *conditional* in nature and emphasise the prevalence of one tendency over another, which operates less forcefully. These two patterns of development are dictated by the unique 'tasks' of the two periods of the cycle; they distinguish reproduction during the period of expansion from reproduction in the depression; they are *superimposed* on the fundamental pattern of expanded reproduction, or the requirement that $v_1 + s_1 > c_2$, which is connected with the process of accumulation both in Department I and in II. As for the mass of inactive and expiring enterprises, from the viewpoint of the reproduction of capitalist relations they represent scrap metal that the 'spirit' of value has abandoned either temporarily or for good.

The moment of crisis, likewise, is not a phenomenon of simple reproduction. In this case, the prevailing tendency is more likely to be in the direction of contracting reproduction. The essential fact is that a cyclical crisis cannot be *strictly* classified in accordance with one or another *type* of reproduction. Its character is much too 'fleeting'. A *revolutionary crisis* is another matter. In that case, the contraction of reproduction is obvious. Its symptoms find *mature* expression in the crash of the system. However, a *cyclical crisis* implies 'stabilisation' of production in the near future and restructuring of the system's ranks so that the productive forces may develop further within the limits of capitalist organisation. The formal indications of diminished reproduction, which are of fleeting significance, are more of a '*memento mori*'[83] for capitalism than an actually realised type of reproduction. Nevertheless, pending a final answer to the direct question [of whether revolution is at hand], we can regard the crisis as a phenomenon of curtailed reproduction.[84]

Thus, we have seen that the period of depression grows over into expansion; and the latter, through overproduction and crisis, turns again into depression. Even a single rotation of the cycle gives birth from within to the forces that provide for its continuous repetition. 'As the heavenly bodies, once thrown into a certain definite motion, always repeat this, so it is with social production as soon as it is once thrown into this movement of alternate expansion and contraction. *Effects, in their turn, become causes, and the varying accidents of the whole process, which always reproduces its own conditions, take on the form of periodicity*'.[85] In another place, Marx posed the problem of the cycle's self-development more concretely: 'The industrial cycle is of such a nature that the same circuit must periodically reproduce itself, once the first impulse has been given. During a period of slack, production sinks below the level that it had attained in the preceding cycle and for which the technical basis has now been laid. In the phase of prosperity, the middle period, it continues to develop on this basis. In the period of overproduction and speculation, the productive forces are strained to the utmost and go beyond the capitalistic limits of the production process'.[86]

The basic mechanism involved in the self-development of the cycle is value, with its numerous drive belts. The inevitability of expansion growing over into crisis results from the character of the capitalist system's 'regulation' when it is under pressure from the massive renovation of fixed capital. This factor, deriving from the uneven progress of technology in a capitalist economy, gives birth to the unique waves of market competition that cause long deviations of market price from the price of production and thus alter the 'proportions' between parts of the developing system. The result of an outbreak

83 ['A reminder of mortality'.]

84 [Maksakovsky is alluding to the debate over capitalist 'stabilisation'. By 1925, Bukharin thought that capitalism was stabilising and no further revolutions were immediately pending in the West. The issue of 'stabilisation' played a central role in Bukharin's political downfall. See Day 1981, Chapters 3–5. Maksakovsky played no direct role in this debate.]

85 Marx 1961, p. 633.

86 Marx 1962, pp. 477–8.

of generalised overproduction in the market is a crisis, which signifies conclusively that the laws of 'equilibrium' have asserted their 'right', thus driving the social system towards restoration of the disturbed 'proportionality' of its parts.[87] The 'disproportionality' that has broken out, both within production and between production and consumer demand, is surmounted by an adjustment of values during the post-crisis period of depression. The diminished magnitude of value (expressed in the market price of production) changes the relationship between market demand and supply and once more attracts market prices to its own level and diminishes their fluctuations. This process, which is associated with enormous moral-technical depreciation, represents transition of the productive forces to the next level of technological development within the limits (for the time being) of capitalism. Capitalism has already become impossible on the old technological basis – it is unable to 'create' its own internal demand and has completed one of the orderly stages of its history. A new level has been reached in the development of labour productivity, which becomes the basis for the ongoing reproduction of capitalist relations.

Thus, the beginning of a new cycle is a new *technological* level, which is 'created' by the law of value in its capitalist form and causes a new 'cyclical' stage of development to unfold. This is how the periodically maturing conflict, between the materially embodied process of production and the *antagonistic* framework of capitalism, is resolved. A change in the *quantitative nature* of value, in its measurement, while the *qualitative* form remains constant, creates the turning point from depression to expansion. The impulse comes from the fall of market prices below the price of production during the post-crisis period, a situation that is impossible to overcome simply through redistribution of capitals because it prevails in all the branches of production. Given the inability of competition to rectify the disturbed relation, the only way out becomes creation of a new focus for 'equilibrium' – that is, a new, lower level of values. On the basis of this new level, both the materially embodied proportions of production and the relative significance of each branch take shape differently. The catalyst for a new 'equilibrium' is technological growth, which is inevitably objectified in a rise of the social average organic composition of capital and thus increases the relative significance of the productive market.

---

[87] [The analogy is with the role of law in Hegel's *Philosophy of Right*.]

This is the origin of the massive increase of demand for elements of productive capital, which then initiates a new cycle and leads the system inevitably to expansion, crisis, depression, etc.

It follows that the 'cause' of the cycle's self-development lies in the mechanism of the law of value, with its capitalistic transmission through the price of production, which 'automatically' resolves the unfolding contradictions of capitalist society so that the *most developed anarchy of economic growth assumes the form of cyclical, law-governed regularity*. The periodically recurring impulses that emanate from the law of value – a unique *perpetuum mobile*[88] – impose a necessary unity upon the anarchic whole of capitalism's dispersed 'parts' and bind them together as the complex 'molecules' of an economic totality. The condition for such unity is continuous disunity. An endless struggle takes place between these two principles of capitalism. Its form of expression is the *wave-like* history of capitalist development, wherein each cycle is the *completed* phenomenon that results from this struggle – until 'spontaneity' once again emerges victorious in this permanent one-on-one combat. The 'alienating' forces of capitalism, being rooted in the antagonism between its relations of production and distribution, at a certain stage 'devour' the forces of 'attraction', thus posing the problem of replacing capitalism with the next social formation, wherein the absence of anarchy will also be associated with elimination of the cyclical lawfulness of the reproduction process.

88 ['Perpetual motion machine'.]

Chapter 3
The Role of Credit in the Conjuncture

In the previous chapter we presented a general theory of the cycle. In accordance with the task that we set for ourselves, we excluded the influence of credit and of the money market on capitalist reproduction. That approach was appropriate because it permitted us to discern the basic moving principles of the capitalist dynamic and to show the mechanism whereby the separate phases of the cycle follow one another. We presupposed that credit, and the money market in general, is not the origin of the law-governed cyclical movement. 'The superficiality of political economy shows itself in the fact that it looks upon the expansion and contraction of credit, which is a mere symptom of the periodic changes of the industrial cycle, as their cause'.[1] As our point of departure, we dealt with forces different from those that play the central role in bourgeois economics. The validity of this methodological approach had to be demonstrated in the theoretical analysis of the cycle as whole. But our approach by no means discounted the significance of credit in *fermenting* the conjunctural process. We have now reached the level of analysis where we must take into account the unique influence of this crucial factor upon the *concrete* conjuncture. The cycle is nothing but the result of a certain changing relationship between the separate

[1] Marx 1961, p. 633.

moments of reproduction on the basis of value, in which credit plays a significant role. Credit and the money market are *not qualitative* factors or fundamental moving forces in the cyclical dynamic, but they do have considerable importance as *quantitative* elements that impart specificity to its successive phases.

Credit is especially important in bringing each high conjuncture to ruin. While the turning point of a high conjuncture results from contradictions that have matured in relations of production and distribution – contradictions that occur even without the involvement of credit – it remains a fact that credit and speculation impart to this turning point the fully concrete character of a crisis. Credit is, therefore, a *quantitative* element with regard to the general course of the cycle, but it becomes a *qualitative* moment in the crisis phase and determines its specific features. Were it not for credit, there would be no capitalist crisis as the intervening stage in the transition from expansion, with its distinguishing feature of overproduction, to depression.

This is the case because credit plays an essential role in the production of 'overproduction', that is, in detaching production from its base in effective demand and in postponing, with all of the ensuing consequences, a timely expression of the contradictions that have already matured in the market. Credit is also an important factor in the growing over of depression into expansion, a process that requires a much greater increase of money capital than would be possible if only the monetary resources of individual capitalists were available.

To clarify the role of credit in the conjuncture, and to trace its activity as an integral moment in the real course of capitalist reproduction – which derives its cyclical form from the moving principles of the system – we must outline *the cycle as a whole* not merely in *qualitative* terms, but also in terms of the *quantitative* determination of its features and conditions.

Marx excluded the influence of credit from the general theory of reproduction. He omitted its effect both on monetary circulation and on the speed with which capital passes through its phases of circulation. As a result, Marx also omitted the influence of loan capital on the reproduction process. In other words, Marx's analysis of reproduction left out (what Hilferding calls) circulation credit and capital credit.[2] Let us now examine the influence of

[2] [Hilferding distinguished between the two kinds of credit this way: 'Circulation credit . . . simply consists in the creation of credit money. Thanks to the service it

these two kinds of credit on capitalist reproduction in conditions of its 'moving equilibrium'.[3]

The laws of simple commodity circulation determine the quantity of money needed to serve reproduction at any given moment. This quantity is directly proportional to the mass of circulating commodities and their prices, and inversely proportional to the velocity of money itself. The latter, in turn, depends upon the speed with which the aggregate social capital passes through its phases of 'circulation'. In the 'normal' course of capitalist reproduction (excluding, for the moment, all disruptive circumstances), a growing mass of circulating commodities is usually accompanied by an increase in the velocity of money, thereby slowing the rate of increase in the quantity of money compared with the circulating commodity values. This spontaneous process of 'economising' on money is simply a consequence of the fact that the functioning industrial capital is undergoing expansion.

What does the functional role of money amount to if we regard it from the point of view of social reproduction? Money is a necessary moment in the distribution of newly produced commodity capital. It is necessary in order that the individual components of social capital might assume the value forms that enable them to function in the production process. In the continuous turnover process, each 'individual' capital, and the social capital as a whole, must assume the irrational, monetary form, which is the initial moment in the turnover of capital and in the further growth of values. Inability to take on the monetary form, or the impossibility of so-called realisation, signals the onset of acute disruptions in values, which are expressed in massive

performs, production is not limited by the amount of available cash. . . . But circulation credit as such does not transfer money capital from one capitalist to another; nor does it transfer money from other (non-productive) classes to the capitalist class, for transformation into capital by the latter. If circulation credit is merely a substitute for cash, that credit which converts idle money of whatever kind (whether cash or credit money) into active money capital is called capital (or investment) credit, because it is always a transfer of money to those who use it, through the purchase of the various elements of productive capital, as money capital' (Hilferding 1981, p. 87). On p. 88 Hilferding adds: 'Capital (investment) credit . . . involves the transfer of a sum of money from the owner, who cannot employ it as capital, to another person who intends to use it for that purpose. . . . Investment credit thus transfers money and converts it from idle into active money capital. . . . Its primary purpose is to enable production to expand on the basis of a given supply of money. The possibility of investment credit arises . . . from the fact that in the cycle of capital money periodically falls idle. Some capitalists are always paying such funds into the banks which, in turn, make them available to others.']

[3] [This condition means prices are assumed to be equal to prices of production.]

stoppages of sales, in falling prices, and so forth. These kinds of problems do not occur so long as we assume exchange according to values.

The main source of the money that serves the turnover of social capital is workers' wages, which are continuously being advanced by capitalists as the monetary form of their variable capital. When these sums are spent on means of subsistence, they realise a significant part of the commodity capital, which can then easily assume the productive form that it requires in order to function (in terms of the scheme, this accounts for half of all distribution).[4] The capitalists themselves advance the money needed to realise the remaining values.[5] They do so in anticipation of future revenues, which are still fettered in a natural integument unsuitable for personal consumption. In these ways, social value assumes the form in which it can continue its process of self-expansion.

A particular feature of these monetary advances is that they return after a certain interval to their owners. The monetary form of Department I's variable capital, after realising an enormous quantity of commodities and facilitating exchanges in Department II, returns to its starting point in Department I. Similarly, the money advanced by the capitalists of both Departments returns to its owners. This is what happens when commodities exchange according to values. But these are not the only monetary resources involved in the sphere of the social turnover. There is also money capital as a special form of industrial capital. So long as the movement of money capital, at any given moment, is simply the conversion M-C (the money form into elements of productive capital, to which C-M, conversion of commodity capital into money capital, corresponds), it takes place within the form of simple commodity circulation and fulfils the simple functions of money, just like the previous sources of money. The difference between money capital and money is that the former is the bearer of capital values as capital sequentially passes through its metamorphoses, whereas wages and the consumed part of surplus-value, as they participate in the realisation of commodity capital, represent the circulation of revenues, which are both formally and *in terms of content* a matter of simple commodity circulation.[6]

Commercial credit exerts an enormous influence over the course of social reproduction in *two* ways: 1) it accelerates the turnover of social capital; and

[4] [See Marx 1957, pp. 510–11.]
[5] [See Hilferding 1981, p. 69.]
[6] [See Marx 1962, pp. 438–9.]

2) it reduces the quantity of money required for commodity circulation. Commercial credit's sphere of activity is found in the phases of circulation. Insofar as the turnovers of individual capitals, representing sequential links in the total social turnover, do not coincide with one another, there is an inevitable slowing down of the passage of capitals through their 'circulation' phases. A smaller portion of the social capital assumes the productive form at any given moment, and the process of the self-expansion of value proceeds more slowly. On the surface of the market, it is clear that all the dispersed elements of the capitalist system are only roughly stitched together. This rough form, in which the 'fates' of separate capitals are first drawn together, is *smoothed over* by commercial credit.

Every capitalist who produces means of production alienates his commodities to another capitalist before their value is replaced by money.[7] This means that all the restrictions inherent in the condition where 'one can buy only after selling' fall away.[8] For the social turnover as a whole, commercial credit eliminates the negative effect of lack of correspondence between the separate phases in the movement of individual capitals. Thus the 'classical' formula C-M-C is transformed into C-C (M).[9] The turnover of social capital significantly

---

[7] [See Marx 1962, pp. 438–9.]

[8] Hilferding 1981. [The footnote refers to Hilferding, but Maksakovsky gives no page number. His comment appears to be a paraphrase of the following remark by Hilferding: 'Now a commodity can be sold and paid for later. It can be transferred to another owner before its value is converted into money. The seller thereby becomes a creditor, and the buyer a debtor. As a result of this hiatus between sale and payment money . . . becomes a means of payment [as distinct from a medium of circulation RBD]. When this happens commodity and money do not necessarily have to appear simultaneously as the two parties to a sales transaction. . . . The commodity is handed over and perhaps even consumed long before its value is realized in the form of money. The contraction of a debt and its repayment are separated by a period of time. . . . Thus when M becomes a debt in the process C-M-C the seller of the first commodity can proceed with the second part of the cycle M-C only after debt M had been repaid. What was previously a simple transaction is now divided into two component parts, separated in time' (Hilferding 1981, p. 60). Compare Hilferding's remarks with those of Marx: '. . . with the development of circulation, conditions arise under which the alienation of commodities becomes separated, by an interval of time, from the realisation of their [values]. . . . One sort of article requires a longer, another a shorter time for its production. . . . Commodity-owner No. 1, may therefore be ready to sell, before No. 2 is ready to buy. . . . The vendor becomes a creditor, the purchaser becomes a debtor. Since the metamorphosis of commodities, or the development of their value-form, appears here under a new aspect, money also acquires a fresh function; it becomes the means of payment' (Marx 1961, pp. 134–5).

[9] [The process C-C (M) denotes commodity exchanges through deferred payment, or through the mediation of credit, in place of C-M-C, where the exchange is mediated by cash money. Following the comments in the preceding note, Hilferding makes the

accelerates. A larger part of social capital values remains in the productive form – the form of 'self-expansion'.

But one must immediately add that credit does not alter the nature of the capitalist relationship. Just as before, the market adjustment of individual capitals remains the fundamental condition of the system. Every disruption of adjustments in terms of value, taking the form of general overproduction, inevitably severs the ties of credit, and the system of capitalist production again reverts to its 'natural' form in order once again to build up a superstructure of credit and then to destroy it in a new periodic disruption. Credit, therefore, does not create a *new*, rational capitalist relationship. It is merely a *secondary* factor in capitalist reproduction, superimposed on the activity of the laws of equilibrium and accelerating the reproduction process at certain stages while alleviating its frictions.

Credit economises on the money in circulation. Appearance of credit arrangements is connected with the development of money beyond its function as medium of circulation to its function as means of payment. This process occurs in direct correspondence with the development of capitalist production. The result is that the market requires less money. Because mutual provision of credits for elements of productive capital is a *two-sided* process, it embraces all functioning capitalists taken together (with some minor exceptions, which we shall deal with later), and to that extent it decreases even further the need for money in the mutual settlement of credit obligations. Gold becomes the medium for a final 'balancing' of credit transactions. The more commodities exchange on the basis of credit, and the greater is the concentration of payments in terms of time and place, the less need there is for gold because the velocity of means of payment increases. Economising on the amount of money in circulation, commercial credit also reduces the number of points at which money continuously enters into the sphere of circulation.[10] But the 'worker'

same point: 'Needless to say, the seller has an alternative course. He can proceed with the purchase M-C by contracting, in turn, a debt for the M in anticipation of repayment for the original sale of his commodity. . . . The function of money as a means of payment, therefore, presupposes a mutual agreement between buyer and seller to defer payment' (Hilferding 1981, p. 61). See also Hilferding's comments on commercial credit on pp. 82–3.]

[10] [Marx writes: 'Credit-money springs directly out of the function of money as a means of payment. Certificates of the debts owing for the purchased commodities circulate for the purpose of transferring those debts to others. . . . [T]o the same extent as the system of credit is extended, so is the function of money as means of payment. . . . Gold and silver coin, on the other hand, are mostly relegated to the sphere of retail trade' (Marx 1961, pp. 139–40).]

and capitalist points of entry do not contract to the same extent. Because of the way in which the value of labour-power is replaced, the source of money represented by the income of the working class cannot contract. Its 'absolute' magnitude does not depend directly upon commercial credit. Matters are different, however, with the sums advanced by capitalists as they take into account future revenues that are not presently in a form suitable for consumption. Because, on the one hand, the monetary volume of variable capital cannot contract through commercial credit, and since, on the other hand, commercial credit does significantly reduce the dependence of commodity circulation on money, it follows that credit's *economising* effect is expressed mainly through decreasing the monetary advances by capitalists. In concrete terms, this means that development of commercial credit makes it unnecessary for individual capitalists to keep large reserves of money on hand. But that is not all. Commercial credit also reduces the need for money *capital* as one of the forms of existence of industrial capital. To the extent that commodity credits balance out between the capitalists, C^1 of each capitalist is converted into the productive form without passing through the monetary form.[11]

This process is theoretically conceivable for social reproduction as a whole. It also expresses a real tendency. A significant part of the circulating value of industrial capital moves 'directly' from the form C^1 to the form C^2. Looking at the entire social turnover in its 'normal' course, we see that the amount of money capital that is needed declines dramatically. Thus, commercial credit, while it does not affect the magnitude of worker 'advances', does reduce both the monetary advances by capitalists and the role of money capital as a component part of the industrial turnover.

Two conclusions follow. *In the first place,* the more credit develops, the greater is the significance of the fund v (variable capital) in realisation and distribution. This means that the consumption fund of the working class becomes not only the *final* condition for 'proportionality', but also the *basis* of monetary circulation in the service of realisation. *Secondly,* the monetary 'hoards' that have been freed up then strive to take on the form of their own

[11] [Marx writes: 'Within circulation, the metamorphosis of industrial capital always presents itself in the form C_1-M-C_2; the money realized by the sale of produced commodity C_1 is used to purchase new means of production C_2. This amounts to a practical exchange of C_1 for C_2, and the same money changes hands twice' (Marx 1962, p. 297). Maksakovsky's point is that credit obviates the need for money to change hands at the time of these exchanges.]

'self-expansion', that is, the productive form.[12] But their 'pure' money component consists of sums advanced by the capitalists against revenues, while the other part is freed up money capital. An interesting phenomenon ensues. Credit not only economises on the circulation of money – it also encourages the money that is freed from circulation by credit, much of which represents the 'existence' of circulating capital values, to take on the *productive* form. As a result, credit changes the *relation* between the separate elements of reproduction. The productive form of social capital's 'existence' expands through contraction of its monetary form. Expansion of the scale of production is accompanied by a sharp reduction of the cash funds of society. One form of industrial capital's 'existence' devours the other. The result is a disproportion 'created' by the simple inclusion of credit, which will inevitably find expression in overproduction. But it is also true that credit 'curtailed' the monetary elements of reproduction in order to occupy the space being vacated. Disrupting the 'proportions' between the parts of 'pure' reproduction, credit also becomes the yoke of 'equilibrium', *replacing* through its economic functions the insufficiency of money. It fulfils this role quite successfully and facilitates more rapid growth of the productive forces. In the conditions that we have postulated – exchange according to values – this greater complexity of the social turnover, as a result of credit, never erupts in the form of a crisis.

[12] [Marx writes: 'The development of money into a medium of payment makes it necessary to accumulate money against the dates fixed for the payment of the sums owing. While hoarding, as a distinct mode of acquiring riches, vanishes with the progress of civil society, the formation of reserves of the means of payment grows with that progress' (Marx 1961, p. 142). Marx notes that money accumulated by one capitalist, in anticipation of future investment, is transformed through the credit system into productive capital for another capitalist: 'The money-capital which the capitalist cannot as yet employ in his own business is employed by others, who pay him interest for its use. It serves him as money-capital in its specific meaning, as a kind of capital distinguished from productive capital. But it serves as [productive] capital in another's hands' (Marx 1957, p. 321). The size of the 'hoard' that the individual capitalist must set aside, and which can be converted into productive capital by another capitalist, is also related to the longevity and volume of fixed capital, the value of which is realised gradually over the course of several years of production. Marx says: 'This money is therefore the money-form of a part of the constant capital-value, namely of its fixed part. The formation of this hoard is thus an element of the capitalist process of reproduction; it is the reproduction and storing up – in the form of money – of the value of fixed capital . . . until the fixed capital has . . . given off its full value to the commodities produced and must now be replaced in kind' (Marx 1957, p. 451). In *Capital*, Volume III, pp. 310–15, Marx deals with transformation of individual 'hoards' into 'money-dealing capital', which becomes fully developed through credit operations. Hilferding deals with the same issues in his chapters on 'Money in the Circulation of Industrial Capital' and 'The Banks and Industrial Credit' (Hilferding, 1981, pp. 67–98).]

We saw in the preceding chapter, however, that the inevitability of a crisis is lodged in the very character and conditions of the law of value's activity during the capitalist epoch. Social reproduction passes sequentially through the stages of the cycle: expansion, crisis, and depression. Hence, the 'regeneration' that credit brings to capitalist reproduction must *intensify* even further the critical moments of the cycle. Breaks in the conjuncture, resulting from the fundamental elements of reproduction, become more acute thanks to the involvement of credit. Intensifying the 'basic' contradiction between production and consumption, credit also intensifies its specific expression – the contradiction between production and the money market. Let us look more closely at how this process matures.

We have established that expansion begins with a massive renovation of fixed capital that is reflected in extension of the whole scale of production and, correspondingly, of the market for consumption. Credit intensifies this expansionary process. Commercial credit reduces the time that capital spends in the phase of circulation, accelerates its turnover, and thus increases the accumulation fund, the annual profit. This means that the tempo of expanded reproduction increases and that society's production apparatus also grows rapidly. 'A mutual interaction takes place here. The development of the production process extends the credit, and credit leads to an extension of industrial and commercial operations'.[13] Moreover, commercial credit 'helps to keep the acts of buying and selling longer apart and serves thereby as a basis for speculation'.[14] This second feature plays an important part in the onset of overproduction. A third feature is the reduction of reserve funds, 'which may be viewed in two ways: as a reduction of the circulating medium on the one hand, and, on the other, as a reduction of that part of capital, which must always exist in the form of money'.[15]

These are the three main ways in which commercial credit affects the reproduction process during an expansion. Commercial credit expands as the production process expands. It is a means for further expansion of production

[13] Marx 1962, p. 470.

[14] Marx 1962, p. 427.

[15] Marx 1962, p. 427. [Hilferding says: 'Credit causes the available supply of money to do a larger volume of work than would be possible in the absence of credit. It reduces idle capital to the minimum which is necessary to avoid unforeseen changes in the capitalist cycle. It thus tries to eliminate, for the benefit of the whole social capital, the idleness of money capital which an individual capital experiences for a certain period of time in the course of the cycle' (Hilferding 1981, p. 89).]

because it reduces the time needed for the turnover of capital and thus increases the profit that it yields. Detaching the possibility of renewing production from direct dependence on the reflux of money, it is also a source of speculation in production. If we look at the whole expansion process in terms of the factors that influence it, it takes the following form. The massive renovation of fixed capital disrupts the value proportions of expanded reproduction. This condition is expressed in the detachment of prices from prices of production, which each capitalist interprets as a *command* to undertake further massive expansion of production. Credit, by shortening the time needed for the turnover of capital, increases the mass of profit being realised and thus increases the rate of capitalisation. But it also facilitates increased capitalisation in another manner. By making possible a prolonged separation in C-M, or between the scale of production and cash on hand, it becomes a natural basis for speculation, which causes production to expand even further.

Marx says that 'with the development of the productive power of labour, and thus of production on a large scale: 1) the markets expand and become more distant from the place of production; 2) credits must, therefore, be prolonged; 3) the speculative element must thus more and more dominate the transactions'.[16]

Credit's ability to expand the scale of production is anticipated by creation of new enterprises and branches of industry. Individual capitalists and their associates, given favourable market indicators, are able to increase the scale of new capitalisations far beyond the limits of the surplus-value currently being realised. Consequently, the element of overproduction *results* organically from the nature of credit and from the emergence of its complex superstructure during the period of cyclical expansion. The intensifying influence of credit on the growing scale of production, expressed in the accelerating turnover of capital, inevitably grows over into a speculative detachment of the scale of production from the mass of surplus-value currently at the disposal of capitalists.[17]

---

[16] Marx 1962, pp. 469–70.

[17] Marx writes: 'The credit system appears as the main lever of over-production and over-speculation in commerce solely because the reproduction process, which is elastic by nature, is here forced to its extreme limits, and is so forced because a large part of the social capital is employed by people who do not own it and who consequently tackle things quite differently than the owner, who anxiously weighs the limitations of his private capital in so far as he handles it himself' (Marx 1962, p. 431).

As we see, the growing influence of commercial credit is closely interwoven with credits in the form of *loans*. The first moment of this mutual interaction comes with the fact that both money and money capital, once freed from the sphere of circulation by expansion of commercial credit, return to the turnover process through loans in the form of additional capital, which strives to assume the productive form as quickly as possible.[18] Commercial credit creates a 'surplus' of money, and loan capital 'liquidates' this surplus by driving it into production. The result is a 'disproportion' between the separate components of circulating capital values, which is 'plugged' by the use of credit. More precisely, credit becomes a *constituent* element of 'proportionality'. The increased volumes of productive and commodity capital are now 'balanced' by the current volume of money capital *plus* credit.

However, credit money, functioning in place of gold, is not a socially meaningful equivalent in relation to commodity values. It has value only so long as, and to the extent that, each of the circulating commodities can potentially be replaced by gold. This presupposes that individual capitals sequentially pass through their phases both in time and in space. The latter condition, in turn, is a function of value adjustments between individual branches and enterprises, that is, of production circumstances in which the commodities of these branches exchange according to market value. Any prolonged deviation of market prices from market values will inevitably be expressed in disruption of the growing system's proportionality. Commercial credit and its consequence – credit money – while painlessly standing in for money capital so long as 'values adjust', *loses* its significance as a constituent element of social proportionality as soon as exchange according to values is disrupted. At this point, the increased magnitudes of social production must be equated exclusively with 'real' money, that is, with gold. Insofar as the volume of cash on hand, including money capital, was sharply reduced through the activity of commercial credit, the general disproportion that has matured between production and consumption finds its specific expression in *lack of correspondence* between the amount of cash money in the hands of the capitalists and the volume of productive and commodity capital in social production. The concrete market expression of this condition is a shortage

---

[18] [See Hilferding 1981, p. 187: The function of loan capital is to make 'sums of money suitable for industrial investment which would otherwise not have functioned as industrial capital'.]

of the money required for each capital to complete normally the exchange C^1-M, which is always the most difficult phase of capital's movement.

Credit money is not able to smooth over this disproportion; on the contrary, it has the effect of making it more acute. The available cash money mainly represents sums that are temporarily freed up by the sequential *turnovers* of the capitalist machine itself,[19] plus 'accumulation' by petty-bourgeois strata and by the working class due to the way in which they spend their wages.

The increased growth of production during the expansion, which is characterised by an excess of demand over supply, is inevitably connected with mobilisation of the entire production capacity. This is what creates the increased demands for credit money to expand the scale of production. These demands originate mainly in branches whose production is in greatest demand, those that are furthest from the control exercised by the consumer market and which, as a result, experience the most severe overproduction. This means that most of the money capital is attracted into the productive and commodity form found in Department I. It is precisely here that the most intense speculation emerges and causes the greatest *detachment* of the scale of production from the immediate resources of this Department. As a result, loan credits *intensify* the disproportion between the scale of production and the money capital on hand, which is needed to service social reproduction.

But, since loan credit concentrates in its institutions the entire sum of capitalist society's monetary accumulation,[20] the impression results that it is always in a position to balance the growing demand for money with increased credit whenever the market might signal problems with production. This is an illusion. It results from failure to understand the nature and origins of

[19] This consists of the following: 1) a reserve fund of money that can enter into the turnover process in case of need but which does not take the form of productive capital (*n* . . . *n*), that is, does not influence the volume of production; 2) accumulated *s* (surplus-value) connected with expanded reproduction; 3) sums that are freed up by the way in which the value of fixed capital circulates; 4) sums freed up by the length of time during which parts of the circulating capital are expended; 5) sums freed up by cheapening of the elements of production; and finally, 6) sums freed up by any reduction in the time required for capitals to circulate. (See Marx 1957, Parts I and II).

[20] Marx says that in providing credit to the capitalist, the banker advances 'the money-capital of his depositors. The depositors consist of the industrial capitalists and merchants themselves and also of workers (through savings banks) – as well as ground-rent recipients and other unproductive classes. In this way every individual industrial manufacturer and merchant gets around the necessity of keeping a large reserve fund and being dependent on his actual returns' (Marx 1962, p. 473).

loan capital. The primary source of loan capital is money that is freed up in the *'normal'* course of capitalist reproduction. This money accrues in the hands of the capitalists and is temporarily put at the disposal of the banks. Any disruption of the 'normal' course of reproduction is expressed first and foremost in difficulties with the sale of commodities and thus in the problems that each capitalist experiences in converting the commodity form of circulating capital into the money form. If there is not a return flow of money (leaving commercial credit aside for the moment), the result must be failure to replace that part of the fixed capital that has worn out, failure to replace fully the circulating capital, and failure, either completely or partially, to acquire surplus-value. Instead of replenishing the diminished fund of loan credits, every capitalist seeks more money credit for himself in order that he might complete his capitalist function at such a difficult moment. 'In this case free capital is needed not for further capitalisation, but to support the reproduction process – both production and consumption – and the existing distribution of capital'.[21] Growing recourse to a contracting money market, at the end of a high conjuncture, is the unique way in which hypertrophied capitalist reproduction *appeals* against the lack of effective demand, which is another expression of this same hypertrophied condition.

Until the end of the end of the high conjuncture arrives, the availability of idle capital, in addition to growing profits, is one of the most important conditions for preserving the *ostensible* 'equilibrium' of the different parts of the system. Idle capital facilitates a temporary conjunctural 'equilibrium' in the sense that through credits the lagging production can be adjusted to effective demand. At the moment when the break in the high conjuncture arrives, there arises a new need to establish 'equilibrium' in the opposite direction; that is, to reverse the fall in demand relative to the growing supply of commodities. This would only be possible if 'the annual mass of surplus-value reached such magnitude that demand for means of production, resulting from productive accumulation, replaced the demand resulting from capital that has already worn out'.[22] In reality, however, such replacement cannot occur; the increased demand for money credit at the end of the expansion simultaneously represents a sharp reduction both of the surplus-value currently

[21] Bouniatian, *Ekonomicheskie krizisy*, p. 192.

[22] Bauer, *Problema rynka i krizisov*, p. 87 [In this condition, new investment exceeds saving for eventual replacement of depreciating fixed capital.]

being realised and, above all, of entrepreneurs' revenues. The essence of the matter is that the movement of loan capital and its sources do not correspond to the movement of industrial capital. They are, in large measure, exact opposites. Marx writes: '. . . the movement of loan capital, as expressed in the rate of interest, is in the opposite direction to that of industrial capital. The phase wherein a low rate of interest, but above the minimum, coincides with the "improvement" and growing confidence after a crisis, and particularly the phase wherein the rate of interest reaches its average level, exactly midway between its minimum and maximum, are the only two periods during which an abundance of loan capital is available simultaneously with a great expansion of industrial capital. But at the beginning of the industrial cycle, a low rate of interest coincides with a *contraction*, and at the end of the industrial cycle, a high rate of interest coincides with a *superabundance* of industrial capital'.[23]

The volume of loan capital, therefore, is inversely proportional over the course of the expansion to the volume of industrial capital. For that reason, loan capital *cannot* be the instrument for restoring the disrupted 'equilibrium'. A drying up of the sources of loan capital is the very first consequence of maturing overproduction. Capitalist credit (in both the commercial and monetary form), which initially serves as a lever for expanded reproduction of the capitalist system, becomes instead a lever for the outbreak of overproduction once 'value proportions' are disrupted between the growing parts of the system as a result of the compulsion to accumulate. This is the common 'fate' of all the organisational factors of capitalist economy (credit, joint-stock companies, and monopolistic organisations), which, in the context of the system's fundamental moving forces, necessarily produce an *irrational* outcome that intensifies the periodic spasms through which the system inevitably passes.[24]

Now let us summarise.

1.) In the previous chapter we established that overproduction means primarily overproduction of the production apparatus of Department I and of its commodity capital. Does credit change anything here? No. On the

[23] Marx 1962, p. 477.

[24] [The reference to 'fate' signifies the absence of self-determination through 'reason'. Maksakovsky is responding to Hilferding's expectation that 'organised capitalism' would develop institutional forms capable of moving the system in the direction of greater rationality. See Hilferding 1981, p. 234. Hilferding thought of capitalist rationalisation as a *tendency*, although he denied that it might be completed (Hilferding 1981, pp. 296–7).]

contrary, it magnifies the problem. The reasons are twofold. *First*, profits are higher in this Department than elsewhere during the expansion because there is a greater lag of supply behind demand. Consequently, there is a massive scale of capitalisation and of establishing new undertakings, together with an increased demand for new capital, which is willingly met by a corresponding supply. *Second*, there is a greater development of commercial credit in this Department than anywhere else. Every 'businessman discounts, in order to anticipate the money form of his capital and thereby to keep his process of reproduction in flow . . . in order to *balance* the credit he gives by the credit he receives'.[25] This is obligatory behaviour for every capitalist: he would not dare behave otherwise, for his sales would *come to a halt*.

The character of production ties between the different branches of Department I is especially suitable for a maximal development of commercial credit. Here, each branch represents a market for the other and, at the same time, is customer for a third, and so on. Insofar as consumption has a productive character, there are no branches that cannot, to one degree or another, provide credits to all the others. For example, the iron and steel industry can be the creditor of all the other branches; the same is true of the machine-building industry, of coal, oil, etc. Here, the network of mutual credits becomes most extensive and complex, binding together into a single knot all the branches of Department I and even, to a significant degree, Department II. Accordingly, the need for cash to settle accounts is also *minimised* by comparison with the value of commodity exchanges occurring on the basis of credit.[26] As a result, the need for reserve funds is reduced here to a minimum; they are 'overstocked'. It is another matter with the branches in Department II, where commercial credit encounters serious *restrictions* resulting from the very nature of the consumer

---

[25] Marx 1962, p. 416.

[26] Marx writes: 'As concerns the circulation required for the transfer of capital, hence required exclusively between capitalists, a period of brisk business is simultaneously a period of the most elastic and easy credit. The velocity of circulation between capitalist and capitalist is regulated directly by credit, and the mass of circulating medium required to settle payments, and even in cash purchases, decreases accordingly. It may increase in absolute terms, but decreases relatively under all circumstances compared to the expansion of the reproduction process. On the one hand, greater mass payments are settled without the mediation of money; on the other, owing to the vigour of the process, there is a quicker movement of the same amounts of money, both as means of purchase and of payment. The same quantity of money promotes the reflux of a greater number of individual capitals' (Marx 1962, pp. 437–8).

goods market. Because production encounters consumer demand directly, there is no possibility for the broad use of credits.[27] Generally speaking, the mutual character of credit exchanges diminishes the closer are the branches of production to Department II: '. . . the circuit of transactions, and, therefore, the turn about of the series of claims, does not take place at the same time. For example, the claim of the spinner on the weaver is not settled by the claim of the coal-dealer on the machine-builder. The spinner never has any counter-claims on the machine-builder, in his business, because his product, yarn, never enters as an element in the machine-builder's reproduction process. Such claims must, therefore, be settled by money'.[28] In such cases, significant monetary reserves are always needed, and they cannot be replaced by feebly developed and *unilateral* credit.

Thus, commercial credit develops primarily in Department I, and the same tends to be the case with loan credits. Credit reinforces the basic causes of overproduction in Department I and intensifies the effects. In qualitative terms, the same effect is felt in Department II, although to a lesser extent, as the volume of production becomes detached from cash transactions and the disproportion between production and consumption deepens. But insofar as the influence of credit is weaker in Department II, that fact, together with all the other fundamental causes, becomes another condition accentuating the disproportionality between Departments I and II.

2.) The immediate prelude to the crisis is a slowdown in the turnover of capital, especially in its 'circulation' phase. This is the first sign of maturing overproduction. The slowdown is accompanied, on the one hand, by contraction of the volume of profits and thus fewer opportunities for accumulation, and, on the other hand, by exhaustion of commercial credit. 'On the eve of a crisis, and during it, commodity capital in its capacity as potential money capital is contracted. It represents *less* money capital for its owner and for his creditors (as well as security for bills of exchange and loans) than it did at the time when it was bought and when the discounts and mortgages based on it were transacted. Every capitalist receives a smaller quantity of money from the sale of commodities than he has to pay on his promissory notes'.[29] At the end

[27] [In view of the time when he was writing, Maksakovsky could not anticipate the modern growth of consumer credit.]

[28] Marx 1962, p. 469.

[29] Marx 1962, p. 479. [Maksakovsky's italics. The final sentence of this quotation does not appear in the edition of Capital, Volume III that I am using.] See also Marx

of an expansion, when entrepreneurial revenues have fallen sharply, hardly any capitalist is in a position to settle his credit obligations with cash. The demand for means of payment grows rapidly. The burden of commercial credit is transferred to the shoulders of money credit. 'In times of stringency, the demand for loan capital is a demand for means of payment and *nothing* else; it is by no means a demand for money as a means of purchase. At the same time, the rate of interest may rise very high, regardless of whether real capital, i.e., productive and commodity capital, exists in abundance or is scarce'.[30] In other words, at the moment when overproduction appears in the market, loan capital is no longer used for capitalisation and speculation, but as a substitute for commodity and commercial credits that have evaporated. But the same causes that determined the collapse of commercial credit – the slowdown in the turnover of capital, rising costs of production due to higher prices of materials, rising wages, and the wearing out of equipment – have also weakened money credit and sharply curtailed the sources from which it originates. Hence, money credit is unable to carry the burden of commercial credit. This circumstance is revealed in a sharp rise of the interest rate. The latter, in turn, contributes to a further weakening of commercial credit, which slows down all the more the turnover of capitals and thus creates the prospect of even higher demand for money capital. Then the interest rate rises still further. The owners of commodities are forced to sell for whatever price they can get. 'This sale has nothing whatever to do with the *actual* state of demand,' Marx writes. 'It only concerns the *demand for payment*, the *absolute* necessity of transforming commodities into money. Then a crisis breaks out. It becomes visible not in the direct decrease of consumer demand, but in the decrease of exchanges of capital for capital, in the contraction of the process of capital's reproduction'.[31]

In the period of expansion, therefore, commercial credit was a powerful lever for extending the scale of capitalist production and, by the same token, for preparing overproduction. Once overproduction is revealed in the market,

1962, p. 249: 'This confusion and stagnation paralyses the function of money as a medium of payment, whose development is geared to the development of capital and is based on those presupposed price relations. The chain of payment obligations due at specific dates is *broken* [Maksakovsky's italics] in a hundred places. The confusion is augmented by the attendant collapse of the credit system, which develops simultaneously with capital, and leads to violent and acute crises ...'.

[30] Marx 1962, p. 503.

[31] Marx 1957, p. 76. [My translation follows Maksakovsky's text.]

commercial credit then greatly increases the supply of commodities. Intensifying competition between sellers to the extreme, it expands supply and reduces the role of the existing effective demand in realisation. Finally, having replaced a gradual decline in prices with their catastrophic drop, it destroys the last foundations upon which the whole grandiose superstructure of credit rested. The credit superstructure falls apart, bringing foreclosures, massive destruction, and – ultimately – the collapse of money credit. 'It is precisely the enormous development of the credit system during a prosperity period, hence also the enormous increase in the demand for loan capital and the readiness with which the supply meets it in such periods, which brings about a shortage of credit during a period of depression'.[32]

3.) We have established that the use of credit makes disproportions of social reproduction more acute in terms of the relation between the scale of production and the money market. How does this process develop concretely?

We clarified above how commercial credit sharply reduces the need for money and money capital, replacing them with credit money. Correspondingly, the reserve funds of capitalists for overcoming difficulties in circulation also decline. But commercial credit cannot squeeze money out of circulation entirely. A certain amount of money must remain as the final means for balancing credit arrangements. But the greater is the mutual extension of credits, the smaller is the demand for money as means of payment. Because mutual credits are most developed in the branches of Department I, as a result of the character of the market for means of production, it is here that demand for cash money declines most markedly. An enormous circulation of commodities is served by an insignificant quantity of gold in its capacity as means of payment. But the same does not hold true in Department II. Here, there are far fewer possibilities for *mutual* credits. This means that a high demand for cash remains, and that credit has much less effect in economising on the circulation of money. Normally, money is paid when the commodity is alienated. The credit links between Departments I and II also have, for the most part, a one-sided character. For example, the machine-building industries might (and do) provide machines on credit to most branches producing means of consumption. But the latter, by virtue of the character of their production, cannot fully offset the credit they receive. Thus, Department II must retain

[32] Marx 1962, p. 440.

more money for circulation as means of purchase and of payment. In this Department, the fund of money 'operates' both for wage payments and for advances by the capitalists.[33] In order for reproduction to proceed without interruption, Department II capitalists must have at their disposal a greater monetary reserve relative to the total turnover of values than is required in Department I.

How does the process of realisation proceed during the period of expansion? The whole social income is concentrated in money form in Department II, fulfilling in the first stage of its metamorphosis (M-C, C-M) the role of means of purchase (circulation) through an enormous number of exchange transactions. Within Department II, a part of this money also plays the role of means of payment, serving transactions completed on credit. Thus, the production of Department II, as the objective embodiment of the social income, concentrates in its channels sufficient money resources for realisation. Now, the question arises: How can the realisation process be completed in Department I, where the commodities produced are (with few exceptions) not consumed as social income? If the commodity circulation between Departments I and II were completed on credit, and if the credit transactions were *mutual in character*, then these transactions would be 'balanced' mainly by the reserve fund of Department I. But credit transactions between Departments I and II have a predominantly *one-sided* character. Only the branches of Department I can be net creditors. Thus the branches of Department II, receiving means of production on credit, replace the commodity values alienated [by Department I] with money. In this way, Department I receives, in addition to its own reserves, a monetary fund adequate for realisation, which appears mainly as means of payment.

As the total sum of money needed for circulation declines due to the economising effect of commercial credit, the relative importance of the money form of variable capital increases in the process of social realisation. This sum, together with the consumed surplus-value, is the only monetary source that *cannot* be reduced through commercial credit. If we abstract from the income of the capitalists, which is a diminishing sum relative to the total wages, then the growing income of the working class, in the form of money, becomes the *fundamental* 'basis' for the money in circulation. It is precisely this source that

[33] [The advances represent purchases of means of production, whose value is to be realised subsequently through sale of the resulting consumer goods.]

provides a continuous stream of money to serve commodity circulation. Working-class incomes, in money form, become the *fundamental condition* for realising the social product. They fulfil the function of means of circulation and of means of payment in settling the differences arising from credit transactions. Therefore, putting aside loan capital, the money form of incomes is the foundation upon which the complex system of credit is erected. The fund of incomes – wages and the consumed part of surplus-value – determines the possibility of unimpeded reproduction and is the ultimate condition for growth of the entire social system. The unavoidable lag of consumer demand behind the growing scale of social reproduction, which we have already shown, becomes the basic condition for overproduction and thus for the crisis. The revelation of overproduction, in turn, is connected with the sudden appearance of a shortage of money. Therefore, to the same degree that disproportionality grows up between social production and the consumer market, the base of money income becomes inadequate for realising the social product.

In this way, the emergence of social disproportionality becomes manifest in the disproportionality between the given scale of production and the money mass available to participate actively in circulation. This is the *money-and-credit* aspect of disproportion, which is associated with the collapse of credit because of a shortage of the circulating money needed to settle an increased volume of credit obligations that come due at different times.

Credit money, as we have seen, is not capable of preventing overproduction. The same causes that determine the onset of the disproportion between production and consumption also cause a sharp curtailment of the flow of loan capital. When the fund of incomes was approximately sufficient to serve realisation, the demand for money credit for purposes of *circulation* was *minimal*. The significantly reduced reserve funds of the capitalists were adequate to overcome the temporary disruptions that arise mainly from the breaking of individual links in the chain of credit. Loan capital was used primarily to increase the *productive* capital of society, which was expanding at a feverish pace. But when the lag of consumer demand behind social production caused tremors in the credit network, in the form of a money-credit disproportion, that same moment coincided with a weakening of the market for loan capital and, because of the high interest rate, thwarted its mission as 'saviour'. Things could not turn out otherwise.

The credit system cannot compensate for the reduction in personal demand by consumers. The monetary resources of the credit system cannot replace the continuously reproduced share of the working class in the total product, expressed in monetary form. The lag of this share behind the growth of the production apparatus of society during the expansion is an irresistible law-governed process, at the basis of which is the characteristic activity of the system's laws of 'equilibrium'. But, insofar as this share (the consumer demand of society) is simultaneously the foundation for the monetary base of reproduction, determining the possibility for realisation and thus for distribution, and insofar as it also serves to 'balance' credits, thereby reducing the reserve funds of the capitalists, the lag of incomes behind production must inevitably mean the collapse of commercial credits. That collapse, in turn, sharply intensifies overproduction and the capitalist competition between sellers, who temporarily refuse to buy and endeavour instead to sell the commodity no matter what happens in order to avoid shouldering the cost of credit in the form of foreclosures, etc. The C-M-C process for individual capitalists separates into two halves. Every capitalist attempts to realise C-M. And since the capital of one capitalist can enter into circulation only if another capital returns to production, it follows that a simultaneous, one-sided process of C-M for all capitalists becomes absolutely impossible. Within the confines of the capitalist system there is not, nor can there be, any purchaser for the whole sum of commodities that the capitalists have on offer. It is impossible within the limits of the system to mobilise the monetary resources needed to provide new and sufficient purchasing power. Neither any single bank nor all of them together can prevent the collapse of social production from a high conjuncture into a depression. Undermined by the disproportionality that has developed in social production, credit cannot find within itself the power to ease the market character of the fully matured disproportion. Marx writes: 'Aside from the prospect of return flow of capital, payment can only be possible by means of reserve capital at the disposal of the person drawing the bill of exchange, in order to meet his obligations in case the return flow of capital should be delayed'.[34] But the reserve capital has, to a great extent, already taken on the productive form due to the efforts of the capitalist himself, or of the banks in providing credit. The remaining sum of money is not adequate to restore 'equilibrium' to the shattered credit system. The monetary resources of the banks suddenly dry up.

[34] Marx 1962, pp. 468–9.

For this reason, Hilferding was mistaken when he put forth the idea of halting the slide by strengthening the credit of the most prominent banks through a whole system of credit and financial measures undertaken by the state.[35] If the central bank and an entire network of banks, ignoring the risk of collapse, began to satisfy the increased demands of the money market by issuing currency, by acceptances, by extending the dates for bad loans, by preserving the convertibility of banknotes into gold and of bills of exchange into banknotes, and by expanding their discount operations in response to needs rather than curtailing them, they would still not 'save' the situation. On the contrary, despite their intentions and plans, this response would only provoke greater 'overproduction'. By enabling the capitalists to avoid cutting production while prices remained high, they would drive capitalist production even further off its rails and aggravate the already developed disproportionality. Every new turnover of capital would be accompanied by even higher demands for money credits as a necessary condition for the preservation of capital values. If we pursue this thought to its logical conclusion, then social reproduction – as an economic whole – would swallow up all the money resources of society; that is, it would swallow one of its own parts, causing even greater overproduction of both productive and commodity capital. As if anticipating Hilferding's formulation of the matter, Marx provided the following response: 'The entire artificial system of *forced* expansion of the reproduction process cannot, of course, be remedied by having some bank, like the Bank of England, give to all the swindlers the deficient capital by means of its paper and having it buy up all the depreciated commodities at their old nominal values'.[36] The sole means for curtailing the inordinately inflated production is a collapse of the high price level, which also entails

---

[35] [Hilferding wrote: 'A monetary crisis is not an absolutely necessary feature of the crisis, and may not always occur. Even during a crisis the turnover of commodities continues, even though on a much reduced scale. Within these limits circulation can be carried on with credit money, all the more so since the crisis does not affect all branches of production simultaneously or with the same force. Indeed, the slump in sales seems to reach its lowest point only when the situation is complicated by a monetary and banking crisis. If the necessary credit money is made available for circulation the monetary crisis can be averted; and even a single bank whose credit position is unimpaired can do this by advancing credit to industrialists against their collateral. In fact, monetary crises have been avoided wherever such an expansion of the means of circulation was possible, and on the other hand they have always occurred when banks whose credit remained unimpaired were prevented from making credit money available' (Hilferding 1981, pp. 274–5).]

[36] Marx 1962, p. 479 [Maksakovsky's italics].

destruction of a part of the redundant production apparatus and of commodity capital. In that way, the crisis, regardless of how highly developed the economic and organisational factors may be, remains the inevitable transition stage from expansion to depression. The intervention of credit for the purpose of *preventing* the activity of forces that determine the reversal of the conjuncture – forces that are 'not subordinated' to credit – can only result in further aggravation of disproportions and, as a result, in the increased severity of the crisis.

But none of this means that credit institutions, once they have set aside the idea of preventing the crisis, are unable to exert any influence on how it develops.

By conducting a preventive policy, credit institutions can somewhat ameliorate the catastrophic reversal of the conjuncture and moderate its effects in quantitative terms, even if they cannot prevent it in qualitative terms. They could do this with all the more success if, at the moment when the market reveals its disproportions through a slowing down of C-M-C, they conducted a highly '*individualistic*' policy of quickly and significantly raising the interest they charge, thus decisively refusing to jeopardise the money funds concentrated in their hands. In that manner, they would reduce the severity of overproduction and guarantee to the capitalists the return of their reserves, on the one hand, while preventing the further growth of overproduction on the other. With that kind of policy, and forgetting about any idea of changing the structure of the cycle, they would turn out to be more capable of conducting a 'reformist' attempt to diminish the consequences of the existing overproduction for national economic life. But even this policy, when conducted with the greatest far-sightedness and understanding of the inevitable reversal in the conjuncture, cannot be completed by the credit network – even if it is organised to the highest degree and fully committed to the conduct of a 'rational' policy. The existence of modern banks is determined not only, and not so much, by the function of commercial credit, but by the ever-increasing role of money (capital) credit. A decisive refusal to extend credit to the industrial system at the moment when the break comes in the conjuncture would mean surrendering to the 'arbitrariness of fate' the bank's own capital funds that are immobilised in industry. This circumstance, together with competition and the appetites for money capital, which grow in direct proportion to the increasing difficulties in industry, makes it impossible for the credit system to separate its own 'fate' from that of industrial capital. The ever-deepening connections between them, and the growing profits of money capital once the difficulties of industrial capital appear, determine the inevitability of a simultaneous crisis in both industry and the banking system.[37]

The condition of credit, in turn, undermines the stock market and the movement of fictitious capital. The activities of speculation and conditions on the stock market are simultaneously determinate manifestations of the movement of the conjuncture and factors in its fermentation. The fundamental movements of value, which are the basis of the cyclical movement of reproduction, also find expression at the *extreme limit* of capitalist circulation through trade in securities. This extremely volatile part of total social reproduction is its most sensitive membrane, registering the reversal of the conjuncture but, like credit, not determining its fundamental causes, which lie in the cyclical dynamic. The securities market is both an agent in fermenting the conjuncture and an expression of its condition at a certain level of social reproduction. It exerts a reverse influence on the 'base' by accelerating the appearance of acute disproportions, which have already matured between production and consumption, and by accentuating their expression in the crisis.

The determinate condition of the securities market is expressed in the

---

[37] [Prior to World War I, Hilferding emphasised more than any other Marxist the integral connection between modern industry and the banks, attributing it to the rising organic composition of capital and describing it in terms of the new category of *finance capital*. In *Finance Capital* Hilferding wrote of the new organisational form as follows: 'An ever-increasing part of the capital of industry does not belong to the industrialists who use it. They are able to dispose over capital only through the banks, which represent the owners. On the other side, the banks have to invest an ever-increasing part of their capital in industry, and in this way they become to a greater extent industrial capitalists. I call bank capital, that is, capital in money form which is actually transformed in this way into industrial capital, finance capital. So far as its owners are concerned, it always retains the money form; it is invested by them in the form of money capital, interest-bearing capital, and can always be withdrawn by them as money capital. But in reality the greater part of the capital so invested with the banks is transformed into industrial, productive capital (means of production and labour power) and is invested in the productive process. An ever-increasing proportion of the capital used in industry is finance capital, capital at the disposition of the banks which is used by the industrialists' (Hilferding 1981, p. 225). Hilferding thought this integration of industrial and money capital might help to *rationalise* capitalism and even mitigate cyclical crises (see note 35 above and the corresponding comment by Maksakovsky). The point of Maksakovsky's response here is that finance capital entails its own contradiction: the potential for mitigating crises is negated by the banks' interest in protecting their investments against the threat of industrial capital being devalued in a stock-market crisis.]

following sequence: growth of disproportions; a slowdown of the turnover of capital; increased stress in the credit system; reduction of credits for stock-market speculation; a corresponding increase in the supply of securities; and eventual collapse of the exchange.

Conversely, the influence of the bourse on reproduction follows this course: a general decline of security prices; the bankruptcy of speculators, capitalists, and of the banks themselves in their role as shareholders; collapse of bank credit; inability to support circulating credit; and the ensuing aggravation of disproportions in production. The beginning of prosperity then brings a rapid speculative rise of the markets due to the low interest rate, which, in turn, compels enterprises to raise dividend payments in order not to precipitate another reversal. This means the scale of production must be forced. For society as a whole, it leads to rapid emergence of a new disproportion, one of the manifestations of which is a new contraction of the money market.

Consequently, one expression of the growing disproportion of social production is the emergence of disproportion between the growing demands of social reproduction for money capital – at a time when reproduction is already slowing – and the money market, which is itself contracting. This contraction is due to: 1) the rise in prices of fictitious capital; and 2) an ever-increasing tendency for money capital to take on the industrial form. The latter process results, on the one hand, from individual capitalists spending their money for industrial purposes, and, on the other hand, from the fact that the money market is drained by the realisation of a growing volume of industrial values and by intensive activity on the part of the banks in extending credits. The disproportion between social production and the money market is revealed first at the uppermost level of the reproduction process – in the securities market – from which social production acquires an important part of the financial resources needed for its expansion. The disproportion next appears at the level of circulating credit, which, being unable to acquire the necessary monetary resources for its 'salvation', contracts sharply and imposes on the capitalists a panicky attempt to complete the process C^1-M^1 at any cost. On a *third* plane, the matured contradictions appear as a commercial crisis, which spreads to production and becomes manifest in numerous ways, including a sudden contraction of the volume of social capital and curtailment of the operations of the production apparatus.

In these ways, the forces that determine the inevitable emergence of production disproportions are expressed at every level of capitalist reproduction.

The further any stage of the reproduction process is from its foundations in production, the more rapidly it experiences the devastation that is occurring in the depths of production. In credit and the money market, the forces that determine the inevitability of overproduction find not only expressions of the existing cyclical tendency, but also factors that precede the disproportion in production, *anticipate* its onset, and *magnify* its final outcome. The inevitability of general overproduction, and thus of the crisis itself, is given by the characteristic activity of the laws of 'equilibrium' in conditions of the massive renovation of fixed capital. The influence of credit and the money market is superimposed on the activity of the law of value. It is a secondary influence and does not determine the character of the capitalist economy's dynamic or the levers of its reproduction. But, insofar as credit and the money market are on the periphery of value relations, they intensify the expression of its inherent tendencies. We see, therefore, that in the theoretically conceivable conditions of exchange according to value, credit *intensifies* the growth of production and makes the capitalist machine operate more rapidly, but it does not, on its own, disrupt 'proportionality'. Since the real course of capitalist reproduction involves limitations on the activity of the law of value over practically the entire course of the expansion, the result is that credit and the money market – as the superstructural levels of reproduction – promote even greater detachment of prices from value (the price of production) and generally have the effect of amplifying overproduction.

Credit may be a 'rational' factor of capitalist economy, but not in the sense that it can eliminate capitalism's cyclical, law-governed anarchy. By mobilising the resources of a capitalist economy and 'economising' on the system's expenses, it *accelerates* the operation of the capitalist machine and at any given moment expands the possibilities for economic development. But despite all its weight and significance, its effect is to amplify *existing* tendencies. The period of expansion is one of massive expansion of the productive forces and simultaneously of the production of 'overproduction'. Credit amplifies overcapitalisation and delays its consequences until the moment when the explosion occurs. The period of depression is then one of restoring the ruptured 'equilibrium' and of preparing for expansion through changing the magnitudes of value, a process accompanied by massive renovation of fixed capital. Credit 'encapsulates' existing tendencies of cyclical development and becomes the most important secondary factor in the growing over of depression into expansion. Restoration of commercial credit and a massive supply of loan capital at a low interest rate represent the yeast that facilitates speedy return to the expansion.

'Credit, on its own, cannot divert economic life onto a false road'.[38] It merely deepens the tendencies already inherent in values. If exchange according to value is disrupted, credit magnifies the consequences for reproduction, actively driving its individual components apart despite their external appearance of being closely interwoven. When it attempts to overcome the spontaneous organisational activity of value, the pivot of the system's movement, it emerges (in the period of high conjuncture) as an alienating force and one of the factors that ferment capitalist anarchy. During the period of depression, price realigns itself with the price of production or else fluctuates around it, and in these circumstances credit assumes an opposite role as the most important factor in promoting growth of social production without significantly disrupting the foundations of 'proportionality'. During the period of prosperity, the picture changes again as prices become dislocated. In this 'two-faced' activity, credit clearly reveals its nature as a 'secondary' factor in the cyclical dynamic.

Insofar as it disrupts exchange according to value, credit is a force both of attraction and of repulsion in the capitalist economy. Value is the capitalist system's law of gravity, but its real activity can only occur through uninterrupted interaction with the disorganised spontaneity of economic phenomena. The dialectical contradiction inherent in the nature of the law of value, which can exert its organising force only in conditions where 'proportionality' is disrupted, determines the *two-sided* activity of credit in the course of capitalist reproduction. Regarded in the context of capitalism's total dynamic, credit's role is to reinforce the law-governed, cyclical course of the reproduction process and to give actuality to its successive phases. Credit and the money market impart a finished relief to the cycle, whose main contours are established beforehand by the 'interaction' between the laws of 'equilibrium' and the massive renovation of fixed capital.

---

[38] Bouniatian, *Ekonomicheskie krizisy*, p. 106.

Chapter 4

The Problem of Crises in the Works of Marx

In the preceding discussion we saw that Marx elucidated the principal moments of the theory of the conjunctural cycle. Not a single important question concerning capitalism's cyclical dynamic was left out of Marx's works: 1) in methodological terms, he specified the appropriate level of analysis for the cycle by constructing the scheme of 'pure' capitalism; 2) he provided the initial theoretical foundations for cyclical analysis in his theory of social reproduction; 3) he established the historical link between the 'appearance' of the cycle and the 'mechanisation' of production, that is, the growing significance of fixed capital and the corresponding development of capitalist competition; 4) he demonstrated the 'autogenesis' of the conjunctural cycle as a result of the dialectical interaction of the system's fundamental economic factors, which act simultaneously as cause and effect; 5) among the totality of factors, he distinguished the basic moving forces of cyclical development and defined the action of 'secondary' factors, such as credit and the money market; 6) he clearly set out the structure of the conjunctural cycle, its separate phases, and the inevitability with which each of them grows over into the next; and 7) he comprehensively worked out the theory of the capitalist crisis, the most important moment of the conjuncture, which brings into focus the specific essence and lawfulness of the system's cyclical dynamic. In other words, long before present-day investigators of the conjuncture, Marx provided everything necessary both for a more comprehensive theoretical elucidation and for a concrete study.

Nevertheless, Marx's work did not provide any *systematic* theory of the cycle. Its elements appear mainly as separate fragments, widely scattered throughout his numerous economic works and without any coherent presentation, for they emerged in connection with other questions that Marx was examining. It is this circumstance, above all, that leads bourgeois economists to criticise Marx for dealing primarily with the 'statics' of capitalism and with omitting the 'dynamics', which they regard as the most difficult part. We have already seen what these allegations are worth.

In the Marxist analysis of the problem of crises, we find two interpretations of the question that are consistently connected. Above all, Marx associated the problem of the crisis with the character of capitalism's relations of production, which, in turn, determine its relations of distribution. 'Let us suppose,' he wrote, 'that the whole of society is composed only of industrial capitalists and wage workers. Let us furthermore disregard price fluctuations, which prevent large portions of the total capital from replacing themselves in their average proportions. . . . Then, a crisis could only be explained as a result of a disproportion of production in various branches of the economy, and as a result of a disproportion between the consumption of the capitalists and their accumulation. But, as matters stand, the replacement of the capital invested in production depends largely upon the consuming power of the non-producing classes; while the consuming power of the workers is limited partly by the laws of wages, partly by the fact that they are used only so long as they can be profitably employed by the capitalist class. The ultimate reason for all real crises always remains the *poverty and restricted consumption* of the masses as opposed to the drive of capitalist production to develop the productive forces as though only the absolute consuming power of society constituted their limit.'[1] In another place, Marx wrote: 'The limits within which the preservation and self-expansion of the value of capital, resting on the expropriation and pauperization of the great mass of producers, can alone move – these limits come continually into conflict with the methods of production employed by capital for its purposes, which drive towards unlimited

[1] Marx 1962, pp. 472–3 [Maksakovsky's italics].

extension of production, towards production as an end in itself. . . . The capitalist mode of production is, for this reason, a historical means of developing the material forces of production . . . and also involves a permanent contradiction between this, its historical task, and the corresponding relations of social production'.[2]

It is perfectly clear that in these passages Marx portrays the problem of crises in its *sociological* aspect. Even omitting the real course of capitalist reproduction (the dynamic of prices, competition, and credit) the inevitability of crises is already given by the character of capitalism's relations of production. On the one hand, the specific expression of growing labour productivity is the rising organic composition of capital and the resulting decline in the significance of the consumer market; on the other hand, capital values endeavour to grow at any cost. These conditions already establish the permanent possibility that the development of social production will surpass effective demand, which is restricted by the antagonistic conditions of capitalist distribution. Concretely, this fact can be expressed by saying that the capitalist employs more capital than is warranted by consumer demand, which can never overcome the activity of the laws of wages. 'If more [labour-time] is used (in a given branch – P.M.) then, even if each individual commodity only contains the necessary labour-time, the total contains more than the socially necessary labour-time; in the same way, although the individual commodity has use-value, the total sum of commodities loses some of its use-value under the conditions assumed'.[3]

The problem is initially posed here on a sociological plane, beginning with the character of capitalism's relations of production. On the one hand, these relations continuously drive the development of the productive forces forward because they assume the form of the 'self-expansion of capital value'; on the other hand, they simultaneously erect barriers to this process through the relative curtailment of social consuming power. This means that the very existence of capitalist relations is connected with an ultimate severance of production from consumption. The unity of these opposites is realised through the mediating link of profit. The striving for maximal profit, which expresses the tendency for rapid growth of the productive forces within the limits of their capitalist organisation, *must* inevitably come into conflict with the narrow

[2] Marx 1962, p. 245.
[3] Marx 1975a, p. 521.

base of consumption, which cannot be detached from its 'result' – the value of labour-power. In the period of expansion, *exceptional* circumstances are created for receiving the maximum profit; but for this reason social production, in its growth, also dramatically outpaces the less dynamic volume of consumer demand. Then the crisis erupts.

This is Marx's point of departure and his initial formulation of the problem of crisis. While it does not provide a theory of crisis in the proper sense of the word, it does provide the methodological foundation upon which the latter can be constructed. Analysis of a *real* crisis presupposes the competition of capitals and the dynamic of price and credit. The fundamental condition for its coming to maturity is the fully developed mechanism of price formation: value – prices of production – market prices. Marx understood this perfectly well: 'Insofar as crises arise from *changes in prices and revolutions in prices*, which do not coincide with *changes in the values* of commodities, they naturally cannot be investigated during the examination of capital in general, in which the prices of commodities are assumed to be *identical* with the *values* of commodities'.[4] A real crisis, one that takes concrete form, can be regarded only as a component of the cyclical development, in which the activities of the precipitating forces are objectified. The forces giving rise to the crisis are simultaneously the basic 'causes' of the cyclical dynamic. The result is that the general theory of crises, which Marx provides at the level of sociology, *grows over* at the following, more *concrete* stage of analysis, into the theory of the conjunctural cycle. Only at that level does the inevitability of crisis, first set out in a general sociological analysis, become concrete and take on flesh and blood.

The moving principle of the capitalist dynamic is the law of value. In conditions of the massive renovation of fixed capital, it is the action of this law that imparts to capitalist anarchy the character of a law-governed cyclical movement. Accordingly, we can give the following general definition of the 'causes' of the crisis. A capitalist crisis is the 'offspring' of *capitalist anarchy*, which, as a result of the activity of the law of value (price of production), is manifested on two planes: 1) the maturing of 'disproportion' between social production and consumer demand; and 2) the emergence of a more particular disproportion between Departments I and II. Both disproportions come to a

---

[4] Marx 1975a, p. 515.

head *simultaneously*. They emerge during an expansion on the basis of the upward deviation of market prices from value (the price of production); that deviation, in turn, becomes the precondition in both Departments for the 'self-expansion' of value occurring more rapidly than the growth of effective demand. Because prices, and thus profits, are highest in Department I, and because there is greater application here of technical improvements and more use of commercial and money credits, the growing scale of production in Department I not only becomes detached from the consumer base of society, but also outpaces development in Department II, which receives less profit and fewer credits and is directly connected with the consumer market. Fully developed overproduction appears with particular force in Department II once difficulties with the sale of production, involving reduction in the number of employed workers, have already begun in Department I.

Capitalism's relations of production determine its relations of distribution. The reproduction of social relations invariably reproduces the cyclical dynamic of the capitalist system. That dynamic is possible only in circumstances where production is periodically detached from consumption; that is to say, *real* reproduction of the capitalist system is only possible through periodically erupting conflicts with its relations of distribution. These conflicts express the anarchy of capitalist economy, which is revealed in its law-governed cyclical movement. Therefore, *the fundamental 'cause' of the capitalist crisis is capitalist anarchy. Its real expression includes the inevitability of periodic detachments of production from consumption, whose particular expression is fully developed overproduction in the form of disproportion between Departments I and II.*

Now let us say a few words concerning changes in the character of crises as capitalism develops. The great majority of bourgeois investigators, up to and including Tugan, speak of the moderation of crises in recent decades. To them the implication is that the basic contradictions of capitalist economy are being *smoothed over*, mainly under the influence of its organisational and organising forms.[5] That interpretation is fundamentally mistaken. The growth

---

[5] [Bourgeois economists were certainly not alone in this regard. In his Preface to the 1885 edition of Marx's *Poverty of Philosophy*, Engels considered the possibility that 'chronic stagnation would necessarily become the normal condition of modern industry, with only insignificant fluctuations' (Marx 1963, p. 18). When he published Volume III of *Capital*, in 1894, Engels elaborated in his footnotes. The productive forces of capitalism, he claimed, were beginning to 'outgrow the control of the laws of the capitalist mode of commodity exchange'. Two factors were held responsible for this trend: 'the new and general mania for a protective tariff' and the related growth of

of contradictions in the capitalist system is directly *proportional* to the development of capitalism itself; they are reproduced on a continuously widening and deepening scale, which is shown by the ever-increasing antagonism between capitalism's relations of distribution, on the one hand, and its possibilities for rapid and massive expansion of production, on the other. This contradiction finds its fundamental expression in the relative decline of the absorptive capacity of consumer demand compared with social production. If the social system's 'equilibrium' is possible only when consumer demand is contracting in relative terms, it is also the case that fluctuations of consumer demand have a steadily increasing effect upon social production. Even a small contraction or deceleration in the rate of growth of consumer demand is enough to ensure, in the final analysis, that an ever-increasing part of the production apparatus loses its 'right to exist'. Moreover, contraction of the consumer market is accompanied by the most impressive expansion of the market for means of production. The production apparatus of Department I grows rapidly and in inverse proportion to the absorptive capacity of the consumer market. As a result of the growing linkages of productive consumption, the individual branches of Department I more and more escape control by consumer demand. The productive forces become, as it were, temporarily 'independent' of capitalism's relations of distribution; they endeavour to use this independence 'to the utmost' both to promote their own development and to advance in the most rapid way possible. That is what

---

trusts, 'which regulate production, and thus prices and profits' (Marx 1962, p. 118). On p. 478, Engels thought 'most of the old breeding grounds of crises and opportunities for their development have been eliminated or strongly reduced'. He summarised on pp. 477–8: 'The acute form of the periodic process, with its former ten-year cycle, appears to have given way to a more chronic, long drawn out alternation between a relatively short and slight business improvement and a relatively long, indecisive depression – taking place in the various industrial countries at different times.' Hilferding's *Finance Capital*, with its anticipation of 'organised capitalism', was one consequence of this trend of thought, although it implied stable growth rather than 'stability' in depression. In turn, Hilferding's work significantly influenced many other Marxist writings on the theory of imperialism, including, in different ways, those of V.I. Lenin and N.I. Bukharin (Day 1981, Chapter 1). In 1931, E.A. Preobrazhensky provided an elegant argument to explain why, rather than being moderated, cyclical crises had become more severe in conditions of monopoly capitalism. Preobrazhensky's work concentrated on capitalism's institutional changes and the distortion of market spontaneity due to monopolistic 'planning' for reserves of production capacity. What Maksakovsky calls 'overcapitalisation' reappeared all the more centrally in Preobrazhensky's theory as a consequence of attempts by monopolies to anticipate and foreclose the possibility of new competition (Preobrazhensky 1985).]

accounts for the extraordinary power of 'overcapitalisation' and overproduction, which is expressed with particular force in the overproduction of materials for fixed capital. A law-governed conclusion logically follows: the closer we come to capitalism's pre-war decades, the more acute must be the overproduction of means of production and *the more destructive must be the interruptions in the curve of conjunctural development.*[6]

Modern crises appear on the surface to have a less devastating character than those that occurred during the first half of the nineteenth century. However, this still does not signify any easing of capitalist contradictions nor any 'growth into harmony' such as bourgeois economists profess to see. Hilferding cited the *first* obstacle to such a development, namely, the increase of the minimum commodity circulation that is necessary for the system's existence.[7] Today, when small-scale, non-capitalist production has been squeezed out, this minimum has to be provided by capitalist enterprises. The *second* obstacle is the growing economic might of concentrated and centralised social production and credit, all of which enable capitalists more successfully to resist and adapt to breaks in the conjuncture. The result is that the increasingly acute contradiction between social production and consumption does *not always* and with the same force manifest itself at every level of capitalist reproduction. The highest levels – credit and the financial 'indices' – do not collapse headlong at the first appearance of overproduction in the market. *Thus production disproportions, while they are more clearly discernible, are also manifested less strikingly on the surface of capitalism, on the stock exchange and in finance.* But credit and financial markets are only the 'superstructural' levels of capitalist society. They can never eliminate the moving forces that determine the system's cyclical development, nor can they overcome its anarchy. The widening and *deepening* contradictions between development of the productive forces of labour, on the one hand, and capitalism's relations of distribution on the other, must inevitably find their most tangible expression. In their 'current' market manifestation they are hemmed in by concentration and centralisation, but this only means they have the potential to become even more acute. Neither the increasing might of capitalist production nor its

---

[6] [This conclusion was identical to Trotsky's in his debate with N.D. Kondrat'ev over the 'long cycle' (Day 1976). Maksakovsky's remarks contradict the theory of capitalist 'stabilisation' that was associated with Bukharin in the latter half of the 1920s (Day 1981, Chapters 3–5).]

[7] [Hilferding 1981, pp. 288–9.]

organisational forms can abolish anarchy; in the final analysis, they both intensify it. Capitalism's immanent contradictions become more acute with every cycle. The forces of alienation are stronger than the forces of attraction. They create conditions in which it is impossible to 'equilibrate' social production with consumer demand. Ultimately, all the postulates of 'equilibrium' collapse; the system comes apart at its seams; *the cyclical crisis – a 'normal' part of capitalism's physiology – becomes a revolutionary force.*

Let us now say a few words concerning the cycle – and especially the crisis – in the circumstances of state capitalism, which is said to be 'an organised whole in antagonistic form'.[8] To the extent that planning takes into account the demand of each branch in relation to the other, as well as the consumer demand of both workers and capitalists, state capitalism is supposed to exclude the possibility of general overproduction and thus of the cycle.[9] The spontaneous attempts of capitalist production to leap periodically out of its own relations of distribution are supposed to become impossible. In other

---

[8] [Maksakovsky gives no footnote, but in this and the following paragraph he is referring to comments by Hilferding concerning the possibility of a 'general cartel' and a planned capitalist economy. Hilferding believed cartels and finance capital were developing a potential for planning, but he concluded that capital could never universalise itself in the manner of Hegelian Spirit. The most that capital could achieve would be a consciously regulated society 'in an antagonistic form': 'Capital now appears as a unitary power which exercizes sovereign sway over the life process of society; a power which arises directly from ownership of the means of production, of natural resources, and of the whole accumulated labour of the past, and from command over living labour as a direct consequence of property relations. At the same time property, concentrated and centralized in the hands of a few giant capitalist groups, manifests itself in direct opposition to the mass of those who possess no capital. The problem of property relations thus attains it clearest, most unequivocal and sharpest expression at the same time as the development of finance capital itself is resolving more successfully the problem of the organization of the social economy' (Hilferding 1981, p. 235).]

[9] [The reference here is to Bukharin. In *Imperialism and the Accumulation of Capital* Bukharin wrote: 'Let us imagine . . . the *collective-capitalist social order* (state capitalism), in which the capitalist class is united in a unified trust and we are dealing with an organized, though at the same time, *from the standpoint of classes*, antagonistic economy. . . . Is accumulation possible here? Of course it is. Constant capital grows, the consumption of the capitalists grows, new branches of production continually arise in response to new needs, the consumption of the workers grows even though it is confined within definite limits. *Despite* this 'underconsumption' of the masses, crises do not occur because the demand of *each branch of production in relation to the others*, the *consumer demand* of the capitalists, and that of the workers, is determined in advance (there is no 'anarchy of production', but a rational plan from the viewpoint of capital) . . . Thus *no crisis of overproduction can occur here*. The course of production, in general, is planned' (Luxemburg and Bukharin 1972, p. 226). For the context of this comment, see Day 1981, p. 75 *et passim*.]

words, expanded reproduction is to develop on the basis of value, which is now to assume a *constitutive* role.[10] Price, as the specific expression of capitalist anarchy, ceases to exist, thereby also eliminating the possibility of periodic price movements that propel the social system into overproduction. In these circumstances, the spontaneous mass renovation of fixed capital also disappears. In place of competition, technological progress will find a new way to be implemented in production, and the renovation of fixed capital will assume a more planned character. The movement of the whole capitalist machine will follow the lines that Marx established in his theory of social reproduction.[11] Intensification of production through credit, in circumstances where value is 'in repose', will no longer have the 'disturbing' effect of driving production out of its 'proportions'. In these conditions, credit will reveal its *true* nature as a factor acting to 'rationalise' the system. In sum, development of the economic system of state capitalism will be confined within the limits of a smoothly rising curve, leaving behind the law-governed pattern of the cycle.

But state capitalism, on the scale of capitalist production in its totality and transcending 'national' limitations, is historically impossible. It is confounded by the growth of anarchy, which is directly proportional to the growth of capitalism in all the many forms of its 'existence'. Therefore, the theory of a 'non-cyclical' and 'crisis-free' development of state capitalism has merely *theoretical* significance in two senses: 1) it throws clear light on the nature and interaction of the forces that give birth to the capitalist cycle in real capitalism; 2) it also anticipates the *non-cyclical* character of socialist reproduction, which will be freed from all antagonisms in the relations both of production and distribution. In a society where the laws of 'equilibrium' lose their specific character as economic laws that act independently of the will and consciousness

---

[10] [The *regulative* role of value is completed in the crisis when deviations of market prices from prices of production are corrected. To speak of value having a *constitutive* role is to contemplate the rule of Hegelian Reason in capitalist society. When Marx spoke of the law of value as capitalism's 'social reason', he indicated that it always expresses itself *post festum* (Marx 1957, p. 315). Capitalist society is driven to cyclical crises by its dialectical contradictions; if, on the contrary, value, as 'social reason', were to *constitute* the capitalist mode of production, the implication would be 'an organised whole in antagonistic form', a formulation that Maksakovsky obviously regarded as nonsense.]

[11] [The reference is to the reproduction schemes in Volume II of *Capital*, which involve a level of abstraction logically prior to Marx's more concrete comments on crises and the economic cycle.]

of 'economic subjects', where they emerge instead in the form of a conscious knowledge of historically conditioned social development – in that kind of society there will no longer be any need for capitalist crises as the forms for reconstructing a disrupted 'equilibrium' that has overstepped the boundaries of the social system.

Chapter 5

In Place of a Conclusion

Our attempt to present a Marxist interpretation of the problem of the conjuncture by no means pretends to be the last word on the question. It is only a preliminary outline of the problem based upon Marx's fragments. The analysis incorporates materials from modern economics, but they play no significant part in the work. Thus, our work completely omits any concrete analysis of the conjuncture's morphology, as revealed in the totality of its external expressions. These materials were not used because they would significantly complicate the exposition and disrupt the logical flow of the analysis. The necessary information concerning the external course of the conjuncture has been indirectly interspersed in the theoretical investigation. We also worked within several other methodological and systematic constraints. As a result, we have set out only the fundamental and most general contours of the problem. A more concrete analysis must be the work of future studies. The potential for such studies must always be connected with a critical assessment of existing ways of observing the conjuncture and existing criteria for making judgements; more precisely, what will be needed is coordination of a methodical apparatus of observation and systematisation with the foundations of the Marxist methodology of conjunctural studies. This work is genuinely necessary, especially with reference to the analysis of our own Soviet economy.

The next crucially important task will be to open a critical front in opposition to prevailing bourgeois theories of the conjuncture, both in the West and in their Russian variants, which are represented by the work of Kondrat'ev, Pervushin, and others. Victory in the battles on this theoretical front will mean driving bourgeois economics from its last fortified strongholds and eliminating the possibility that bourgeois economic ideas might penetrate into our own Soviet economic construction.[1]

General questions of the economic dynamic already are, and will continue to be, a focus of bitter theoretical struggle. Capitalism's post-war condition; elements of economic stabilisation; external signs of the beginning of expansion in several leading capitalist countries, incorporating the latest changes in technology; growing processes of capitalist rationalisation and concentration – these concerns, in all their magnitude, pose the problem of the economic dynamic in relation to the most modern forms of capitalism. Whether or not post-war capitalism remains confined to its procrustean bed of law-governed cyclical movement; whatever specific features may appear in the general dynamic of the capitalist whole or in individual countries; whatever may be the influence of capitalism's latest organisational forms on the character of its dynamic; and whatever may turn out to be the relation of that dynamic to the Leninist theory of imperialism, as dying capitalism, to the law of uneven capitalist development, etc. – in their totality these questions are not merely of theoretical interest, involving the next stage in the advance of Marxist thought in response to the structural changes of capitalism's physiology and its particular features, but they are also of *direct*, practical importance for the revolutionary struggle of the proletariat in the West and for the existence of our Soviet system.

The general theory of the conjunctural cycle is the prelude to meeting this challenge and a vitally necessary part of our work. It is dictated by 'the spirit of the times'.

---

[1] [The reference is to Bazarov's theory of the 'levelling-off curve', which implied a declining rate of growth in output as the Soviet economy reached the limits of existing production capacity in the 1920s and faced the growing need for new accumulation. See the discussion in Erlich 1960, Chapter 3.]

Bibliography

Aftalion, Albert 1913, *Les crises périodiques de surproduction*, 2 volumes, Paris: Rivière.

Bauer, Otto [no date], (An article in an edited collection [title unknown]), *Problema rynka i krizisov*, Moscow [publisher unknown].

Bazarov, Vladimir A. 1927, *Kapitalisticheskie tsikly i vosstanovitel'nyi protsess khozyaistva SSSR*, Moscow [publisher unknown].

Bazarov, Vladimir A. 1926, 'Krivye razvitiya kapitalisticheskovo i sovetskovo khozyaistva', *Planovoe khozyaistvo*, 4–5: 87–119.

Bouniatian, Mentor 1922, *Les crises économiques, essai de morphologie et théorie des crises économiques périodiques, et de théorie de la conjoncture économique*, translated by J. Bernard, Paris: M. Giard.

Bouniatian, Mentor [no date], *Ekonomicheskie krizisy*, Moscow [publisher unknown].

Bukharin, Nikolai I. 1928, *Imperializm i nakoplenie kapitala*, Third Edition, Moscow and Leningrad: Gosudarstvennoe Izdatel'stvo.

Bukharin, Nikolai I. 1982, *Selected Writings on the State and the Transition to Socialism*, edited and translated by Richard B. Day, Armonk: M.E. Sharpe.

Cassel, Karl Gustav 1925, *Teoriya kon'yunktury*, Moscow [publisher unknown].

Day, Richard B. 1976, 'The Theory of the Long Cycle: Kondrat'ev, Trotsky, Mandel', *New Left Review*, I, 99: 67–82.

Day, Richard B. 1979–80, 'Rosa Luxemburg and the Accumulation of Capital', *Critique*, 12: 81–96.

Day, Richard B. 1981, *The 'Crisis' and the 'Crash': Soviet Studies of the West (1917–1939)*, London: NLB.

Erlich, Alexander 1960, *The Soviet Industrialization Debate, 1924–1928*, Cambridge, MA: Harvard University Press.

Hilferding, Rudolf [no date], *Finansovyi capital*, Moscow [publisher unknown].

Hilferding, Rudolf 1981, *Finance Capital*, edited by Tom Bottomore and translated by Morris Watnick and Sam Gordon, London: Routledge and Keagan Paul.

Hutchison, Terence W. 1966, *A Review of Economic Doctrines, 1870–1929*, London: Oxford University Press.

Kautsky, Karl 1924, '*Finansovyi kapital i krizisy*', in *Osnovnye problemy*, Moscow [publisher unknown].

Kondrat'ev, Nikolai D. 1922, *Mirovoe khozyaistvo i evo kon'yunktury vo vremya i posle voiny*, Vologda: Gosudarstvennoe Izdatel'stvo.

Kondrat'ev, Nikolai D. 1923, 'Spornye voprosy mirovovo khozyaistva i krizisy', *Sotisalisticheskoe khozyaistvo*, 4–5: 50–87.

Kondrat'ev, Nikolai D. 1924, 'K voprosu o ponyatiyakh ekonomicheskoi statiki, dinamiki i kon'yunktury', *Sotsialisticheskoe khozyaistvo*, 2: 349–82.

Kondrat'ev, Nikolai D. 1925, 'Bol'shie tsikly kon'yunktury', in *Voprosy kon'yunktury*, edited by Kondrat'ev, Moscow: Finansovoe Izdatel'stvo NKF SSSR.

Lenin, Vladimir I. 1960, *Collected Works*, Volume 1, Moscow: Foreign Languages Publishing House.

Livshits, Boris 1929, Review of Maksakovsky's book in *Mirovoe khozyaistvo i mirovaya politika*, 11/12: 222–7.

Luxemburg, Rosa 1963 [1951], *The Accumulation of Capital*, translated by Agnes Schwartzschild, London: Routledge and Keagan Paul.

Luxemburg, Rosa and Nikolai Bukharin 1972, *Imperialism and the Accumulation of Capital*, edited with an introduction by Kenneth J. Tarbuck and translated by Rudolf Wichmann, London: Allen Lane/The Penguin Press.

Maksakovsky, Pavel V. 1928, 'K teorii tsikla i dinamika sovetskovo khozyaistva', *Bol'shevik*, 6: 8–28 and 7: 9–19.

Mandel, Ernest 1975, *Late Capitalism*, London: NLB.

Mandel, Ernest 1980, *Long Waves of Capitalist Development*, Cambridge: Cambridge University Press.

Marx, Karl 1957, *Capital*, Volume II, Moscow: Foreign Languages Publishing House.

Marx, Karl 1961, *Capital*, Volume I, Moscow: Foreign Languages Publishing House.

Marx, Karl 1962, *Capital*, Volume III, Moscow: Foreign Languages Publishing House.

Marx, Karl 1963, *The Poverty of Philosophy*, New York: International Publishers.

Marx, Karl 1970, *A Contribution to the Critique of Political Economy*, Moscow: Progress Publishers.

Marx, Karl 1973, *Grundrisse*, translated with a foreword by Martin Nicolaus, New York: Vintage.

Marx, Karl 1975a [1968], *Theories of Surplus-Value*, Part II, Moscow: Progress Publishers.

Marx, Karl 1975b [1971], *Theories of Surplus-Value*, Part III, Moscow: Progress Publishers.

Mendel'son, Abram S. 1928, *Problema kon'yunktury: Diskussiya v Kommunisticheskoi Akademii*, Moscow: Izdatel'stvo Kommunisticheskoi Akademii.

Mombert, Paul 1921, *Einfuhrung in das Studium der Konjunktur*, Leipzig [publisher unknown].

Mombert, Paul 1924, *Vvedenie v izuchenie kon'yunktury i krizisov*, Moscow [publisher unknown].

Moore, Henry Ludwell 1914, *Economic Cycles, their Law and Cause*, New York: Macmillan.

Moore, Henry Ludwell 1923, *Generating Economic Cycles*, New York: Macmillan.

Osinsky, N. [Oboloensky, Valerian] 1925, *Mirovoe khozyaistvo i krizisy*, Moscow: Izdatel'stvo Kommunisticheskoi Akademii.

Pervushin, Sergei A. 1925, *Khozyaistvennaya kon'yunktura*, Moscow: Izdatel'stvo 'Ekonomicheskaya Zhizn'.

Pigou, Arthur C. 1920, *The Economics of Welfare*, London: Macmillan.

Preobrazhensky, Evgeny A. 1985, *The Decline of Capitalism*, translated and edited with introduction by Richard B. Day, Armonk: M.E. Sharpe.

Röpke, Wilhelm 1922, *Die Konjunktur*, Jena: G. Fischer.

Röpke, Wilhelm 1927, *Kon'yunktura*, Moscow [publisher unknown].

Röpke, Wilhelm 1963, *The Economics of the Free Society*, Chicago: Henry Regnery Company.

Say, Jean-Baptiste 1803, *Traité d'économie politique; ou, Simple exposition de la manière dont se forment, se distribuent, et se consomment les richesses*, Paris: Deterville.

Spiethoff, Arthur [no date], (An article in an edited collection [title unknown]), *Problema rynka i krizisov*, Moscow [publisher unknown].

Tugan-Baranovsky, Mikhail 1913, *Les crises industrielles en Angleterre*, Paris: M. Giard & É. Brière.

Index

Aftalion, Albert, 8, 15, 37
Aristotle, xiii, xliii

Bauer, Otto., x, 98n, 118n
Bazarov, Vladimir A., x, 10n, 32n, 34–7, 99, 144n
Bouniatian, Mentor, x, 8, 15, 37, 73–4, 118n, 132n
Bukharin, Nikolai I., 28n, 33, 52n, 71n, 88n, 103n, 138n, 140n

Cassel, Gustav, x, 6, 8, 15n, 37, 62, 64n, 72n, 77, 94

Engels, Frederick, xxxix, 31, 137n
Erlich, Alexander, 144n

Hegel, Georg Wilhelm Friedrich, xiii–xxxviii, xliii–xlvi, 97n, 104n
Hilferding, Rudolf, x, 7n, 87n, 89–90, 107, 109n, 110n, 113n, 114n, 116n, 119n, 127, 129n, 138n, 139, 140n

Kant, Immanuel, xiv–xvi
Kautsky, Karl, x, 66, 87n
Keynes, John Maynard, 83n
Kondrat'ev, Nikolai D., x, 9–10, 21–4, 34n, 35n, 54n, 139n, 144

Lenin, Vladimir I., xiii, xxix, 26n, 138n
Livshits, Boris L., 21n, 80n, 82, 94n
Luxemburg, Rosa, x, 26n, 28n, 33n, 52n, 53, 64n, 80n, 92

Maksakovsky, Pavel V., x–xii, xxxvi–xlvii, 3–4
Marx, Karl, x, xii, xxii–xlvii, 14n, 16, 19–21, 23n, 26, 28, 34n, 36, 37n, 39–40, 42–6, 49–61, 64, 73, 75n, 76n, 77–8, 79n, 80, 91, 96–8, 100, 103, 106–7, 109n, 110n, 111n, 112n, 113n, 114–15, 117n, 119, 120n, 121n, 122, 123n, 126–7, 133–6, 141, 143
Mandel, Ernest, 9n
Mendel'son, Abram S., xi–xii, 3–4
Mombert, Paul, x, 7n, 8
Moore, Henry Ludwell, 32–3

Osinsky, N., x, 23n, 40

Pervushin, Sergei A., x, 8, 21–2, 24, 30, 32, 144
Pigou, Arthur C., 30n
Plato, xiii–xiv, xvii, xx, xliii
Preobrazhensky, Evgeny A., x, 63n, 138n

Ricardo, David, 42
Rodbertus, Karl Johann, 67
Röpke, Wilhem, x, 6, 8, 15n, 30n, 37
Rubin, Isaak I., x

Say, Jean-Baptiste, 38, 39n
Sombart, Werner, 6
Smith, Adam, xviii, xxv, xli, 42
Spiethoff, Arthur, x, 8, 73, 78, 83n, 94n
Trotsky, Leon, 9n, 139n
Tugan-Baranovsky, Mikhail I., x, 68, 90, 137